# ADVANCE PRAISE FOR
## *MEDIOCRE*

"Oluo's *So You Want to Talk About Race* has been one of the most recommended books during the ongoing racial justice movement. Her new offering is a nuanced analysis of white male America—and how white supremacy has affected politics, football, and more. Oluo deftly combines history and sociological study with personal narrative, and the result is both uncomfortable and illuminating."

—*Washington Post*

"Ijeoma Oluo's sharp yet accessible writing about the American racial landscape made her 2018 book, *So You Want to Talk About Race*, an invaluable resource for anyone looking to understand and dismantle racist structures. Her new book, *Mediocre*, builds on this exemplary work, homing in on the role of white patriarchy in creating and upholding a system built to disenfranchise anyone who isn't a white male."

—*TIME*

"Ijeoma's revelatory and visionary new book confronts disturbing hidden histories that vibrate throughout our institutions and communities today. The connections and insights in *Mediocre* make it an essential read."

—Austin Channing Brown, *New York Times*–
bestselling author of *I'm Still Here*

"There is no one more adept at parsing the toxic effects of white male privilege and systemic oppression than the immensely talented Ijeoma Oluo. Her brilliant book is a master class in understanding how systems of domination working relentlessly in the service of white male patriarchy not only harm all women and people of color, but ultimately hinder white men themselves from reaching greatness."

—Michael Eric Dyson, *New York Times*–
bestselling author of *Long Time Coming*

"Simply put, *Mediocre* is required reading and I'm not-so-secretly envious of every person who gets to read this intelligent, well-written, and engrossing book for the first time. Oluo is one of our great voices and her writing not only educates us, moves us to be more compassionate and analytical about our roles in society, but it inspires us to act and change the world for the better. But first, I need to read this book again. It's just that damn good."

—Phoebe Robinson, *New York Times*–bestselling
author of *You Can't Touch My Hair*

"Ripped, tragically, from yet another and another and another set of headlines, *Mediocre: The Dangerous Legacy of White Male America* breaks ground and forces a bold, startling, and necessary conversation about the implications of institutional supremacy, and its crushing impact on people of color and women."

—Patrisse Khan Cullors, cofounder, Black Lives Matter,
*New York Times*–bestselling author of *When They Call You a
Terrorist*, and joint recipient of the Sydney Peace Prize

"Oluo masterfully maps and diagnoses the pervasive plague of white mediocrity as a long-standing yet substandard model for American success. *Mediocre* brilliantly serves as a pressing call to action for every person, regardless of race or gender, to examine one's relationship with white male mediocrity, to understand its harmful effects, and to actively resist its hold."

—Kimberlé Crenshaw, executive director, African American Policy Forum, and professor, UCLA and Columbia Law Schools

"With *Mediocre*, Ijeoma Oluo gives us another book of profound and important truth in service of liberation. Her skillful, straightforward, and accessible writing style cuts to the heart of white male supremacy and holds it up for us to reckon with. With a deep love for humanity, she shows us how the legacy and current ubiquitousness of this system is life-destroying for people of color and even for white men ourselves."

—Matt McGorry, actor, *How To Get Away With Murder* and *Orange is the New Black*, activist, and cofounder of Inspire Justice

"In her illuminating new book, Ijeoma Oluo unpacks how 'mediocrity' is a privilege created and perpetuated by our obsession with white male superiority. Oluo deftly balances the cultural history of white western male mythmaking with contemporary cultural criticism of the aggrieved white American man. It is a deft and thought-provoking book that contextualizes public discourse on race, class, and gender in America."

—Tressie Mcmillan Cottom, author of the National Book Award finalist *Thick*

"Once again, Ijeoma Oluo uses her elegant voice to speak directly to the root issues at the core of the United States' seeming inability to reconcile who we have been with who we had hoped to be. This book goes beyond how we got here, and digs into where we are, what we're going to do about it, and what's at stake if the people with the most power refuse to do better."

—Ashley C. Ford, writer

"*Mediocre* is urgent, powerful, and laced with an acidity that forces us to contend with our own complicity in a culture that systematically oppresses women, people of color, and especially, women of color. America is a nation that aspires to greatness but refuses to acknowledge how its laws and conventions instead protect white male mediocrity. Both *So You Want to Talk About Race* and *Mediocre* are necessary reads, because few writers are as vital to understanding our present moment as Oluo."

—Jeff Yang, author, CNN contributor, and
cohost of the podcast *They Call Us Bruce*

# MEDIOCRE

## ALSO BY IJEOMA OLUO

*So You Want to Talk About Race*

# Ijeoma Oluo

# MEDIOCRE

## The Dangerous Legacy of White Male America

SEAL PRESS

New York

Seal Press
Hachette Book Group
1290 Avenue of the Americas, New York, NY 10104
www.sealpress.com
@sealpress

Printed in the United States of America

First Edition: December 2020

Published by Seal Press, an imprint of Perseus Books, LLC, a subsidiary of Hachette Book Group, Inc. The Seal Press name and logo is a trademark of the Hachette Book Group.

The Hachette Speakers Bureau provides a wide range of authors for speaking events. To find out more, go to www.hachettespeakersbureau.com or call (866) 376-6591.

The publisher is not responsible for websites (or their content) that are not owned by the publisher.

Print book interior design by Amy Quinn.

Library of Congress Control Number: 2020944625

ISBNs: 978-1-58005-951-0 (hardcover), 978-1-58005-950-3 (ebook)

LSC-C

Printing 1, 2020

*This book is dedicated to Black womxn: You are more important than white supremacy.*

# CONTENTS

# INTRODUCTION

## *Works According to Design*

I was at an idyllic women's writing retreat. I spent my days in a charming cabin surrounded by trees, kept warm by a little wood-stove. As I looked out the window to the giant evergreens surrounding my cabin, I was supposed to feel the spark of inspiration. But I wasn't feeling inspired yet. This setting was quite a change for someone like me: a single mom of two boys used to writing over the din of crashes and bangs and shouts and her own attention deficit disorder. I had adapted to being creative even with a teenage boy regularly interrupting to tell me that he needed more snacks and, yes, was still incapable of finding them himself.

But this writing retreat was designed to get women away from the cries of "Mom!" or "Honey?" that so often compete for our brain space. We were supposed to be honoring our creativity by giving it the time and space it deserved. No children, no men, no internet, no television.

So we worked each day in solitude, and then every evening, at around six p.m., all five of us writers would leave our individual

cabins and gather for dinner in the main farmhouse. Over a lov-
ingly prepared meal made with vegetables freshly pulled from the
farmhouse garden, we would discuss our writing projects, asking
each other questions and offering support and encouragement. We
talked about the work we were doing: the books we were writing,
the plays we wanted to write. We floated ideas, asked for advice
about agents and editors. We laughed and drank wine.

But more than anything, we talked about men. Not our part-
ners or friends or brothers—we talked about shitty dudes. And
even though we came from diverse racial, ethnic, and socioeconomic backgrounds, we all had plenty of dudes to talk about. We
talked about the white men in publishing who were constantly
devaluing our work. We talked about the male writers who would
grab your ass at book fairs or offer to give you feedback on your
work and then try to sleep with you. We talked about how much
time we had spent writing about shitty white dudes. Because if we
weren't writing about the president, we were writing about how
men without uteruses should not control our reproductive choices,
or about how rapists should actually go to jail for rape—even if
they were gifted athletes.

Every evening, we would come together and talk about how we
were trying to write and live in a world run by men who seemed
pretty determined to stop us from having a voice, from experienc-
ing success—from having our own free and independent lives.
And I know this isn't a problem that's particular to the writing
industry. I've participated in similar conversations when I worked
in advertising and when I worked in tech. These are conversations, I'm sure, that women find themselves having in just about
any job they have, in every school they attend, and in every community where they live. There is an abundance of bad guys to be
found just about everywhere, and we can't seem to stop talking
about them.

"Works according to design."

This is a comment that I and many of my fellow racial justice commentators have made when truly horrible things happen, just as they were intended to. A police officer shot an unarmed Black man, and a grand jury decided that the officer didn't even need to face trial? Works according to design. A kid of color selling weed will be sentenced to years in prison while a wealthy white man receives house arrest for his second DUI? Works according to design.

Although the phrase may seem alarmingly coldhearted, it is our way of reminding ourselves that the greatest evil we face is not ignorant individuals but our oppressive systems. It is a reminder that the deaths of Trayvon Martin and Sandra Bland are not isolated cases. It is a reminder to refuse to let our shock and outrage distract us into thinking that these incidents do not all stem from the same root source, which must be dismantled. That source is white male supremacy.

White men lead our ineffective government with almost guaranteed reelection. They lead our corrupt and violent criminal-justice system with little risk of facing justice themselves. And they run our increasingly polarized and misinforming media, winning awards for perpetrating the idea that things run best when white men are in charge. This is not a stroke of white male luck; this is how our white male supremacist systems have been designed to work.

And when I say "white supremacy," I'm not just talking about Klan members and neo-Nazis. Blatant racial terrorists—while deadly and horrifying—have never been the primary threat to people of color in America. It's more insidious than that. I am talking about the ways our schoolrooms, politics, popular culture, boardrooms, and more all prioritize the white race over other races. Ours is a society where white culture is normalized and universalized, while cultures of color are demonized, exotified, or erased.

The average Black household in the United States has one-thirteenth of the net financial worth of the average white household; the average Hispanic household has one-eleventh. One-third of Black men in America are expected to be imprisoned in the course of their lives. As stark as these numbers seem, we people of color—especially women of color—live with these realities every day. Our entire society is built to ensure that white men hoard power. And it's important to remember that the women and people of color most violently harmed by these systems are those who are also queer, transgender, or disabled.

The "male supremacy" in white male supremacy has been in place in white culture since before white people thought of themselves as white. For centuries, women were not allowed to own property, to attend university, to vote. Whatever degree of freedom women and girls had in their public and private lives was determined by men.

Women still spend a large portion of their lives battling men for their basic dignity and safety. They face the persistence of the gender wage gap, the fact that one in five women is a victim of sexual assault, and the ongoing debate about whether male abusers should keep their jobs and even their status.

These injustices are not passed down by God; they are not produced by any entity greater than ourselves. These oppressive systems were built by people—with our votes, our money, our hiring decisions—and they can be unmade by people.

So, at this beautiful dinner table in a farmhouse in the woods, as we continued talking about these white men and their unchecked anger, fear, and irresponsibility—this phrase kept popping into my head: *works according to design.*

I thought about the white men who talked over me in meetings. I thought about the white male lead in a movie who sits in his cubicle and laments his lot, bemoaning that he was supposed to be so much more. I thought about the white men wearing swastikas in

Charlottesville, angry about their own failures and shouting about the people they blamed for them.

I thought of every think piece published since the 2016 election trying to explain the new angry white man. He was disillusioned, he was afraid. He was dissatisfied with his job and his elected representatives. He felt forgotten and left behind. Our modern, pluralist world's focus on diversity had harmed white men in some real way, leading to this age of white male anger. At least, that is what the pundits said.

And here we were, a group of accomplished women talking about these white men as if they were a problem that had recently fallen upon us from the sky, instead of the predictable product of centuries of cultural, political, and economic conditioning.

And suddenly, my anxiety of the last few days faded, because I knew that I was going to write this book.

"Lord, give me the confidence of a mediocre white man."

When writer Sarah Hagi said those words in 2015, they launched a thousand memes, T-shirts, and coffee mugs. The phrase has now become a regular part of the lexicon of many women and people of color—especially those active on social media. The sentence struck a chord with so many of us because while we seemed to have to be better than everyone else to just get by, white men seemed to be encouraged in—and rewarded for—their mediocrity.

White male mediocrity seems to impact every aspect of our lives, and yet it only seems to be people who aren't white men who recognize the imbalance.

I am not arguing that every white man is mediocre. I do not believe that any race or gender is predisposed to mediocrity. What I'm saying is that white male mediocrity is a baseline, the dominant narrative, and that everything in our society is centered around preserving white male power regardless of white male skill or talent. I also know that many white men accomplish great things. But I will argue that we condition white men to believe not only that the best they can hope to accomplish in life is a feeling of superiority over women and people of color, but also that their superiority should be automatically granted them simply because they are white men. The rewarding of white male mediocrity not only limits the drive and imagination of white men; it also requires forced limitations on the success of women and people of color in order to deliver on the promised white male supremacy. White male mediocrity harms us all.

When I talk about mediocrity, I am not talking about something bland and harmless. I'm talking about a cultural complacency with systems that are horrifically oppressive. I'm talking about a dedication to ignorance and hatred that leaves people dead, for no other reason than the fact that white men have been conditioned to believe that ignorance and hatred are their birthrights and that the effort of enlightenment and connection is an injustice they shouldn't have to face.

When I talk about mediocrity, I talk about how we somehow agreed that wealthy white men are the best group to bring the rest of us prosperity, when their wealth was stolen from our labor.

When I talk about mediocrity, I am talking about how aggression equals leadership and arrogance equals strength—even if those white male traits harm the men themselves and the kingdom they hope to rule.

When I talk about mediocrity, I talk about success that is measured only by how much better white men are faring than people who aren't white men.

When I talk about mediocrity, I am talking about the ways in which we can't imagine an America where women aren't sexually harassed at work, where our young people of color aren't funneled into underresourced schools—all because it would challenge the idea of the white male as the center of our country. This is not a benign mediocrity; it is brutal. It is a mediocrity that maintains a violent, sexist, racist status quo that robs our most promising of true greatness.

By defining greatness as a white man's birthright, we immediately divorce it from real, quantifiable greatness—greatness that benefits, greatness that creates. White men have assumed inborn greatness, and they are taught to believe that they alone have seemingly infinite potential for greatness. Our culture has shaped the expectation of greatness exclusively around white men by erasing the achievements of women and people of color from our histories, by excluding women and people of color as heroes in our films and books, by ensuring that the qualified applicant pool is restricted to white male social networks.

But the expectation of accomplishment is not an accomplishment in and of itself. By making whiteness and maleness their own reward, we disincentivize white men from working to earn their privileged status. If you are constantly assumed to be great just for being white and male, why would you struggle to make a real contribution? Why take a risk or make a determined effort that might fail when you can be rewarded for keeping your head down? Societal incentives are toward mediocrity.

Most women and people of color have to claw their way to any chance at success or power, have to work twice as hard as white men and prove themselves to be exceptional talents before we begin to entertain discussions of truly equal representation in our workplaces or government. Somehow, we don't think white men should be required to shoulder any of the same burden for growth and struggle the rest of us are expected to work through in order to accomplish anything worthwhile.

How often have you heard the argument that we have to slowly implement gender and racial equality in order to not "shock" society? Who is the "society" that people are talking about? I can guarantee that women would be able to handle equal pay or a harassment-free work environment right now, with no ramp-up.

I'm certain that people of color would be able to deal with equal political representation and economic opportunity if they were made available today. So for whose benefit do we need to go so slowly? How can white men be our born leaders and at the same time so fragile that they cannot handle social progress?

What we have been told is great, thanks to the mediocre-white-man-industrial complex, just isn't always that great. The image of the ideal white man—the bold and confident ones we end up idolizing, giving promotions to, electing to office—that image is often the epitome of mediocrity. And when entrusted with these positions of power, such men often perform as well as someone with mediocre skills would be expected to: we see the results in our floundering businesses and in our deadlocked government. Rather than risk seeming weak by admitting mistakes, white men double down on them. Rather than consider women or people of color as equally valid candidates for power, white men repeat that a change in leadership is somehow "too risky" to entrust to groups that they have deliberately rendered "inexperienced."

This discrepancy between our limited definition of greatness and what we're left with comes in part from our insistence that our system is a meritocracy, when it clearly is not. There are all sorts of systems and institutional barriers that have worked for centuries to ensure that large segments of our society—regardless of talent, skill, or character—will never be allowed to rise out of poverty or powerlessness.

This country's wealth was built on exploitation and violence, and those who worked hardest to build it were not empowered or enriched by its successes—they were enslaved people, migrant laborers, and domestic workers. Much of this country's early infra-structure, for example, was built with slave labor, and then with grotesquely underpaid immigrant labor and prison labor. Many of our business and political leaders were freed to dedicate their time and energy to their professional success by the unpaid labor of wives and mothers and the underpaid labor of nannies and housekeepers.

Those who profited off that labor did little more than be born with a whip in their hand. But nevertheless we crafted a story of greatness around them. We say that they earned greatness, and that if we emulate them, these cruel and powerful white men, we will one day rise to where they stand.

When I say "we," I don't mean me. I am a Black woman. True, I have been told time and time again that my best chance of success is to emulate the preferred traits of white maleness as much as possible. Still, mine is not the image of the great leaders in our history books, nor that of the heroes in our stories. For someone like me to expect any greatness without having exceptional talent and luck was, at best, foolish and, at worst, dangerous. This is not my birthright.

There has always been a nagging discrepancy between the promise and the reality of white maleness. White men have often had the sneaking suspicion that the American dream is a fiction. At the same time, white men have always feared the potential of losing that one great superiority—the *better than*. If all you have is *better than*—better than women, better than people of color, no more and no less than that—why would you willingly give up the one prize you never had to earn?

And so these white men often end up clinging to a disturbing construct and blaming those with less power for its shortcomings. This seems for some like a better option than questioning the promised great reward ahead of them. After the wealthiest white men take their cut, there is never enough left for the average white man to have his crown. But we, as a society, continue to tell white men that their coronation is just around the corner.

Too many women and people of color have experienced the rage of a white man who had been patiently waiting in line to be the next president or CEO. When he finally realizes that his turn may never come, he looks around to see who is to blame for taking his place—he thinks his loss is the cost of opportunity for others. But he never looks up at the elite white men he has been striving to emulate. If we look under the feet of many of the white men to whom we grant so much power, we will see the masses crushed by their failures—including other white men.

While we would like to believe otherwise, it is usually not the cream that rises to the top: our society rewards behaviors that are actually disadvantageous to everyone. Studies have shown that the traits long considered signs of strong leadership (like overconfidence and aggression) are in reality disastrous in both business and politics—not to mention the personal toll this style of leadership takes on the individuals around these leaders. These traits are broadly considered to be masculine, whereas characteristics often associated with weakness or lack of leadership (patience, accommodation, cooperation) are coded as feminine. This is a global phenomenon of counterproductive values that social scientists have long marveled over.

The man who never listens, who doesn't prepare, who insists on getting his way—this is a man that most of us would not (when given friendlier options) like to work with, live with, or be friends with.

And yet we have, as a society, somehow convinced ourselves that we should be led by incompetent assholes.

This patriarchal elevation of incompetence has a special flair, however, in capitalist and individualist societies like the United States. When wealthy white men hoard power among themselves, they also need a cost-efficient way to keep the masses from threatening the status quo. How do you keep the average white male American invested in a system that disadvantages him?

You give them whiteness. You give them maleness. You give them an identity that will provide a sense of victory in good times and bad. All you need to be successful as a white man is to be better off than women and people of color. And all you need to do to distract white men from how they are actually faring is to task them with the responsibility of ensuring that people of color and women don't take what little might be theirs.

White male identity is not inborn—it is built. This identity is not designed to be its most intelligent, most productive, most innovative self. The aspirational image of white maleness is meant to be far less than that. Elite white men don't need actual competition from rising and striving average white men. Instead, this status becomes a birthright detached from actual achievement. It is an identity that clings to mediocrity.

I don't think it has ever been easy to be a woman of color in America, but these last few years, since the election of Donald Trump in 2016, have been harder. Every day, we face a new onslaught of white male anger, aggression, fear, or incompetence. My friends and I stare at each other in wonder over it. *How did we get here?* is the question everyone seems to be asking. *Is it Trump? Are all these men just angry at Obama? Is it the internet? Is it the decline of public education? Is it going to get worse? How did we go so wrong?* These questions kept bubbling up at the dinner table at our writing retreat.

What I do know is that the impact white men have been having on my life and the lives of so many others is not new. What we are seeing in our political climate is not novel or unexplainable. It works according to design. Yes, of course the average white man is going to feel dissatisfied with his lot in life—he was supposed to. Yes, of course our powerful and respected men would be shown to be abusers and frauds—that is how they became powerful and respected. And yes, the average white male voter (and a majority of white women voters whose best chance at power is their proximity to white men) would see a lewd, spoiled, incompetent, untalented bully as someone who best represents their vision of America—he does.

Sitting at the dinner table with those women, talking about angry, entitled white men, I started to see part of these men's design. Part of the road that was deliberately laid down before the angry white men we see today. I saw them encouraged by every hero, every leader, and every history book to be what they became. And I saw that the path that began far before our last presidential election, far before any of our current political leaders were born, extends into the future regardless of who wins the next elections. And I wanted to see the entire map. I wanted to see if there was a way for us to pick a different path before it was too late.

And so I looked. I started with today's titans of white male mediocrity—the arrogant, entitled, irresponsible, willfully ignorant bullies who have risen to power and prominence while dragging us into disappointment—and I worked backward. I started looking for their earlier incarnations, through each generation, at every turn of our country's past.

I started looking for where and how we, as a society, have encouraged and idealized the traits of these white men, even at great political, economic, and social cost.

As I looked back through our history, I started to see patterns. I started to see how time and time again, anything perceived as a threat to white manhood has been attacked, no matter how necessary that new person or idea may have been to our national progress. I started to see how reliably the bullying and entitlement we valued in our leaders led to failure. These are traits that we tell our children are bad, but when we look at who our society actually rewards, we see that these are the traits we have actively cultivated.

In sharing some of these stories here, I aim to draw a portrait of what white male mediocrity in the United States looks like and how it attempts to perpetuate itself—in our education system, our sports teams, our businesses, and our politics. I want to show the ways in which we have been trapped in cycles of self-harm that have cost countless lives and have held us back economically and socially. With a clear view of our past, we may then consider trying something new for our future.

Looking through these stories, I saw parts of myself as well—not only where I had suffered at the hands of those in power, but also in my attempts to fulfill the role assigned to me in the hopes of gaining my own personal power. We've all been instructed to value and strive toward the white male version of success. I saw how strong the messaging has been, and how susceptible we all are to it.

When we consider the privilege hierarchies of race, gender, and class, it's clear that some of us have played a larger role than others in perpetuating this harmful image of white maleness. But I also think that all of us, regardless of demographic, have played a part in upholding white male supremacy. We are all told to aspire to the largest bite of our piece of the pie—no matter how meager our piece may be.

The mediocrity of the constructed white male identity is not only disappointing for them, but devastating for those of us who are the first to be sacrificed when the predictable fruits of mediocrity come to bear. Those of us who are not white men are the labor to be exploited, the scapegoats to blame, the bags to punch. All this anger distracts us from noticing how we've built a system that has never benefitted anyone except the most powerful white men, the select few who hoard the profits made from the systems of race and gender and class. We must realize that whom we look up to and what traits we cultivate as a society can change, and they must if we are to survive.

For now, let's journey through the creation of the white male America we are living in today. Let's look at how today's results come from our past decisions. Let's look at how the glorification of white male aggression brought about the brutality of westward expansion, how the disdain of women workers exacerbated the Great Depression, how the fear of racial integration drove the Great Migration, and many more examples of how white male America was built and solidified at a devastating cost. We can then see how the decisions that were made decades—even centuries—ago in the desperate preservation of white male supremacy have led us to the brink of social and political disaster.

Let's tell these stories, so that we may learn how to write better ones to come.

# CHAPTER 1

# COWBOYS AND PATRIOTS

## *How the West Was Won*

We all have that one relative, the one whose name is never said without a sigh of frustration or a groan of dread. The one relative who is always quick to offer inappropriate commentary, in his outdoor voice, at the dinner table. For our family it was someone I'll call Brian. Brian was one of the rare Fox News viewers in the family. He would spout conservative talking points that he heard on cable news, and when he ran out of memorized semi-factoids, he would make up arguments to defend his point. Sometimes he didn't seem to have a point beyond "I disagree loudly with whatever it is you are saying."

You didn't have to be talking about politics in order to suddenly find yourself dragged into a convoluted political debate. You could be talking about your new cell phone and everyone would be commenting on what a nice phone it was, and suddenly Brian would interject with how his cell phone provider was better than yours and how the reason you were with such and such company was because of a vast liberal news conspiracy designed to "fuck you over." Brian was pretty sure that a lot of things were trying to fuck us all over—cell phone companies, banks, car companies, universities—and somehow it was all liberal media's fault.

Luckily for us, Brian was a distant relative; we only had to endure him at weddings, funerals, and occasional Christmas celebrations that brought the extended family together. We could give our fake smiles and try our best to change the subject, knowing that we would be able to return home, far away from Brian, and forget about him until someone else in the family died.

This all changed with social media. Suddenly, Brian was everywhere, and he was so much *more* Brian online. Everything was amped up—the conspiracy theories, the forced debates, the made-up talking points—all in caps lock. I didn't think it was possible that online Brian could be more annoying than real-life, interrupting, bloviating, creepy-joke-telling Brian, but—here he was, somehow even worse.

As my writing career began to take off, Brian decided that I would make the ideal sparring partner for online debate. I had muted his posts early on, so I was no longer subjected to his daily rants about illegal immigration or his fearmongering about how Obama was going to take away all of our rights, but he insisted on bringing his very loud opinions to my social media pages. He would show up on random status updates to challenge me to a debate of wits (literally, saying: "I challenge you") on issues I had no desire to debate. Every time, I would either ignore him or politely decline and wish him a good day. Sometimes he would try to debate others who interacted with my social media posts, and I would ask him to please go away.

I couldn't understand what Brian was getting from all this on-line antagonism. Almost nobody took him up on his debate challenges; nobody thanked him for his uninvited opinions. The sexist, xenophobic, homophobic, racist politicians and policies he supported were not only in stark contrast to the beliefs of the family he seemed to genuinely love; they also hurt many members of our family and put many of them (especially those who were queer, Muslim, or people of color) at risk.

One day, after he left a particularly long comment on my Facebook page telling me that he supported Trump because all the Democratic candidates were weak on immigration and terrorism, I took the bait. I asked him how he could support someone who literally put his family in danger, why he insisted on spouting Fox News nonsense even when some of his closest family members had made it clear that his doing so hurt them. He responded that his own family—even the brown, Muslim family members—weren't at risk because they weren't the terrorists Trump was after. He talked about how liberal media had blinded me to the dangers that were out there waiting for me if Democrats gained control of the government.

Weeks later, after yet another horrific mass shooting in the United States, he showed up on my social media page again, this time in defense of gun rights. The story he shared was quite illuminating. He told about a fateful night when he was walking alone to his car and a "thug" with a "hoodie" confronted him with a gun. "It was him or me," he said. But luckily, Brian was packing. If it weren't for Brian's weapon at the ready, he would have been dead. He insinuated that the "thug" got what was coming to him and that he would always do what was necessary to protect himself and his family.

What made this story so revealing is that I'm pretty sure none of it happened. Lemme draw you a picture of Brian. Brian is a late-middle-aged white dude who lives in the Midwestern suburbs. He tucks his Disney T-shirts into his jean shorts and pulls his white socks up to his knees. Brian is a dude who has had few adventures in life, and even fewer friends. I've never seen him in the general vicinity of a gun. And if he ever shot a "thug" in the street, I'm sure I would have heard about it before then.

But none of Brian's so vigorously defended political beliefs were based in reality. No "thug" had tried to take his life in the street, and yet he still clung to his belief that he needed access to guns in order to protect himself. He had never encountered any Muslim terrorism in his Midwestern suburb, but he was still convinced that there were terrorists eager to cross the border to bomb his subdivision. From these made-up horrors, these fictionalized ene- mies, he had created a villain worthy of the violent bravado that he imagined he would display if confronted by said villain. This web of racist lies was what he needed to make himself seem like a man. He invented a story about bad guys who were out to get him, and he repeated it to himself and others until he believed it. Then he made up another story—of himself as hero, defending himself and his family against this violent threat—and he repeated that one until he believed it too. Brian wrote himself into his own Amer- ican western, a world of cowboys and Indians, cops and robbers. And for a man with no job, few friends, and a family that couldn't stand him, pretending to be a main character in violent American mythology was as close to belonging as he was ever going to get.

I thought about every Black person who has had the cops called on them for trying to cash a check at a bank, for trying to shop at a store, for trying to exist in public—and I wondered what stories the frightened white people must have told themselves to justify their fears. I thought about the story that George Zimmerman must have been telling himself as he shot seventeen-year-old Tray- von Martin for simply walking around a gated neighborhood as a Black teen. I thought about what story Michael Dunn must have been telling himself as he opened fire on a car filled with Black teenagers because their music was too loud, killing seventeen-year-old Jordan Davis. I thought about what story Wade Michael Page (who was likely radicalized by anti-Muslim propaganda while he served in the US Army)[1] must have been telling himself as he opened fire on a Sikh temple in Wisconsin, killing forty-one-year-old Paramjit Kaur, sixty-five-year-old Satwant Singh Kaleka, thirty-nine-year-old Prakash Singh, forty-one-year-old Sita Singh, forty-nine-year-old Ranjit Singh, and eighty-one-year-old Suveg Singh.

I'm so glad that Brian probably doesn't actually carry a gun, and I hope he never will. Mediocre white men who want to be heroes too often feel the need to fabricate villains to justify their imagined role—even if that means vilifying entire populations of people. Their dreams of grand adventures are mere whims and fantasy, but the violence such white men visit upon others is often very, very real.

## A COWBOY IS BORN:
## BUFFALO BILL TAKES THE STAGE

Buffalo Bill is onstage engaged in fierce battle. He and his scouts are fighting a ferocious group of Cheyenne warriors. The audience holds its breath as the terrifying Cheyenne appear to be gaining the upper hand. But just when it seems all hope is lost, Buffalo Bill—dressed in an elegant black velvet, lace-trimmed, Mexican vaquero suit—takes aim at the Cheyenne war chief Yellow Hand and fires. Their chief shot dead, the Cheyenne are defeated. Buffalo Bill walks over to Yellow Hand's lifeless body, takes out his knife, and removes Yellow Hand's scalp. Buffalo Bill triumphantly raises the scalp in the air. "For Custer!" he declares.

The audience erupts into wild applause and cheers. "For Custer!" they cry.

In Buffalo Bill's stage show *The Red Right Hand: or The First Scalp for Custer*, the scalping of Yellow Hand was an act of justice.

George Armstrong Custer was the celebrated army general who was killed, along with his entire command, during the Indian Wars at the Battle of Big Horn in June of 1876. The infamous battle would become known as "Custer's Last Stand." Custer was beloved in white American culture for his leadership in battle, but he was known to many Native people for his role in their forced removal from their land onto reservations. In July 1876, just days after the Battle of Little Big Horn, Buffalo Bill had taken revenge against the brutal Indians for killing Custer, using their own barbaric methods against them. He had scalped one of their leaders to avenge the death of one of his own.[2] By the end of the year, Buffalo Bill would begin reenacting the scalping of Yellow Hand for the entertainment of paying audiences.

The idea of scalping as a Native act of barbarism is one that persists. But the act of scalping one's enemies had existed in European cultures for over two thousand years before European colonizers arrived on the shores of this continent. And since the early days of European colonization in the Americas, the scalping of Native people by European settlers was not only encouraged but rewarded.

In Canada, the American colonies, and Mexico, governments paid a handsome sum for the scalps of Native men, women, and children.[3] In eighteenth-century New Hampshire, you could earn one hundred pounds for every male Native scalp you turned in, fifty pounds for each scalp of a Native woman, and twenty-five pounds for the scalp of each Native child.[4] These were not individually named Native people who were wanted for particular crimes—the reward was for any Native scalp, for no other reason than the act left the world with one less Native person.

While both Natives and Europeans used scalping as a weapon in battle, the European use of scalping as one of their many tools of genocide would be largely erased from textbooks. In place of this gruesome history, Americans are widely taught half truths glorifying the supposed suffering and heroism of European colonizers.

The story of Buffalo Bill's scalping of Yellow Hand would become a part of that mythology—a story that he largely invented, just as he had invented his own legend. Before William F. Cody was Buffalo Bill, he was a lot of other things. Cody had worked as a farmer, a teamster, a trapper, a driver, and a soldier. But throughout much of it, Cody maintained dreams of taking the stage as a successful actor.

Cody was given the name Buffalo Bill for his talent in slaughtering buffalo (now known as American bison). Buffalo were plentiful around the country, and hunting them was a popular sport, but Cody was obscenely prolific in killing—claiming to have shot dead 4,280 buffalo in just eighteen months.[5] At first, Cody hunted buffalo for food. He got a job with the railroad companies to kill buffalo in order to feed railroad workers. But quickly, the work became about more than killing buffalo; it became a part of killing Indians.

As American colonizers looked to expand their territory westward with the building of railroads in the mid- to late nineteenth century, they came into direct conflict with the Native people who had lived on those lands for centuries. Prime railroad territory was often prime grazing territory, and valuable resources like gold were found in places where the Sioux hunted. The US government had declared de facto total war against Native people wherever they stood between the United States and its expansion west. The United States attacked Native people in every way it could—fighting combatants on the battlefield, killing women and children in their homes, spreading disease, forcing relocation—nothing was off limits. But still, Native communities fought to maintain their lands, and fought well.

"Cheyenne people, Lakota people, and Arapahoe people at that time were basically freedom fighters trying to defend themselves, their homelands, and their way of life," Russell Brooks, a Cheyenne filmmaker, scholar, and educator explained to me.[6]

In 1869, facing a protracted battle with Native tribes like the Sioux, President Ulysses S. Grant appointed Phillip Sheridan as commanding general of the army and asked him to help solve the "Indian Problem" once and for all. Sheridan reached out to William Tecumseh Sherman, who had distinguished himself with his scorched-earth battle tactics during the Civil War, for advice. Sherman observed that wherever buffalo existed, there would be Native people, and they would continue to fight for land wherever the buffalo roamed. Sherman's advice to Sheridan was simple: remove the buffalo in order to remove the Indian. "I think it would be wise to invite all the sportsmen of England and America there this fall for a Grand Buffalo hunt, and make one grand sweep of them all," Sherman wrote to Sheridan.[7] No more buffalo, no more Indians.

As Cody gained a reputation as a skilled hunter, he went to work for Sheridan, killing as many buffalo as he could. Buffalo hunting became a wildly popular sport for white people in the West—well, "sport" is far too generous a term, because there was little sportsmanship involved. Men from all over the country boarded trains headed west in order to shoot buffalo with .50-caliber rifles from train windows. They killed thousands of buffalo a day, leaving the animals' lifeless bodies where they fell on the plains to rot.

Wealthy and powerful men from the East Coast and even Europe rode west to join in on the fun, guided by William Cody, by this point known as Buffalo Bill. As journalists traveled with the wealthy men to document the hunts for newspapers across the country, Cody saw his first real opportunity for fame. As Buffalo Bill started featuring in major newspaper stories as a symbol of the adventures to be had in the Wild West, Cody capitalized on the attention. He began partnering with the authors of dime-store novels and started commissioning plays about his exploits. Soon,

Cody was regularly traveling back and forth—east to star in stage shows, and then back west to continue the wholesale slaughter of buffalo.[8]

As famous hunters like Cody popularized buffalo hunting and countless men joined in the killing, they found that they had to travel farther west in search of buffalo as numbers dwindled. The excitement following the widespread slaughter of buffalo began to wane. Cody, now having tasted celebrity, went in search of greater fame and found it in battle. An experienced scout with the US Army, he signed on to join in the Plains Wars in 1876, announcing from the stage of one of his shows that he was leaving "play acting" in search of the "real thing." He packed his costume and went off to war.

Opportunity struck a little over a month after Cody joined the 5th Cavalry in southern Wyoming. A small band of Cheyenne warriors had been spotted heading west in pursuit of two US military couriers. Cody gained permission from his superiors to take a small group of fighters to engage the warriors. Before leaving, Cody changed out of the typical sturdy, rough clothing that the rest of the cavalry wore and into his costume. Dressed in black velvet pants and a red silk shirt trimmed with silver buttons, Cody rode out to meet fame and fortune.

The fight itself was unextraordinary. Cody's men exchanged shots with the Cheyenne warriors. Cody and one Cheyenne warrior fired at each other, the warrior just missing Cody, and Cody shooting the warrior in the leg and felling his horse. Then Cody's horse tripped in a hole and went down too. Cody and the warrior both took aim again, and Cody once again proved the better shot, killing Hay-o-wei, his adversary. The name Hay-o-wei translates to "Yellow Hair," which the young warrior was named due to his blonde hair. Yellow Hair was not a war chief; he was just a warrior of no particular rank. The entire confrontation was over in a few minutes.[9]

The rest of the Cheyenne warriors fled the scene, and as Cody's men left in pursuit, Cody walked over to Yellow Hair's body, scalped the dead warrior, and took his warbonnet and weapons as trophies. According to Cody, he thrust the scalp in the air and shouted, "The first scalp for Custer!" Nobody else at the skirmish remembered him doing that. None of the warriors that the men fought had been at the battle of Little Big Horn or had likely ever encountered Custer.

Within a week of his killing Yellow Hair, stories of Cody's bravery under fire began to reach the newspapers. The first to write about Cody's heroism was his friend Charles King for the *New York Herald*. The quick fight became much more dramatic in the retelling. Other papers picked up the exciting tale of Cody's first scalp for Custer. The cavalrymen who were with Cody when they engaged the small group of Cheyenne warriors were surprised to see what had been such an inconsequential fight suddenly spun into an epic battle.

Cody made the tales even taller in a letter to his wife, Louisa, which was meant to precede a package of his war trophies. In the letter he wrote, "We have had a fight. I killed Yellow Hand, a Cheyenne chief, in a single-handed fight. [I am going to] send the war bonnet, shield, bridle, whip, arms, and his scalp. . . . The cheers that went up when he fell was deafening." The package reached Louisa before the letter; when Louisa opened it, expecting a gift from her husband and instead finding a human scalp, she fainted.[10]

A few months after killing Yellow Hair, Cody left the cavalry to return to the stage. *The Red Right Hand: or The First Scalp for Custer* scandalized and excited audiences. Each night, Cody took the stage in the very outfit that he wore in battle to reenact a wildly dramatized version of the killing of Yellow Hair, now renamed by Cody as Yellow Hand and promoted to the position of chief, instead of simple warrior. Sometimes Yellow Hand would go down due to a gunshot wound; sometimes he would die in hand-to-hand combat with Cody. While papers denounced the blatant glorification of violence, audiences packed the theater to see Cody wave the scalp of Yellow Hand in the air in victory.

This was not the first time that Cody had tried to claim fame from violent confrontation with the Cheyenne people. "He was no friend to the Cheyenne," Russell Brooks told me. Cody had long been involved in US Army campaigns to forcibly remove Cheyenne and Lakota people from their lands. Cody was involved in what is known to Americans as the Battle of Summit Springs but is known to Brooks and other Cheyenne as the Battle of White Buttes. In that battle, in which the US Army ambushed a band of Cheyenne who were resting on their way north to join up with Lakota people, twenty warriors, seven women, and four children were killed. Cody shot and killed a Cheyenne warrior and claimed that he had shot Cheyenne chief Tall Bull. Others at the scene testified that Tall Bull had been killed at the beginning of the battle by another soldier, and Cody had instead killed somebody else who was riding Tall Bull's horse.[11]

Cody would go on to develop more stage productions showcasing the violent masculinity of the West to great success, leading to the 1883 debut of his most famous show, *Buffalo Bill's Wild West and Congress of Rough Riders of the World*. The timing of Cody's show was perfect. In the mid-nineteenth century, white men in England and the United States began to worry about their young men. These young men had it too easy; their wealth and comfort had made them soft. In the United States, a country still fighting to retain the land it had stolen from Native people, this softness could threaten the expansion of America across the continent. The call for white men of America to maintain physical power was not just political; it was a spiritual calling. The rise in popularity of Muscular Christianity in the United States and Europe during this time gave white male elites a religious mandate to conquer both rugby fields and battlefields. According to practitioners of Muscular Christianity, physical softness in men had undermined traditional masculinity and had led to intellectual and moral softness.

As the wives and daughters of these wealthy white men began to make strides in social and political life, men felt an even greater threat to their masculine identity. This fear of the "feminizing" of young American elite men led to calls for stories of "strong, brutal men with red-hot blood in 'em, with unleashed passions rampant in 'em, blood and bones and viscera in 'em."[12] "Masculine" theater, dime novels, and adult male fiction steeped in grit and violence known as "red-blooded realism" became increasingly popular, in large part due to the threat of the widespread success of women writers like Harriet Beecher Stowe and Susan Warner (whom author Nathaniel Hawthorne dismissed as a "damn'd mob of scribbling women"),[13] and of plays geared toward women audiences. Young white men popularized dime novels that told wild tales of danger and exploration, hunting and gunfights, first with stories of Daniel Boone and Davy Crockett, and later with fictionalized accounts of the exploits of heroes and outlaws like Kit Carson and Billy the Kid. Buffalo Bill's own stories of adventure would make it into dozens of wildly popular dime novels. Men in search of manhood began to look west.

Cody's *Wild West* show offered everything that white men in search of power and glory were looking for. In Cody's show, white men were noble and brave. They fearlessly tamed animals and fought savages. "Indians," even when Cody allowed them to be something less than mindless killing machines, were seen as great relics of the past, conquered by the superiority of white men. Once-great Native warriors were paraded in front of white crowds like tigers in a zoo to show how great white men must be to have physically bested people built for little more than violence.

The lure of Western adventure did not dissipate as these boys became men. Instead, they set out to star in their own stories of physical dominance. One man who was heavily influenced by cowboy mythology, and in turn shaped an entire generation in its image, was President Theodore Roosevelt. Roosevelt was a poster boy for the manly renewal that Western-themed violence promised. Once known as a scrawny, squeaky-voiced dandy, Roosevelt moved to the Dakota badlands in the late 1880s to remake himself. When Roosevelt returned to the East Coast, tanned, muscular, and brimming with tales of taming wildlife and battles against cattle thieves, he became the American man that every American man wanted to be.

Roosevelt was not just a strong proponent of cowboy mythology and Muscular Christianity; he was also directly inspired by William Cody's image. When Roosevelt fought in the Spanish-American War in 1898, the name given to his regiment, the Rough Riders, was taken from Cody's *Wild West* show. In return, Cody dramatized the Rough Riders' celebrated Battle of San Juan Hill in his stage show.[14] Roosevelt also seemed to believe the same violent, racist stereotypes of Native people that were displayed in the early *Wild West* shows, infamously saying in 1886, "I don't go so far as to think that the only good Indian is the dead Indian, but I believe nine out of every ten are, and I shouldn't like to inquire too closely into the case of the tenth."[15]

As president of the United States, Roosevelt's obsession with the physical supremacy of white manhood would influence his policy decisions. Roosevelt saw the West as a place to be won, and in his view white Americans had already won it—by conquering both the terrain and the Native people. To Roosevelt, it was white Americans' honored duty to preserve and protect the beauty of Western lands for future generations of white Americans to enjoy. Roosevelt claimed for the United States tens of millions of acres previously promised to Native people, land that had been stewarded by Native people for countless generations. They became our national forests and parks.

In an article published in the *American Indian Law Journal*, Native scholar and law professor Angelique Townsend Eagle-Woman noted that while Roosevelt is celebrated today as a great conservationist for his creation of national parks and forests, his actions were actually "an illegal, unconsented-to land grab from the Tribal Nations, and then a reappropriating of those lands owned by tribal peoples to the ownership of the United States on a might makes right basis."[16] Roosevelt made this decision not just callously, but calculatingly. Professor of American history Gary Gerstle described Roosevelt as a man who "expected that they [Native people] would be eliminated, exterminated from America in contest with the white men who were settling the continent, to the people who he hailed as backwoodsmen. And he required the Indians to be there to be the strenuous opponent through which Americans could prove their valor. But he was very clear that in a modern America that he was building, he expected they would be exterminated either through battle or through simply the inability to adjust to modern life."[17]

The white culture of the West was steeped in the expectation of triumph over land and peoples. In fact, Roosevelt shared this belief with Cody, whose stories of white victory over both the West and the people who had previously inhabited it carried a sense of inevitability and paternal racism. "This continent had to be won," Cody wrote. "We need not waste our time in dealing with any sentimentalist who believes that, on account of any abstract principle, it would have been right to leave this continent to the domain, the hunting ground of squalid savages. It had to be taken by the white race."[18] Manly men were quick to sing the praises of a stage show that opened with the scalping of an Indian and then moved through gunfights, horseback riding, cattle roping, and more fantastic feats of masculinity. One reviewer commented that compared with Buffalo Bill's *Wild West*, "all the operas in the world appear like pretty playthings for emasculated children."[19]

Cody himself encouraged this celebration of hypermasculinity. A poster for *Wild West* from 1902 loudly declares that the show is "Standing like an obelisk above and beyond all others. A perfect phalanx of all that is GREAT, GRAND, and HEROIC." It touts "A gathering of extraordinary consequence to fittingly illustrate all that VIRILE, MUSCULAR, HEROIC MANHOOD has and can endure."[20]

Cody expanded his show from a small stage to an extravaganza the size of a small town. He hired real Native warriors to play Native warriors. Gunslingers and cowboys would join the show. Eventually he would add "Zulu warriors," Mexican "vaqueros," Turks, and dozens of other "exotic" performances. Buffalo Bill's *Wild West* became the most popular show in America, and he became one of the wealthiest and most famous entertainers in the world.

Buffalo Bill Cody, Wild Bill Hickok, and many other dime-store-novel heroes would inspire an entire generation of young white men to head west in search of their own Manifest Destiny. With the *Wild West* show gaining in popularity, Cody also strove to increase its respectability. *Buffalo Bill's Wild West* was not a "show"—it was, according to Cody, an educational event. It was a living history. People would come to *Wild West* to learn as much as to be entertained. Few questioned the supposed educational value or legitimacy of his project. And the racist, exaggerated stories of white male American bravery, leadership, and righteous victory became a part of our collective understanding of American history; these misleading legends persist to this day.

After decades of success, *Wild West* was eventually done in by financial mismanagement, Cody's drinking habits, and the rising popularity of movie theaters. Cody died on January 10, 1917, at age seventy. Cody is still remembered as an icon of the American West: a soldier, a showman, a wildlife conservationist, and a friend of the Indian. He deliberately cultivated that reputation. As Cody interacted with the Native people who worked in his show, he became less comfortable with the scalping act that had launched his career. The scalp and warbonnet of Yellow Hair were removed from their stage-side case, never to be displayed again. Cody would eventually speak against the scalping of Native people. In his dramas of the Wild West, Native people were no longer portrayed as bloodthirsty savages and instead became "noble savages": moral, trustworthy innocents who were tricked by evil Mormons into attacking innocent white people—at least until Cody and his friends could show up and save the day.[21]

Cody would also come to regret the massacre of buffalo that had given him his stage name. While the great buffalo hunt featuring live bison would always be a prominent part of Cody's show, he began to speak out against the buffalo hunting that he had popularized. Perhaps one of the most brutal of white male privileges is the opportunity to live long enough to regret the carnage you have brought upon others.

While I had, like many people, heard the name Buffalo Bill, he was not a featured hero in 1980s Seattle, as he has been in places like Wyoming or Colorado. About a decade ago, on a business trip to Cody, Wyoming (named after William Cody, who is considered one of the city's founders), I happened upon the Buffalo Bill Center of the West. I knew very little about Buffalo Bill, but the five-museum complex seemed to take up an entire city block, and I had a few hours to kill before my flight back home. I decided to go inside.

Greeting me at the entrance of the Buffalo Bill museum was a stagecoach filled with memorabilia. There were countless artifacts from the *Wild West* show: Annie Oakley's stage costume, the weapons of Native warriors, even a full-size replica of Cody's personal show tent. I was both dazzled by and uncomfortable with the elaborate spectacle on display in these exhibits. I cringed looking at pictures of the "Zulu warriors" and read about how Cody was apparently very "forward thinking" on race and gender in his time—being a white man who was not afraid to pay the women and people of color who performed in his show (never mind that he paid them less than the white men). The magic just . . . wasn't there for me. But then again, I'm pretty sure that I—as a liberal Black Seattleite who has no dreams of riding horses, shooting guns, or performing any acts of physical bravery or adventure at any time in my life—was not the target audience for this exhibit.

At the end of my time in the museum I almost passed by a display that was not nearly as flashy as the others. On a wall set slightly apart from the rest of the exhibits hung a set of black-and-white photographs. I took a closer look at one of the photos and I saw skulls. Thousands and thousands of buffalo skulls. Buffalo skulls piled dozens of feet high. White men proudly standing on mountains of buffalo carcasses. It was a series of photos acknowledging the massacre of buffalo by white hunters. Surrounding the photos were quotes from Native people lamenting the devastation as their beloved buffalo were hunted nearly to extinction.

Buffalo were a primary food source, but they were more than just food to the Plains Indians. The entirety of the buffalo was integral to their way of life. Bones were used for knives, skin was used for clothing and shelter, dried dung was used as fuel, sinew was used for bowstrings, horns and hooves were used as cups. And the connection to buffalo was not just physical; it was also spiritual. The Lakota view their nation as a sister nation to the Buffalo nation. Oglala Sioux leader Red Cloud tried to explain the importance of the buffalo to Roosevelt in 1903. "We told them that the buffalo must have their country and the Lakota must have the buffalo," he recalled.[22]

There were an estimated thirty to sixty million buffalo in America at the beginning of the nineteenth century. By 1900, there were only around three hundred. Many of those few remaining buffalo were found in Cody's *Wild West* show, where he staged his great buffalo hunts, proclaiming them the "last of the only known Native herd." Crowds came from all over to gaze at the remaining few of the great beasts. Cody would later be praised for helping lead buffalo-conservation efforts by keeping American interest in the animals alive through his shows.[23] The man who earned his name by killing buffalo is now honored for his commitment to their survival.

Other quirks of history abound in the *Wild West* show. When I first read about the scenes in which Native people were portrayed as naïve savages tricked into violence against white people by scheming Mormons, I was amused and a bit confused. The story sounded like a rather ridiculous—and oddly specific—tale of white-on-white crime. Why Mormons? Why were they attacking other white people? Why did they need to trick Natives into doing their dirty work for them? I chuckled to myself at how very outlandish the *Wild West* show must have been and wondered what sort of white people would have been entertained by such tales. But as I was researching the history of Mormon fundamentalism in the West, I came across an event that may well have been the basis for the *Wild West* stories—even if the reality was far too gruesome for any stage reproduction.

In 1857 the Baker-Fancher party, a group of white Christians, was making its way west from Arkansas in a wagon train. When they arrived in the Utah territory, they immediately began to clash with Mormon settlers, who had moved to the territory a few years earlier in hopes of establishing a homeland away from the religious persecution they had experienced back east. After years of being chased from state to state by angry and bigoted Christians, the Mormons were wary of outsiders and perhaps a little quick to the gun. This new land was to be their Zion, and they were required by God to protect it.

By the accounts that exist, the Baker-Fancher party felt that the land was theirs to use as well. They grazed their animals on pasture already claimed by Mormon families. They refilled their water from rivers that the Mormons believed were their own.

The Mormons had an uneasy relationship at best with the Paiute people. They occupied the Natives' land, but they still convinced local Paiutes to help them scare off the Baker-Fancher party with the promise that they'd get to keep whatever livestock was left behind. I imagine that one colonizer was the same as the other to the Paiutes, and so some agreed to join the assault to at least earn some cattle out of the deal.

The Mormons, who darkened their faces with paint in an attempt to blend in with the Paiutes, launched their attack on September 7, 1857. It was supposed to be a quick ordeal—they would shoot a few interlopers who would then run away and leave the Mormons to the land they had rightfully stolen, and if anyone came asking, the entire thing could be blamed on the Paiutes. But the Baker-Fancher party did not run away, even though they were outnumbered. Fueled with the fervor of Manifest Destiny, just as the Mormons were filled with religious zeal, the Baker-Fancher party dug in for a fight. As the days dragged on, many of the Paiutes who had been promised a quick profit of cattle abandoned the battle, seeing that it was not worth the trouble.

Now, with fewer Natives to blame the attack on, the Mormons decided that the risk of being identified as the attackers was too high. The Mormons raised the white flag, calling for a cease-fire. The Baker-Fancher party laid down their weapons and came out of their shelters. They were then shot and hacked to death. James Lynch, a migrant traveling through Mountain Meadows a year after the massacre, documented the grizzly sight left behind: "Human skeletons, disjointed bones, ghastly skulls, and the hair of women were scattered in frightful profusion over a distance of two miles."[24] Every person over the age of six—120 innocent people in total—was brutally murdered in what is now known as the Mountain Meadows Massacre. The surviving children were kidnapped by Mormon families.

Only one of the attackers would face justice, a man named John Lee. Nephi Johnson, a Mormon who was at the Mountain Meadows Massacre, would testify that he saw Lee and "the Indians" murder the Baker-Fancher party. He testified that he himself hadn't taken part in any killing and couldn't recall seeing any other Mormons take part in the killing.[25] Lee, in a long and very detailed confession, stated that "the Indians" who participated in the massacre were recruited by Nephi Johnson himself, and that they, Lee, and many other Mormon men had massacred the Baker-Fancher party on direct order of Mormon leaders who told them to "*decoy* the emigrants from their position, and kill all of them that could talk."[26]

In 1877, twenty years after the massacre, John Lee was found guilty and shot by a firing squad. Despite his testimony of innocence, Nephi Johnson would be forever haunted by what happened on Mountain Meadows. On his deathbed, Johnson asked a young writer to hear his confession. But when she arrived, all he could do was scream, "Blood, blood, blood" over and over.[27]

In the story of the Mountain Meadows Massacre lies the tale of the battle for the West. White men battling other white men for land that was never theirs, leaving nothing but destruction in their wake. This pattern of entitlement and destruction would repeat itself in future generations all across the West, and would grab headlines in 2016 when two brothers, Ammon and Ryan Bundy, walked into the offices of the Malheur Wildlife Refuge, carrying rifles and thousands of rounds of ammunition, and decided to claim it for their own.

## WHOSE AMERICA? THE BUNDY BROTHERS VS. THE FEDERAL GOVERNMENT

Cliven Bundy is proud to trace his lineage back to Nephi Johnson. Johnson, who adopted Bundy's grandfather John Jensen, is Cliven's proof of his claim to the land around his ranch in

Bunkerville, Utah. His adoptive great-grandfather came to the West in search of a uniquely American dream that at times placed Mormon settlers in direct conflict with the US government and often caused them to see themselves as different from "Americans," the non-Mormon whites who had persecuted them and forced them West.

As the Mormon migrants claimed the territory of the Paiute people, their fierce antigovernment stance and religious devotion to protecting their claims to the land would merge with images of the ferociously independent Western cowboy. While Mormon settlers were mocked and villainized in *Buffalo Bill's Wild West*, you would be hard-pressed to find men in the present day who better fit the archetype of a Western cowboy than the Bundys and their rancher community.

Cliven Bundy had been raised in the independent American spirit, and he brought up his sons with the same insistence on being free from outside interference and from relying on the government. He also instilled in his sons the willingness to suffer—and make everyone else around them suffer—in order to maintain their independence.

Cliven's son Ryan's first political protest was in the third grade. The target of his protest was his own mother. Cliven had lost money on some cattle, and the family was having trouble making ends meet. To ease their burden, Cliven's wife, Jane, signed up their five children for subsidized school lunch. Ryan, who had been taught by his father to never accept government handouts, refused to eat. In remembering the protest, Ryan stated that it reinforced the lesson that "we're supposed to earn what we have and not to take from others."[28] Each day he sat quietly outside and refused to join his classmates at lunch. After three days, Ryan's mother relented and began making lunches from home again.

Nothing says "American" like a boy making a woman struggle so that he can seem independent.

Cliven is not only against government handouts; he is also against government fees—especially from the federal government. He is a fierce opponent of federal grazing restrictions and fees and has counted the federal Bureau of Land Management (BLM) as an enemy for decades. He stopped paying the grazing fees for his cattle in the 1990s. His opposition to the BLM is both religious and personal. Cliven is part of a small sect of Mormons who believe that the Constitution was evidence of a divine plan to restore Zion in the United States. This is a warped patriotism that has designated them as the true interpreters of and heirs to American destiny. They believe that the Constitution invalidates any federal claim to land in the United States outside Washington, D.C. This appears to be a willful misreading of the Constitution, one that the Mormon church itself has rejected.[29] Nevertheless, a sizeable minority of Western Mormons believe that the Constitution proves that the federal government has stolen land that is rightfully theirs, and that any grazing fees are just further theft. When you add in a religious duty to defend land that the Bundys and other Mormons believe is Zion, you get a fierce opposition to any other entity claiming authority over the land.

While the religious aspect of the Bundys' opposition to the federal government might cause many to dismiss them as isolated zealots or weirdos, to do so would be a mistake. Antigovernment beliefs, and the specific belief that the federal government doesn't have the right to dictate land use, are shared among many in the West—Mormon and non-Mormon. The Bundys themselves would show the rest of the country just how popular their opposition to the federal government is.

"When I went to visit the Bundys in 2015, I thought they were sort of an anomaly—an isolated family with radical beliefs that were launching this little regional war," Betsy Gaines Quammen, a Western historian and conservationist who has written the book *American Zion: Cliven Bundy, God, and Public Lands in the West,* told me over the phone. "I'm really surprised at how explosive these ideas have become. It's everywhere now."[30]

The Bundys first rose to notoriety in 2014. After years of Cliven Bundy grazing his cattle on public lands without paying his grazing fees, and after many warnings, the federal government notified Cliven that it was going to round up his illegally grazing cattle and confiscate them.

The Bundy family rallied around Cliven as government trucks rolled into Bunkerville. When Cliven's fifty-seven-year-old sister Margaret Houston tried to block one of the BLM's vehicles, she was thrown to the ground by a BLM officer. The officer's violent actions were caught on video, which went viral online.

Once the footage of a federal officer throwing a white woman to the ground on his way to confiscate a white man's cattle reached other antigovernment groups, "patriot" groups, and militia groups, hundreds of people flocked to Bunkerville to support the Bundys. On April 12, 2014, the Bundy family led hundreds of armed supporters to the federal government's holding pen for the Bundy cattle. They set up armed sniper positions and erected roadblocks. They were, according to Cliven, "ready to do battle."[31] BLM officers, seeing that they were on the edge of a very bloody fight, backed down—leaving the Bundys to reclaim their cattle. The Bundys celebrated their victory and immediately became heroes to whites who held antigovernment sentiments—individuals, militias, and white supremacist groups—throughout the West.

Antigovernment sentiment had thrived throughout the rural West since the time of Nephi Johnson. But the election of Barack Obama to the presidency caused an explosion in popularity of white nationalist and antigovernment groups in the region. People could mask their racist discomfort with a Black president behind a general distrust of the government and a "patriotic" desire to take America "back to its roots." Cliven himself may believe that he is purely motivated by faith, his desire for independence, and his dedication to a misguided interpretation of the US Constitution, but it appears to be very hard for him to hide the racism that informs his beliefs.

In describing his beliefs to a *New York Times* reporter, Cliven went on a long racist tirade, opening with, "I want to tell you one more thing I know about the Negro," which is never a good start. He dug up the common racist tropes about Blacks with nothing better to do than crowd welfare offices. "They abort their young children, they put their young men in jail, because they never learned how to pick cotton," he ranted. In case anyone might have been wondering if they heard Cliven right and he was as racist as he sounds, he added, "I've often wondered, are they better off as slaves, picking cotton and having a family life and doing things, or are they better off under government subsidy? They didn't get no more freedom. They got less freedom."[32]

Anyway, the Bundys and the rest of the white, antigovernment sector of the West celebrated Cliven's victory over the feds—a victory so decisive, they were downright cocky about it. After the feds abandoned their posts to deescalate the confrontation, Cliven demanded that local law enforcement turn over the BLM officers' weapons to them.[33] He felt confident that the feds had been scared away for a while. "They don't have the guts enough to try to start that again for a few years," he said. And he was right. It would be two years before Cliven would face any consequences for his actions.

But Cliven's sons Ryan and Ammon were not content to wait for the feds to come back. Fueled by their victory over the BLM, the Bundy brothers were looking for the next opportunity to take on the federal government. They found it in the 2015 case of the Hammonds.

Like Cliven Bundy, Dwight Hammond had a long-standing dispute with the BLM, mainly over grazing access to the Malheur National Wildlife Refuge in Oregon. The 188,000-acre Malheur refuge required grazing permits in order to take cattle over the protected land, and Hammond, whose property bordered the refuge, greatly resented the inconvenience. Not only did Hammond flagrantly disregard the need for a permit; he also regularly sent the refuge staff threatening letters promising to "pack a shotgun in his saddle and no one will challenge me!" as he took his cattle through the refuge. He even cut holes through the refuge fence to let his cattle through.[34]

The BLM put up with Hammond's antics for the most part, sending him letters and fines but otherwise leaving him alone, until he and his son Steven started setting fires. The Hammonds claim that they were lighting small fires on their land as part of wildfire prevention, but that they lost control of them. The government maintains that the Hammonds were setting fires to cover up their illegal hunting on the refuge. Two fires that the Hammonds set spread beyond their property onto public land—which is extremely dangerous and potentially catastrophic in a region known for its hot and dry climate. The Hammonds were arrested and charged with arson. After they were found guilty, a sympathetic judge sentenced father and son to relatively short sentences of three months and one year, respectively. The US Justice Department appealed the short sentences, and the Hammonds were given new, five-year sentences by a different judge.[35]

The Bundys and many in the ranching and antigovernment community were outraged at the perceived injustice of the Hammonds' sentences. Ammon and Ryan Bundy felt called to take their battle with the federal government to Harney County in Oregon in support of the Hammonds.

The Bundy brothers gathered supporters from all over Washington, Oregon, and Idaho. On January 2, 2016, they converged on Burns, a town near Malheur, for a rally in support of the Hammonds. Without warning, Ammon Bundy and a small group of supporters left the rest of the group and headed to the wildlife refuge. Ammon and his armed crew occupied the refuge offices. The rest of the Hammond supporters—including Ammon's brother Ryan—were surprised and confused by the change of plan. Ammon would later explain that he had been called to Malheur by God. The next day, Ammon posted a video from Malheur stating that they planned to occupy the refuge for the next several years. Ammon and Ryan issued a list of demands, including that the federal government allow ranchers to return to historical grazing practices (basically just grazing wherever and whenever they wanted to), abolish the grazing permit system, and turn over the Malheur refuge to the county. In the video, Ammon summoned other antigovernment groups and supporters to arm themselves and join the fight: "We are calling people to come out here and stand."[36]

Antigovernment groups, militias, white supremacist groups— basically all your angriest of white men—flocked to Malheur to join the struggle. Soon, the locals found their towns overrun with heavily armed strangers, federal officers, and news camera crews. Locals were not happy to be caught in the middle of the standoff, and the Hammonds themselves were not exactly excited about this "help" that they hadn't asked for. The Mormon church publicly condemned the Bundys' actions. But Ammon and Ryan didn't care. For weeks they camped out in the refuge offices, basking in their righteousness and the media attention.

The occupation came to an end shortly after LaVoy Finicum, one of the Malheur occupiers, was killed in a confrontation with federal law enforcement on the way from Malheur to a local rally. Finicum, author of the apocalyptic novel *Only by Blood and Suffering: Regaining Lost Freedom*, was shot on January 26, 2016, shortly after he was recorded on video shouting at officers, "You want a bloodbath? It's going to be on your hands."[37] Officers maintain that Finicum was shot while reaching for a gun. Ryan Bundy was injured at the scene and arrested. Ammon was arrested shortly after.

A few days later, Cliven Bundy was arrested while trying to board a plane to Oregon to join the fight with his sons. On February 12, forty-one days after Ammon first marched his armed group into the Malheur offices, the last holdouts at the reserve surrendered to authorities, and the standoff was over. Law enforcement officers confiscated dozens of guns and over sixteen thousand rounds of ammunition from the site.

Members of "patriot" groups such as the Oath Keepers and the Three Percenters would come from throughout the region to attend Finicum's funeral. He was laid in an open casket, with an American flag draped across his chest.[38]

The Bundys faced multiple charges from both the Malheur refuge takeover and the armed standoff with the feds in Bunkerville two years earlier. The charges were numerous, but the government still had to make its case against the Bundys in court. Instead of freedom fighters, the government maintained that the Bundys were freeloaders. Even though the Bundys enjoyed grazing rights at pennies on the dollar of what the rights would cost if they were leasing private land, they wanted to use and abuse the American landscape for free. The BLM wasn't exactly known as a group of strict conservationists—actual conservationists often said that "BLM" stood for the "Bureau of Livestock and Mining" because of the extent to which the bureau allowed cattle grazing, logging, and mining on protected lands.[39] But despite the low fee and lax rules, the Bundys still sought to violate the scant laws protecting public lands because they felt it was theirs. Further, the Bundys decided on a violent takeover of federal offices in support of two arsonists—a takeover that shut down the Malheur reserve and disrupted the lives of thousands of townspeople for weeks, as well as costing one man his life.

As justified as the federal government believed it was, the first trial against the Bundys—this one for the Malheur takeover—was a disaster. The state bungled evidence and relied too heavily on a hard-to-prove conspiracy charge. In addition, documented anti-Mormon sentiment from BLM officials severely undermined the credibility of the feds' case. On October 27, 2016, the Bundys were acquitted of all charges relating to the Malheur occupation. When they were not immediately released from custody, their lawyer, Marcus R. Mumford, threw a fit and had to be restrained by four US marshals.[40]

The second trial against the Bundys, for their role in the Bunkerville standoff, ended in a hung jury in January 2018. After two years in jail awaiting the conclusion of their trials, the Bundys were free and victorious. Two weeks after Cliven Bundy was freed, he was giving antigovernment speeches in Paradise, Montana. Ryan and Ammon have both been sought-after speakers throughout the West since their release.

Later in 2018, President Donald Trump—who counts many antigovernment, angry white men among his political base—pardoned the Hammonds. As a final insult, the Hammonds' grazing rights were restored. The Trump administration has filled BLM leadership with antiregulation, antienvironmental cronies. In the years since the Bundys were released, BLM oversight of public lands in the West has decreased sharply—with many environmentally sensitive regions left completely to the whims of ranchers.

When I asked her about the consequences of ranchers being allowed free rein over public lands, Betsy Gaines Quammen lamented, "In terms of changing the ecosystem—the water quality is damaged, there's overgrazing and erosion, wildlife species are extirpated. It's really trashing the land." Amid this environmental destruction, the Bundys and other antigovernment groups and militias look for a stage for their next battle.

"The militia movement right now is shopping for a cause, and this pardon means that their focus will likely return to public-land politics," said JJ MacNab, a fellow at George Washington University's Program on Extremism.[41]

Quammen agrees. "Right now, we have social media, so these stories are being told over and over again, and the reach of these militia networks is huge," she explained to me. "They are growing, and they are feeling more empowered. They have people in authority that are either actively supporting them, or you have people who are kind of looking the other way."

And so, while many in our government still see "Black identity extremists" as a top threat to national security, the heavily armed and violent white militias and antigovernment groups continue to grow throughout the West. Their battle with the federal government in their quest for unfettered power for white men will likely only increase as they are emboldened and even aided by sympathetic politicians and government officials.

Lost in this battle between white men is the fact that neither the ranchers nor the federal government has the right to the land around Bunkerville or the Malheur refuge.

For centuries, the land of the region was lived on and tended to by the Paiute nations. It may be clichéd to say that they lived in harmony with the land, but they certainly knew better than to try to graze cattle in the hot, dry desert. The Paiute people followed the buffalo and other wild food sources through this terrain. Their land-management practices ensured that food would be abundant and that the landscape was protected. (In fact, the current recommended practice of setting controlled light burns to prevent larger forest fires in high-risk areas was for many decades dismissed by white Americans as "Paiute forestry.")[42]

The land was promised to the Paiute people by the federal government in 1872. But the government had no interest in keeping white colonizers from settling there. The Paiute people took their grievances to the US government, and they were rebuffed. White settlers were incredulous that the Paiutes thought they had any right to the land. An editorial in the *Idaho Statesman* summed up the popular opinion toward Native claims on land: "The idea that the Indians have any right to the soil is ridiculous. . . . They have no more right to the soil of the Territories of the United States than wolves or coyotes."[43]

Tensions boiled over into open conflict, starting the Bannock War in 1878. The US government used the fight as an excuse to round up the Paiute people and ship them to a reservation in eastern Washington, claiming their millions of acres of land for white America. The remaining Paiute population was decimated by Mormon adoption programs, which took over forty thousand Native children from their families and placed them in Mormon households.[44] When the Bundys took over the Malheur refuge in 2016 and damaged many priceless Paiute artifacts housed there, nobody besides the Paiute people remaining in the area seemed to care, just as few non-Native people seem to care about the damage currently being done to the land the Paiute have called home for hundreds of years.

"I could go to the Bundys where his grandparents are buried," said Jarvis Kennedy, the Paiute tribal council's sergeant at arms, when he was asked how the Paiute people felt about seeing video of Bundy's clan rifling through their sacred artifacts. "How would they feel if I drove over their grave and went through their heirlooms?"[45]

Present-day ranchers like the Bundys are living the Buffalo Bill fantasy of the West: white men, free to do what they please. Ravaging the environment, exploiting and erasing Native people, and pulling a gun on anyone who stands in their way. The idealized American cowboy has been woven through the fabric of American culture, and its impact is keenly felt. The *Wild West* stage shows morphed into Western movies that glorified the tough and noble white man against racist depictions of Native and Hispanic people. The story of the struggle and victory of white colonizers worked its way into school history books, both erasing the crimes committed against Native people and cementing an idea of American heroism that centered on white male power.

The story of the cowboy acted out by stage performers like William Cody also created a persona that white men seeking power could adopt in order to project an image for the American public to relate to. Just as it helped Roosevelt in remaking himself and getting elected, the idea of the cowboy as an honest everyman played a large part in the iconography that made George W. Bush so popular with white men in his presidential campaigns, even if his elite family background spoke to an upbringing that was far from rough and tumble (something he has in common with Roosevelt, after all). Even for those who will never don a cowboy hat, the idea of a white man going it alone against the world has stuck. It is one of the strongest identifiers of American culture and politics, where cooperation is weakness and others are the enemy—to be stolen from or conquered. The devastation that the mythological cowboy of the West has wreaked did not stop with the extermination of the buffalo. It may not stop until it has destroyed everything.

CHAPTER 2

# FOR YOUR BENEFIT, IN OUR IMAGE

## *The Centering of White Men in Social Justice Movements*

A few years ago I found myself at a vegan restaurant/punk music bar in one of the whitest areas of Seattle. I didn't know anybody in the audience except for the one friend whom I had dragged along with me. I didn't see another Black person in the room. I stayed the entire night and even ate a vegan dinner.

Why, you may be asking, was I putting myself through this? I was there to support a comedian. A white, male, vegan, punk rock–singing comedian. If you are guessing that this is not my typical sort of comedy, you would be right. But I was happily there.

I was there because in a sea of white male comedians making jokes in which women and people of color were the punchlines, this dude was making jokes in which those dudes were the punchlines. He mocked the white dudes who couldn't seem to figure out what consent meant. He made fun of the white dudes who believed that brown people were our nation's biggest threat and global warming was a hoax. He got out his guitar and sang songs about these men's fears of their own inadequacy. I, and many others, was grateful to see in his shows evidence that maybe white men didn't have to be so bad.

Occupying this unique space, he was able to build a name for himself. His shows sold well, his radio show was popular, and he was often asked to be a commentator on progressive issues—especially those surrounding feminism.

It is probably less shocking to you than it was to me to find out that this comedian was actually bad. Very bad. First one woman came forward with a story of abuse, then another. Then more stories of sexual impropriety, and just general asshole, misogynist behavior. When we looked to him to explain the allegations, he disappeared.

To those of us who had supported him, the entire situation was both heartbreaking and embarrassing. It was heartbreaking because we had trusted him, and that trust was violated. It was embarrassing because, well—when we really thought about it—he was never really that funny. His jokes were basic, often consisting of nothing more than angry screeds with no punchline. His music was . . . not good. If you ever wondered, "What if Bob Dylan's less poetic brother were a self-righteous, mediocre comedian who tried to get into punk rock?"—this guy would answer your question. Often his jokes and songs spent more time basking in self-glorification about not being one of the "bad guys" than talking about the actual bad guys or their victims. And yet, at the time, we had eaten it up. We were that desperate for a white man to not be trash that we treated mediocrity like it was a masterpiece.

When I brought up this comedian to my brother, he simply groaned and said, "Ugh. I can't believe I once played in his shitty band."

We all had egg on our faces.

A few months after disappearing from the social world, the comedian was back. He had a new schtick, though. He was the "anti-PC" comedian who would talk about how extreme feminism and "wokeness" were the enemy, indistinguishable in their harm from the racism and sexism he once lambasted. He was welcomed into the alt-right/men's-rights activist world with open arms.

Plenty of women have met the "male feminist" who can quote bell hooks but will use those quotes to speak over you. Plenty of people of color have met the white antiracist who is all for Dr. King's dream until people of color start asking white people to make actual sacrifices for racial justice. Ego can undermine even the best of intentions, but often, when things like this happen— when someone we trust as an ally ends up taking advantage of their position and then turning against the principles they once claimed to fight for when that abuse is discovered—we find that the intentions were never that great in the first place.

Whiteness and masculinity are two identities that are built almost exclusively as the inverse of that which their identities oppress. Where whiteness is smart, Blackness is dumb. Where whiteness is successful, Blackness is a failure. Where masculinity is strong, femininity is weak. Where masculinity is analytical, femininity is emotional.

Identities that are oppressed and constrained by whiteness and/or masculinity struggle to free themselves from their oppressors in order to develop independence. The greatest risks to identities of color or womanhood in a white supremacist patriarchy are the white supremacy and patriarchy that seek to control them. There-fore, the amount of safety, security, and freedom that people of color and women (and other nonmale identities) are able to obtain lies in the extent to which they can gain social, political, and fi-nancial independence from patriarchy or white supremacy.

Whiteness and masculinity are threatened both where their sta-tion or behavior begins to approach that expected of Blackness and femininity, and where Blackness or femininity strays from its expected role and no longer serves as a direct contrast to whiteness and masculinity. These dual constraints are important to realize, because while whiteness and masculinity are the two most power-ful identities in a white male patriarchy, they are also wholly de-pendent on the identities they oppress.

Whiteness is not only threatened when it takes on too many traits of identities of color; it is also threatened when communities of color cease to stay below whiteness, where society's scripts say they belong. A white family may feel threatened not only when their daughter brings a Black man home for dinner (breaking from what is expected of her as a white person), but also if that Black man makes the same wage as her father (breaking from the expectations of Blackness that whiteness depends on). The same is true for masculinity. Men may feel threatened not only when their sons declare their love of the color pink, but also when their daughters choose monster trucks over dolls.

Much of this is subconscious, because the mechanisms of whiteness and masculinity are so rarely critically examined. But the feelings of threat to white male identity often make white men act in ways that are counter to their stated morals and beliefs.

So what happens when a white man decides to take up a cause that will directly threaten his identity as a white man? Well, sometimes he will subconsciously work to maintain his position above those he is trying to "help" by elevating himself even further above them with his selfless deeds, by recentering the goals of the group to maintain his social and political power, or by quietly exploiting or abusing individuals he is claiming to help—or perhaps a combination of the three. Sometimes this is the conscious goal of the white man in joining these efforts from the very beginning. Such men are predators. But often these men are completely unaware of their hypocrisy because they are not doing anything out of the ordinary by centering themselves when they've always been centered, or by taking advantage of those who have always been taken advantage of—they're just living according to the norms of society.

But ultimately, if a white man's abuses are discovered and he's no longer able to freely center himself or to elevate himself above those he feels entitled to oppress, he will often completely reject his previous declarations of allyship. When challenged, he will go back to the open misogyny and racism that will always put him first.

## THE EARLY MALE FEMINISTS

Feminism has never been perfect. Even before suffragettes marched the streets in the nineteenth century, feminism has been working out its kinks, only to come up with new ones. We know about the racism, about how early feminists were quick to sell out their Black allies and trade on fears of a fully emancipated Black population in order to try to get the right to vote before Black people. But there are also the classism, the ableism, the transphobia, queerphobia, femmephobia, and a healthy dose of internalized misogyny—just to get the list started. No social justice movement is perfect. Of course one as broad as "equality for women" is going to have myriad different and often competing ideas.

And even in our social justice movements, we will easily replicate many of the oppressive social constructs we've been subjected to—especially when those concepts are deemed "outside" the core focus of the movement. But over generations, feminism has grown and changed. There is still what is called "white feminism"—the tendency for white feminists to center themselves at the expense of women of color—but at least now we have a name for it. And in naming it, we can think about how to move beyond it. Dr. Kimberlé Crenshaw gave us the term "intersectionality" and a framework to bring our feminism into a more inclusive and less harmful space. While we debate what issues we should prioritize, how to avoid harm, and what exactly our end goals are, we also continue to steadfastly push for fundamental issues like ending pay discrimination, interpersonal violence, and sexual assault.

We've agreed and disagreed. We've stood in solidarity by the hundreds of thousands in marches. We've undercut each other when we needed support the most. It is hard to be a woman, and at times it can be even harder to be a feminist woman. And in the midst of it all, we still have to deal with dudes. The dudes who don't want us to have political power. The dudes who don't want us to have jobs. The dudes who don't want us to feel safe. The shitty dudes.

But there are good guys. The male feminists who have read *Sister Outsider* and wear their "This is what a feminist looks like" T-shirts. And they seem really great. Except when they are interrupting us in group discussion, or telling us what they think we should read to become better feminists like them, or trying to sleep with all our friends. And if you look at these good guys and wonder, "Were they always this shitty?" Yes. Yes they were.

Not all male feminists are shitty, but all of them—like all of us—have internalized misogyny that they are (or are not) working through. And working with these men while they process their misogyny can be annoying, harmful, and sometimes downright impossible. It's hard enough with the men who genuinely want to do better, even if their mere existence gives one hope that we might be making progress. But there are also some dudes who clearly got into this whole feminism thing because in it they saw a new opportunity for personal gain. These dudes can do a lot of damage to feminist movements and the women they interact with there, and the ones who can do the most damage are often white men (not because shitty men of color don't exist in feminist movements, but because men of color usually lack the social and political power that allows white men to make everything about themselves).

Although we might think that "woke" bros are a new phenomenon, they've actually been taking credit for feminist ideas and taking up space in feminist circles since there was feminism. Consider Greenwich Village in the early twentieth century. Writer-activists Floyd Dell and Max Eastman were at the center of a new movement in the 1910s: socialist feminism. Born of an elite bohemian age, it melded the desire for female social and political power with the free-love experimentation of the art world and the socialist struggle against capitalist exploitation.

The brother of prominent socialist feminist Crystal Eastman, Max Eastman was a natural fit for this world. Tall, physically attractive, and with the added distinction of prematurely white hair, Eastman turned heads. Once he had your attention, his words were eloquent, passionate, persuasive. He never wasted an opportunity to showcase his sharp intellect and elite education. Eastman was known to be "irresistibly charming, even when on the offensive."[1] He was soon known as one of "the hottest of the radicals" of his time.[2] Floyd Dell was slighter in build and dark-haired, raised in the Midwest rather than on the East Coast. He didn't have the brashness of his friend; instead, he was equipped with the quiet confidence of a self-taught writer. Dell was not, however, a dull sidekick. He had a talent for organizing writers and thinkers, and he was known for his many love affairs with women in the bohemian crowd.[3] Both men were introduced to socialist feminism by women—notably Crystal Eastman and Ida Rauh (whom Eastman would later marry). The new movement deeply appealed to Dell and Eastman; they wanted to demonstrate to other men why they should be socialist feminists as well.

Eastman and Dell had a problem with the patriarchy. And while today we may easily talk in some circles about toxic masculinity and the ways in which the patriarchy hurts men and boys by pulling them away from their true selves in favor of an artificial masculine ideal, there weren't a lot of men who were openly voicing dissatisfaction with the patriarchy in 1910. But Eastman and Dell's problem with the patriarchy was a little different than the issues we talk about today. Socialist feminism—at least how Eastman and Dell understood it—rested on the concept that capitalism was not only exploiting women; more importantly, it was turning them into exploiters of men. By forcing women to depend on men for the financial well-being of themselves and their children, patriarchy was trapping men in the vice of capitalist exploitation. There was no way for men to be free, they argued, if women were not free.

The solution to this problem, Eastman and Dell maintained, was the deconstruction of capitalist exploitation and the removal of the sexist societal restrictions that prevented women from entering the workplace—and carrying their own financial weight. While many feminists today recognize that the restrictions on women in the workplace actually aided capitalism in the exploitation of their labor for the direct benefit of men (why pay women at all when you can make them work for free in the home to provide bedrock support for our economy?), Eastman and Dell saw women's freedom only as a means to men's freedom. Women, the notion went, were the oppressors of men, who were kept in wage slavery.

And what did freedom look like to Eastman and Dell? A lot of what seemed to appeal to their vision of a feminist future revolved around their dicks.

Socialist feminism would be great for men, Dell and Eastman argued at length in many essays with titles like "The Emancipation of Man."[4] Women, obviously intellectually disadvantaged by the capitalist patriarchy, would become more intelligent and interesting in a socialist feminist society. Freed from sexist ideas of marriage and propriety, women would also become more sexual. Imagine: intelligent, beautiful (and yes, Dell and Eastman regularly voiced assumptions that these women would be beautiful), highly sexual women that you could have sex with, make babies with—even make conversation with—without having to buy them dinner?

I am, of course, being slightly reductive here to make a point. Dell and Eastman were on the right side of a lot of feminist issues. They spoke up for women's suffrage and birth control, for civil rights, for people of color. But they also really, *really* liked the idea of feminism that offered them sex with women who were "not like other women," and they used these promises repeatedly to try to recruit other men to socialist feminism. And both men hoped to find the feminist marriages that would bring them their own personal utopias.

For years, Dell had searched for a wife who would fulfill his socialist feminist fantasies and thought he had found her in Margery Curry. Curry was an older woman, experienced, a respected feminist with her own income. The two wed in 1909. Dell was by all accounts very happy at first. Curry was intelligent, connected, and a great wit. But Dell wasn't very physically attracted to her. At least not as much as he was to other, younger, more adoring women.

Luckily for Dell, he was in a liberated marriage. This meant he could have affairs. And boy, did he. Dell quickly fell in love with another woman, and then another, and another. Each time, his wife (whose idea of a liberated marriage did not seem to include lies and infidelity) would be heartbroken. She even offered to divorce him. But Dell didn't want a divorce, as for some reason this marriage with an unhappy woman that he didn't love and wasn't physically attracted to was still working for him.[5] Curry endured

Dell's affairs for years. When he found himself sleeping with not one but two of his friends' wives, he decided that perhaps remaining in a loveless marriage was complicating his life a bit too much. After four years of marriage, Dell left his wife in search of a more fulfilling love.[6]

Max Eastman's marriage had started out even more promisingly than his friend's had. After a long search for the right woman to begin his sexual and intellectual adventures with, Eastman found his partner in Ida Rauh—feminist, artist, socialist, and friend of his sister Crystal. Rauh introduced Max to her socialist friends and helped deepen his understanding of Marxism and feminist theory. They were married in 1911, and Rauh gave birth to their son the next year.

There were a few problems early on. The first was that, although Rauh was the feminist and independent artist and thinker Max was looking for, she didn't seem to adore him enough. She was critical of him, "stingy with praise," and gave him "no admiration at all." The second problem was that Eastman immediately discovered that he (like Dell) wanted to have sex with other women—and girls (apparently one of his first temptations was his seventeen-year-old neighbor, a girl he had watched grow up. Eastman was twenty-seven at the time).[7]

Eastman moved through multiple affairs and, like Dell, was disappointed to find that his wife was not nearly as enthusiastic about his dalliances as he was. Max and Ida separated for a time and then tried living in the same house but with separate quarters. Ida remained unhappy with Max's continued affairs. Max had dedicated so much time and energy to the idea of socialist feminism, and yet here he was, unhappily stuck with a wife and kid.

This chapter in history is not only about how two self-proclaimed male feminists ended up being shitty husbands. They were also kind of shitty feminist leaders. Max Eastman was a founder of the New York Men's League for Woman Suffrage, which sounds pretty cool, right? However, one of the first things Eastman did was make a promise to the men who signed up that "no member would be called upon to do anything. The main function of the league would be to exist."[8] In the battle for women's suffrage, in which women literally fought and died, men become heroes by simply existing.

At the helm of the socialist magazine *The Masses* (founded by the Eastman siblings) and later *The Liberator*, Eastman and Dell provided a platform for socialist feminist writers and thinkers to share their vision of a new future. A lot of great writers and thinkers were published in *The Masses*, like Mary Heaton Vorse and even Langston Hughes. But as editor, when Dell did publish women, he tended to focus on the work of women who he thought exemplified *his* ideal feminism. And that feminism was not nearly as concerned with economic or political rights as it was with sexual and artistic liberation. Dell and Eastman weren't shy about critiquing the politics of other women. Dell wrote about his favorite feminists in his book *Women as World Builders*, in which he differentiated between the women he viewed as serious feminists—those who theorized about how much the world needed to change—and the "courtesans," who were only interested in finding their personal joy. Both Dell and Eastman wrote at length about how feminism would benefit men, but if women focused more on advancing their own needs and causes, the two men openly disapproved.

Eastman and Dell did not see any hypocrisy in critiquing the looks or personalities of their female peers. Both men were huge fans of the dancer Isadora Duncan, who focused on liberating dance from the rigid confines of ballet. Her celebration of the woman's body was certainly a feminism they could appreciate and enjoy. When Duncan was not onstage, however, Eastman found her "didactic" and "assertive."[9] Dell described feminist writer Cornelia Barns as an "elf eyed girl" who "came through the door of The Masses like a child into a playroom."[10]

Their ideal feminist was a woman who was sexually and intellectually liberated for the pleasure of men like Dell and Eastman. She would be beautiful and pliable—open to the teachings of feminist men. In an article for *The Masses* titled "Feminism for Men," Dell wrote not of how patriarchy took away women's agency or denied them economic and political freedom, but of how it made "sweethearts" into "wives"—depriving men of exciting romantic relationships:

> First observe what it means to be a sweetheart. . . . She is not shut out from his society by reason of differences in habits or tastes. The assumption is that their habits and tastes ought to be alike. If she doesn't understand baseball, he explains it to her. If he likes golf, he teaches her how to play. If he loves poetry, he sits up and reads her his favorite poets. . . . If she has been brought up with the idea that it is wicked to drink, he will cultivate her taste in cocktails. He will give her lessons in Socialism, poetry, and poker, all with infinite tact and patience. . . .
>
> When you have got a woman in a box, and you pay rent on the box, her relationship to you insensibly changes character.
>
> When she has left that box and gone back into the great world, a citizen and a worker, then with surprise and delight he will discover her again, and never let her go.[11]

In the end it was marriage that caused Dell to leave feminism behind and join the ranks of the antifeminists. After leaving his unhappy marriage and pursuing various unsatisfying love affairs, Dell was beginning to think that new women weren't for him. He didn't want to marry a woman with her own dreams and passions—at least not dreams or passions that didn't revolve around him. He wanted a woman who would put him and their children above all else. Only one person in a marriage could afford to chase their dreams, and in Dell's marriage, that person would be Dell.

Dell surprisingly found the old-fashioned marriage he was looking for in a thoroughly modern woman: B. Marie Gage. Gage was
a socialist author and feminist activist who had even been arrested
for her pacifist organizing during World War I. But the two fell
quickly in love. They were married ten weeks after meeting and
moved away from the city to start a family.[12] Gage left her writing
and activism behind, and Dell eschewed his feminism to concen-
trate on writing stories and plays. Their marriage was by all accounts a happy one, lasting more than fifty years, until the end of
Gage's life. As Dell settled into domestic bliss, he became further
convinced that if feminism didn't work for him, it wouldn't work
for anyone. Dell still believed in a liberated and valued woman—
as in a woman free to pursue her interests in raising a happy home
and who would be appreciated for her talents in doing so. Dell's
feminism morphed into support of the traditional gender roles
that he had once fought: the man at the head of the household, the
woman running the home.

While Dell may have seemed disloyal in both feminism and
marriage, the truth is that his loyalties never changed. Dell was always loyal to whatever belief system or situation best served his interests, for as long as they served his interests. In his later writing,
like *Love in the Machine Age*, Dell—now established in his traditional heterosexual marriage—stepped further away from socialist
feminism and renounced his former advocacy of free love, homosexuality, and working mothers. These were no longer the ideals
of a free and accepting society; they were the follies of youth, and
they would lead to nothing but unhappiness.

"Do we want to train young people for . . . living happily ever
after in heterosexual matehood, or for living tormented and frustrated lives of homosexuality, frigidity and purposeless promiscuity?" Dell asked.[13] Heterosexual love and family—centered around
content wives and mothers—were where true happiness lay.
Women should only work in their younger years, until they found

a husband, and if necessary to help solidify an early marriage in its lean years. But once her husband got his feet beneath him, a woman should stop working and take on her *real* job, that of wife and mother. This was still, to Dell, a modern marriage, because while on the surface it may have seemed like a regurgitation of patriarchal constraints on the lives of women, it was different because women would be celebrated and supported more than they had been in the past for happily living within those constraints.

Old friends Max Eastman and Floyd Dell ended up becoming quite disappointed in each other. Eastman was vocally critical of Dell's rejection of the feminism he had helped pioneer, wondering how his friend had become such a patriarchal traditionalist. I'm sure that Dell's transition was confusing and surprising, but Dell's disappointment in Eastman ended up being much deeper, a grudge that he carried into old age.

When Eastman finally got away from his wife after six years of marriage, leaving her with their child (whom he would not see again for two decades), he decided to travel to communist Russia to see his beloved socialist revolution in practice. In the two years that Eastman was in Russia, he fell in love with and married Elena Krylenko, the sister of a prominent Bolshevik. Eastman's socialist dream quickly devolved into a nightmare as Stalin and Trotsky battled for power in the wake of Lenin's death. As Stalin consolidated his power and began silencing his enemies through mass imprisonment and executions, Eastman was understandably heartbroken and disillusioned. Stalin ended up being another white man who would distort entire movements to serve his purposes—and would take these distortions to murderous extremes.

As Eastman's Russian friends were imprisoned and murdered, his desperation to make American society aware of what was happening alienated him from the American socialist community. With nothing left to lose, Eastman stopped talking about what needed to change in Russia's socialism and decided that the atrocities in Russia proved that socialism was, in its entirety, untenable. So Eastman stopped writing for leftist, socialist magazines and began writing anticommunist screeds for conservative magazines like the *New Republic*. Anybody who supported communism, according to Eastman, was aiding and abetting the murder and oppression in Russia. Eastman called out the friends and establishments he had worked with in the past. He got really into Friedrich Hayek, an economist whose ideas became favored by archconservatives like Margaret Thatcher. Eastman's betrayal of the ideals he once held was complete when he began to support Senator Joseph McCarthy's persecution of suspected communists.

Eastman's feminism and ethical principles took a back burner as he dedicated his life to crushing communism. "We're in a political fight, not an ethical argument," he said in defense of McCarthy's targeting of American citizens for their political beliefs. "You go into battle like women in silk dresses, more concerned with keeping your skirts clean than defeating the enemy."[14]

Eastman now had no patience for weak-minded liberals who couldn't stomach some oppression in the great battle against the evils of communism, just as he previously had lacked patience for the weak-minded liberals who couldn't stomach revolution in the great battle against the evils of capitalism. In trying to understand his friend's monumental political shift from left to right, Dell theorized that his continual hatred of liberals was his sustaining consistency.[15]

Eastman and Dell had little in common toward the ends of their lives. Eastman was now dedicated to fighting the socialism that had brought him to prominence, and Dell was devoted to subverting the feminism that had brought him fame. The two men had stopped speaking, any friendliness between them frozen over by their ideological differences.

Eastman and Dell are not special outliers. They were two white dudes who came into a movement and made it about themselves.

In their activism, they became momentary rock stars, despite having little skill or dedication to the movement itself. Then they wreaked a little havoc before deciding to set fire to the building as they left.

But in that lack of singularity lies the problem: their story is a common one. Mediocre, highly forgettable white men regularly enter feminist spaces and expect to be centered and rewarded, and they have been. They get to be highly flawed, they get to regularly betray the values of their movement, yet they will be praised for their intentions or even simply for their presence—while women must be above reproach in their personal and public lives in order to avoid seeing themselves and their entire movement engulfed in scandal. Even in today's feminist movements, there is a push to show men what they will get out of supporting feminism. You should be a feminist, we argue, because it will also benefit *you*. And it's true that feminism can help men in many ways. As the mother of two sons, I'm constantly trying to protect them from the damaging patriarchal messages that tell them that their only power is in domination, that the only emotions they can feel are lust and anger. I see firsthand what harm the patriarchy can inflict on men and boys as I watch my children and their peers battle to be whole people in a society that tells them that "men" can only exist in one particularly violent way.

But when I tell my sons that they should be feminists, I don't try to sell it to them based on the benefits they will reap. I tell them what I also tell white people who are looking for reasons to be antiracist: Yes, it will offer some real benefits for you. Your life will be better in many ways when we work to end oppression. But it will not *always* benefit you. Sometimes it may seem like justice is disadvantaging you when the privileges you've routinely enjoyed are threatened. But you have to do it anyway, because you believe that women and people of color are human beings and that we deserve to be free from oppression, even when that means you personally have to give some things up.

When that true commitment to equality isn't there, when white men waltz into social justice movements with their privilege unchecked and expect to feel rewarded and comfortable at all times, they slow us down. They also hurt people, and they compromise the integrity of our movements.

We don't speak a lot about Eastman and Dell these days, but when they are remembered, they are remembered almost universally fondly. Even socialist commentators seem to have found a way to forgive Eastman's betrayals of the movement—even though his support of McCarthy put his former colleagues at serious risk, and even though he spent more of his life trying to destroy communism and socialism than he spent supporting them. Contemporary articles sing the two men's praises while glossing over their later conservative work. Indeed, in articles about Dell's life, when attention is given to his legacy as a proponent of male feminism, almost no attention is paid to the harmful antifeminist and homophobic nature of his later work. History is very kind to the memory of mediocre white men.

## JOE BIDEN IS BOTH FOR AND AGAINST BUSING

When a young Joe Biden was campaigning to represent Delaware in the US Senate in 1972, he was, like many liberals of the time, not openly opposed to busing. After the landmark 1952 Supreme Court ruling in *Brown v. Board of Education*, desegregation efforts were put in motion throughout the South. Black students were bused into white schools, sometimes needing the protection of the National Guard. When the Supreme Court gave federal courts broader power to use busing to desegregate schools across the country in *Swann v. Charlotte-Mecklenburg Board of Education*, busing began to be mandated in Northern cities as well.

In the 1950s and early '60s, busing had primarily been a Southern issue, and images of white parents shouting and spitting on Black students who were desegregating white schools had long painted opposition to busing with a broadly racist brush. When white Republicans tried to pass an amendment ending busing, Biden accused representatives of using busing as a scare tactic to secure white votes. But as more Northern cities faced their own busing orders, many politicians like Biden who had supported busing efforts in the past found that their own white constituents suddenly had a very big problem with the practice.

From the beginning, Biden was in a tricky spot. He had long touted not only his liberal record but also his close connections to Delaware's Black community. By the end of Biden's senatorial campaign, he had created a confusing stance on busing that was all his own. Biden's stance was so convoluted that local papers wrote that he was both "for and against" busing.[16]

Biden stated that he was for busing to correct "de jure" segregation and was against it to correct "de facto" segregation, meaning that he was in support of busing where school segregation had been purposefully built and maintained, and against it where it just happened to occur due to factors outside of racist segregation efforts. In other words, busing was good for the South, where racist laws had been written to keep Black and white kids in separate schools, and was bad in the North, where Black and white kids were apparently separated by coincidence or magic.

But courts had not found much magic in the school-segregation issues in Delaware. In the 1970s, Wilmington, Delaware, was about half Black, half white. Yet Wilmington schools were 82 percent Black, while the schools in the nearby, wealthier suburbs of Newcastle County—which also educated white students living in the wealthier outskirts of Wilmington—were 79.8 percent white.[17] Black parents saw that white schools had more funding, better buildings and learning materials, and better student outcomes than Black schools. But they were unable to enroll their children in these better schools because of strict Delaware laws that had split the urban and suburban schools into separate districts. Black parents sued, and in 1974 federal courts decided that the segregation of the schools around Wilmington violated the law.

Suddenly, liberal white families in Delaware not only faced the prospect of Black kids attending their lily-white schools; they also faced the potential horror of having their white kids sent directly into the heart of darkness that was Wilmington public schools. When the young Biden voted against two amendments in 1974 that would have dismantled busing-desegregation programs, his white constituents rallied against him. In June of 1974, white families gathered at an antibusing event in Newport, Delaware, determined to force Biden to listen to their concerns. When Biden tried to explain the "de-facto/de-jure" reasoning behind his halfhearted support of busing, he was loudly jeered by the crowd.[18] White people stopped Biden around town to accuse him of ruining their children's lives by sending them to Black schools.

Biden got the message. If he continued to defend busing, he ran the real risk of becoming a one-term senator. In 1975, Joe Biden stunned his Senate colleagues by throwing his support behind known segregationist Jesse Helms's proposed antibusing amendment to the Constitution. Speaking in defense of Helms's amendment, Biden told the Senate, "I have become convinced that busing is a bankrupt concept."[19] In a later television interview, Biden warned that if the US government didn't come up with a different solution for school segregation than busing, "we are going to end up with the races at war." Biden explained that the good white people he represented weren't racist, but busing might make them so: "You take people who aren't racist, people who are good citizens, who believe in equal education and opportunity, and you stunt their children's intellectual growth by busing them to an inferior school and you're going to fill them with hatred."[20] Biden's argument was that the white Northerners who had benefitted from schools that consolidated white wealth and excluded Black students from sharing in that wealth with legislation that kept their districts (and the corresponding property taxes and PTA funding opportunities) separate were not racist, but subjecting them to the same education that Black students had long been forced to endure would *make* them racist.

Biden went even further, calling the concept of busing itself racist. Why did Black students need to sit next to white students in order to succeed? How patronizing! Were Black students not smart and talented enough to succeed on their own? Biden argued that they were, and to support busing was to assume that they were not. To Biden, busing spoke to assumptions about the inferior ability of Black culture to succeed without white influence, saying, "It implies that Blacks have no reason to be proud of their inheritance and their own culture."[21]

Now convinced that busing was wrong, likely both for the country and for his reelection chances, Biden made antibusing his cause célèbre. In 1976 Biden introduced his own antibusing amendment, aimed at preventing the Justice Department from pursuing cases that would lead to federally enforced busing. In 1981, Biden partnered with yet another well-known segregationist when he and Strom Thurmond introduced antibusing provisions into the Justice Department's spending bill.[22]

Biden was obsessed with ending busing, stating that, in his first eight years in the Senate, "No issue has consumed more of my time and energies."[23]

When Biden, a young, liberal Northern senator whose star was on the rise, came out strongly against busing, it gave other liberal senators permission to do the same. Instead of a stance taken only by the likes of George Wallace in order to preserve white supremacy, antibusing as framed by Biden became an issue that white liberals could stand behind without questioning their racist motives.

The majority of Black voters at the time still supported busing to desegregate schools, but their concerns were drowned out by the wants of the white majority. Many Blacks felt the same way that NAACP leader Tom Atkins did in 1975 when he said, "An anti-busing amendment is an anti-desegregation amendment, and an anti-desegregation amendment is an anti-Black amendment."[24]

Ed Brooke, representing Massachusetts as the first Black person to win popular election to the US Senate, was a fierce supporter of busing to support desegregation of schools when other measures had failed. He was devastated over the antibusing legislation that Biden helped push through the Senate, calling the vote on Biden's antibusing amendment "the greatest symbolic defeat for civil rights since 1964."[25] Whereas Brooke's support of busing would end his Senate career, Biden's antibusing stance would help ensure his reelection.

Today, busing gets mixed reviews. Busing did integrate schools. Funding for schools was more equalized across racial lines. A larger percentage of Black students were given the same educational opportunities as white students. Some students, both Black and white, later testified to the value and growth they'd received from a more diverse environment. But busing was often traumatic for students who were pulled from their neighborhoods and sent across town to go to school with strangers who were at times openly hostile to their presence. Busing was in many cases more damaging to Black students than white ones, as Black children faced violence from white peers and parents for simply trying to get a better education.

But busing was never supposed to be the ultimate solution to ending school segregation. The reasons behind the "de facto" segregation that Biden talked about—issues like employment and housing segregation—were at the heart of school segregation and school-funding disparities in the North. But that segregation was built by racist housing and employment segregation that white

Northerners valued even more than their educational segregation. History had shown how violently white Northerners opposed true desegregation in housing and employment. When efforts to address the root causes of school segregation failed, all that was left was busing. As Brooke said in his defense of busing programs, "It is not necessarily the best way, but in certain instances busing is the *only* way to achieve desegregation."[26] Busing was the option that was better than nothing. But when it ended, lawmakers decided that it was time to try nothing.

Biden remained proud of his record on busing for decades, even writing about it in his 2007 memoir *Promises to Keep*, calling busing a "liberal trainwreck."[27] His stance would fade into the background during the Obama years, when he served as vice president. But it would come to the foreground again in 2019 when Biden was campaigning for the Democratic nomination for president. The voters that Biden tried to win over in the 2019 presidential primary were quite different from the voters he answered to in 1970s Delaware. Biden would need the support of Black voters in order to secure the Democratic nomination. Suddenly, he remembered his actions around busing much differently. When he was interviewed for the popular podcast *Pod Save America* in March of 2019, Biden decided to burnish his busing record by focusing on the time he voted to support busing in 1974—and not the decade he spent trying to defeat it. "In the middle of the single most extensive busing order in all the United States history, in my state," he said, "I voted against an amendment, cast the deciding vote, to allow courts to keep busing as a remedy. Because there are some things that are worth losing over."[28]

I'm sure there must be some things worth losing over, but Biden has consistently decided that busing was not one of them.

When, in June of 2019, Biden bragged about his ability to rise above partisan politics to get things done in Washington, he highlighted his working relationship with notoriously racist senators like Herman Talmage and James V. Eastland.[29] Eastland was known for reportedly shouting at a White Citizens' Council rally in Montgomery during the bus boycott, "All whites are created equal with certain rights, among these are life, liberty and the pursuit of dead niggers."[30]

Many were shocked and outraged that Biden would brag about being able to work closely with people who proclaimed that the killing of Black Americans was one of white Americans' inalienable rights. Cory Booker, also bidding for the Democratic presidential nomination, voiced his dismay as a Black man upon hearing Biden speak so fondly about virulent racists, and said that Biden should apologize. Biden countered that Booker should instead apologize to *him* for insinuating that Biden was anything but an antiracist crusader, stating, "Cory . . . knows better. There's not a racist bone in my body. I've been involved in civil rights my whole career. Period. Period. Period."[31]

But Biden's tales of reaching across the aisle to segregationists reminded many journalists and commentators about the other times that Biden worked with unapologetic segregationists in pursuit of antibusing legislation. Biden was forced once again to try to explain to the public his support for busing in "de jure" segregation versus busing in "de facto" segregation. His explanation did not grow any more elegant in the decades since he'd first come up with that justification in 1972.

After busing was dismantled nationally, the "other methods" of desegregating schools that Biden insisted were more effective than busing never materialized. Without federal mandate forcing integration, schools slowly resegregated, and their funding followed. A 2019 report showed that nonwhite school districts received $23 billion less per year than their white counterparts. Even when controlled for income discrepancies, the funding was less, with poor white schools still receiving more funds than poor schools where the majority of the students were people of color.[32]

Funding disparities and the concentration of underprivileged students in schools with fewer resources than wealthier white schools have also led to a higher turnover of teachers in nonwhite schools. This all has contributed to persistent testing gaps between white students and Black, brown, and Native students.

Biden's home state of Delaware, like many states that were once ordered to use busing to desegregate their schools, has been resegregating in the years since busing ended. Busing there had been very successful at desegregating schools. In 1989, there were no intensely segregated (i.e., 90–100 percent minority-student) schools in the metro Wilmington area. But by 2010, the number of intensely segregated schools had grown to 15 percent. The average Latinx student in Wilmington attended a school where 61 percent of students were low income, and the average Black student attended a school where 56 percent of students were low income, while the average white student attended a school where only 37 percent of the students were low income.[33] As racial disparities in educational funding and outcomes returned to Delaware, parents of color once again brought their case to the courts in hopes of obtaining equitable educational opportunities for their children. In a 2018 case, the state of Delaware argued in its defense that the Constitution doesn't require that the state provide the children of Delaware with a fair or "adequate" education system.[34]

We find racism in our systems when we look at what the system produces. When we find systems with outputs that negatively affect people of color in a way or to a degree that they do not affect white people, we have a racist impact that can be tied to a racist cause. Often, that racism looks little like the proud hatred professed by the senators whom Biden worked with, and more like that of Biden's white constituents, who couldn't imagine a worse fate for their children than having to go to the same schools that Black children had always attended. Or it looks like the racism of Biden himself, who, in catering to the racism of his white constituents, legitimized the excuses that white people used to hide the sinister reasons for their antibusing stances, severely undercutting the efforts of his Black constituents to provide a better education for their children.

We can find racism in the fact that the "other methods" for desegregating schools and providing equal education for students of color never materialized after busing was defeated. Discussion of the solutions promised by the antibusing crusaders like Biden disappeared the moment busing did. I look at the rising resegregation of schools across the country. I see generations of students of color being denied the quality education they deserve, and I see the heartbreaking racism of a nation that can mobilize to kill the one effective desegregation strategy we've had—and then just walk away, leaving our children behind.

## THE WRATH OF THE BERNIE BROS

In the late spring of 2019, I had a dream about Bernie Sanders. I was doing what I'm normally doing in my waking life—desperately rushing to meet a writing deadline. But this time, Bernie Sanders was in the room. He was following me around trying to explain that his work for Black America was even *better* now than when he had marched with King. If I would just listen to how he had changed his approach since the 2016 election, I would see.

"Bernie," I said, "I have a book due."

I tried to ignore Sanders and focus on my writing, but every time I'd look at my Word document, a message would pop up from somebody on social media saying, "You should listen to Bernie," and, "Did you know he marched with King?"

I woke up and tried to laugh off my anxiety, but I could feel it—the election season was coming.

I wasn't the only person in my circle with Sanders-related anxiety. I asked my friend and fellow writer Imani Gandy how she felt leading up to the 2020 election, and she laughed. "I literally have to pause and think before I say anything about Bernie Sanders, because it will become absolute insanity."

Why was I having anxiety dreams about Sanders? Why was Imani trying to avoid "absolute insanity" from talking freely about Sanders? It is not because of Sanders himself—well, not exactly.

No matter what you think of Bernie, he ran a very progressive campaign. There is no surprise that it appealed to so many young people. And many people who supported Sanders showed the care and respect for others that you would expect from a campaign so focused on social issues.

But for others, especially a group of particularly vocal white men, the support for Bernie took on a sharper edge, a darker tone.

I'm talking about the Bernie Bros.

Perhaps I should have taken Imani's lead and kept my Sanders thoughts to myself, because when I woke up from my dream, I decided to tweet about it. I tweet about pretty much everything (ask my kids; it annoys them to no end), and I felt like the dream was a humorous illustration of both writing anxiety and political anxiety.

Although many people found the tweet funny, others apparently had left their sense of humor at home. Suddenly, my tweet was being shared by pro-Bernie accounts, and the response was far less jovial. A sampling:

"I was recently in the ICU for diabetes. Couldn't keep going at my job after. And you're getting annoyed about a dream [about] Bernie Sanders. Really."

"You're a barren clown."

"I had a dream that politics wasn't a wasteland of rich idiot blue checked dipshits who write about any wine fueled nonsense that pops in their head."

"I dreamt poor people had healthcare and weren't dying of treatable illness and we fixed the economy. I guess that would be inconvenient if you were a real selfish ghoul using politics to try to make yourself feel special while shitting on people with real struggles and heartbreak."

"'Bestselling authors' using their platform to halt momentum towards single payer are threatening to me and others like me the same way Nazis are to you."[35]

Yikes.

What is a Bernie Bro? The term appears to have been first coined by Robinson Meyer at *The Atlantic.* It has come to stand for what some see as the stereotypical supersupporter of Sanders: a young, white man who will vigorously defend Sanders from any negative comment—usually with long lectures explaining how the commenter doesn't understand politics or doesn't care about poor people, people of color, and women if they don't support Bernie, even if the person he is lecturing happens to be a woman of color.

Assholes exist everywhere, and they always seem to come out in force during an election season—for every single candidate. So what made the Bernie Bros so special that they inspired countless think pieces and even a section of this book?

One factor was their anger. The image of white men on the left was usually stereotyped with a hippie-like concern for others and often dismissed as ineffective (and "feminized") due to their dedication to political correctness and overall politeness. So observers were surprised to see the palpable rage coming from many in the Sanders camp. These were white men who felt personally wronged by our system and were dedicated to Sanders's campaign for their own self-interests. The anger they voiced over the cruelties of "establishment" politics, their disdain for "liberal elites," and their feeling of exclusion from modern-day "identity politics" felt like a funhouse mirror of the grievances of white male Trump supporters.

Then there was their use of social media. Rapidly expanding use of the platforms in the years leading up to the 2016 election provided millions of people with countless new opportunities to debate, commiserate, and squabble about their political beliefs. The internet provided an instant political rally at the push of a retweet button. This meant that writers and commentators were constantly and quickly met with a large, vocal response to any of their political opinions—but also that any everyday person who dared speak their mind could find themselves the target of angry political opposition.

And the people they targeted were another factor in generating taxonomical articles and giving these supporters space in the culture. A lot of people who felt besieged by Bernie Bros (especially online) were women and people of color. Feminist writer Sady Doyle, for example, found herself the focus of hundreds of angry and abusive messages after an online confrontation with writer and Sanders supporter Freddie deBoer. She documented her experience on Tumblr: "I am now the subject of blog posts labeling me 'the most extreme opponent of the Bernie Army' (yes, it's an army now) and various gross-out pictures of pig testicles. There have been, I'd estimate, a little over 100 messages on Twitter today alone."[36]

When Senator Jeanne Shaheen endorsed Clinton during the 2016 campaign, she was flooded with comments from Sanders fans who were angry at any Clinton mention:

"Hey Shaheen, if your daughter was raped, would you still stand with Hillary? You do know what rape it [sic], right Jeanne?"

"Hooray for another paid $hillary troll, enjoy the rest of your stay jeanne, your time is up. The revolution will is coming for you. #feelthebern"

"Their vaginas are making terrible choices!"[37]

And then there was the Bernie Bros' fervor. A light critique of Sanders would bring down the wrath of God: immediate, angry responses from Sanders supporters that seemed vastly disproportionate to what was said. In addition, the critiques would have you forever labeled by this group of fans an "enemy" of Sanders and what he represents.

When Imani Gandy spoke up about issues she had with how some Sanders fans were treating Black Lives Matter protesters who interrupted a Bernie Sanders rally, she quickly became a target of the more zealous Bernie Bros. She was hounded online in every space she occupied. Blog posts were written about her. YouTube videos were made about her. They started digging through her past. They found that she had worked as a lawyer in foreclosures for a few months in 2011. That was enough to paint Gandy, even with her years of activism, as the enemy. From then on it was regular insults, threats, and attacks on her character.

"I was the target of them for about two straight years," Imani recalled in a conversation with me, "and it was nasty and it was vicious."[38]

The extreme anger in defense of Sanders didn't just appear online. In 2016, when Clinton won more delegates in a heated Nevada primary than Sanders, chaos erupted. According to reports by attendees, angry Sanders supporters yelled obscenities and threw chairs. Some even had to be escorted out of the room by security when they refused to leave after the convention ended.[39] Even though by the time of the Nevada primary, Clinton already had a pretty insurmountable national-delegate lead, angry Bernie fans still left violent and sexist voice mails and text messages for Nevada Democratic chairwoman Roberta Lange. Here are a few snippets:

> "I just wanted to let you know that I think people like you should be hung in a public execution to show this world that we won't stand for this sort of corruption. I don't know what kind of money they are paying to you, but I don't know how you sleep at night. You are a sick, twisted piece of shit and I hope you burn for this! . . . You cowardless [sic] bitch, running off the stage! I hope people find you."

> "You fucking stupid bitch! What the hell are you doing? You're a fucking corrupt bitch!"

> "Oh Roberta, Roberta, Roberta, you old, old hag. Oh, we watched the whole thing in Nevada. You're really kinda screwed, lady. Um, yeah. Really stupid. Fuck you."

> "You're a cunt. Fuck you!"

> "Bitch answer me! How much did the Hillary campaign pay you for that shit? You weren't a coward yesterday, don't be one now! Biggest cunt in politics next to Clinton"

> "You stupid ass bitch. We're coming for your ass."[40]

Finally, there's Sanders's politics. You might not have expected candidate Bernie Sanders to attract such racist and misogynistic followers. He had a strong record of civil rights activism and a very liberal presidential campaign platform. He was concerned about the environment, he was antiwar, he was prochoice, he wanted free college tuition. If you were to list all the Sanders talking points to someone who was unfamiliar with the candidates and then ask that person who they thought his most vocal supporters were likely to be, chances are the answer wouldn't be "white male millennials who like to yell at women of color on the internet." We were all supposed to be on the same side, so why did it seem so hard sometimes to tell Bernie Bros from Trump supporters?

Sanders did not create these more extreme and sometimes abusive supporters. Each one decided for themselves what to believe and how to act. But Sanders has always carried his white male privilege into his politics, even when discussing issues of race and class. The anxiety over a Black president and over the rising gender and racial political consciousness in America was felt not just by conservative white men. That gender and racial power shift impacted the material conditions in progressive political circles as well, and white men who had long vocally supported a more free and equitable future were becoming uncomfortable with what that future might look like and whether or not they would have a starring role.

The candidacy of Sanders, who prioritized progressive issues of working- and middle-class white men over those of women and people of color (although if you were to ask Sanders or his supporters, they'd likely insist that the issues most important to working-class white men are the same as those facing working-class women and people of color), became an opportunity for white men to still see themselves centered in a new progressive future when the only other alternatives were a woman president or Donald Trump.

Interviews with Black volunteers and staff members of the 2016 Sanders campaign showed that, even within the campaign, many Black people felt as if the Black community was a low priority for Sanders. The *New York Times* highlighted the experience of campaign staffer John Solomon: "When Mr. Solomon joined the campaign in late 2015, he was told his job would include networking with Black voters and planning events in Black communities. But almost immediately he was assigned tasks like keeping itineraries and chauffeuring surrogates that had little to do with outreach—which made him feel like 'support staff,' he said."[41]

When Sanders had a campaign stop at Morehouse College, a historically Black institution (formally known as a historically Black college or university, or HBCU), Black campaign staffers wanted students to get the first chance at tickets, to increase the chance that young Black audiences would get to see Sanders speak. When the campaign refused, the majority of tickets were snatched up by white locals, leading to a majority-white audience and making the local Black community (and Black campaign staffers) feel undervalued.[42]

In an interview with *Splinter News*, campaign staffer Danny Glover, who is Black, detailed some of his difficulties in trying to get the Sanders campaign to reach out to the Black community. He felt that the campaign's efforts at Black outreach were really more lip service than substance: "We threw some resources to it to say we did it, but they didn't put as many people behind it as they should have."[43]

Glover said that stops were cut from Sanders's tour of HBCUs after the South Carolina primary, in late February. He said he was told by superiors that there wasn't enough money to continue them. The Sanders campaign raised $44 million in March, its best performance to date.[44]

The experience for some women on the 2016 Sanders campaign was also disappointing, to say the least. The *New York Times* interviewed women staffers who reported dealing with sexual harassment from their male colleagues. When Giulianna Di Lauro reported sexual harassment to her manager, he apparently told her, "I bet you would have liked it if he were younger." Campaign worker Samantha Davis reported that she was marginalized after she refused to go to her male supervisor's hotel room. Masha Mendieta complained that women in the campaign were treated like personal secretaries for their male managers; they were asked to fetch things and run personal errands instead of doing substantial work. Women campaign staffers also reported dismay at finding out that some of them were paid as little as half the amount their male counterparts earned for the same work.[45]

The women who spoke to the *Times* said that they had reported this harassment and discrimination to superiors in the campaign and that their concerns were dismissed or ignored. After the *New York Times* ran its article in 2019 detailing these allegations, Sanders apologized.[46]

Sanders appealed to younger voters across the board, but he deliberately courted a specific kind of voter—young, white, progressive men—not only by speaking to issues they cared about, but also by making sure to avoid focusing too much on issues that they (and perhaps he) may have felt threatened by. Many people of color questioned Sanders's stance on racial issues because he seemed to routinely focus on class over race. When he was asked directly about racial matters, especially about racial economic topics, the subject often pivoted back to class; we need, the line went, to look at issues that affect us all, and not just a few.

Sanders has always prioritized class over race. In an interview he gave the *Chicago Tribune* in 1990, he discussed his political activism of the 1960s:

> During that period, I became active in the peace movement and the civil rights movement. . . . There were many people who were liberal and they were concerned about poverty, or they were concerned about racism, or they were concerned about militarism but they never put them together or saw the connection. . . . They never saw that the roots of many of these problems lie in an economic system in which 1 percent of the population owns half of the wealth of the country, an economic system in which the rich controls, to a large degree, the political and economic life of the country.[47]

In the young Bernie Sanders, I can see reflections of the modern-day Bernie Bros. There is no doubt that economic inequality is one of the biggest issues this country faces. I'm not arguing against that position, and I agree it's a real problem that demands real solutions. But Bernie's statement (and the words of many progressive white men I encounter) displays the patronizing assumption that poor activists, activists of color, and antiwar activists were ignorant of the role that economic inequality played in the issues they were trying to address. It's an assumption that, even though someone might be focused on a concern that severely impacts their life and therefore is of top priority to them (like, say, Black people fighting for equality in the Jim Crow era), they were unable to see how their issues were connected to those of other activists.

Even while claiming plenty of street cred for his marches with Dr. King, Sanders still felt that the activism of that time needed to pivot away from race. To many people of color, especially Black people, this can feel very disingenuous. And if you are a Black person who agrees with Sanders that economic inequality is a major issue in this country (as I am) but also feels that we must address issues of race if we are going to bring economic equality to everyone (as I do), Sanders can be very frustrating (and he is). He seems to fail to understand that the system of race has been built to ensure that Black and brown people will remain at the bottom of the economic ladder. And if you are a Black person who knows that economic inequality is a major issue, but you also need candidates to speak strongly on issues like police brutality, then hearing Sanders pivot to talk about jobs programs in the Black community as if a job will stop a bullet (as he suggested in a letter to the editor of the *New York Times* after Michael Brown, an unarmed Black teenager, was killed by police in Ferguson, Missouri) can make you want to tear your hair out.[48]

Sanders seemed to also view women's issues as secondary to socioeconomic class. When in 2016 Trump said that women who have abortions should be punished, Sanders replied that his re-marks were a "distraction" from the "serious issues facing Amer-ica."[49] To many women (and anyone with a uterus, regardless of gender), especially on the left, the assault on reproductive rights *was* a serious issue facing America. Sanders further alienated many women when he endorsed an antichoice congressional candidate, Marcy Kaptur, in 2016, and then an antichoice gubernatorial can-didate, Tom Perriello, in 2017.

Often, when issues of gender were brought directly to Sand-ers, his answers were awkward, if not dismissive. When a young woman at an event asked him what she should do to become the second-ever Latina senator, he replied, "It is not good enough for somebody to say, 'I'm a woman, vote for me.' No, that's not good enough. What we need is a woman who has the guts to stand up to Wall Street, to the insurance companies, to the drug compa-nies, to the fossil fuel industry. In other words, one of the struggles that you're going to be seeing in the Democratic Party is whether we go beyond identity politics."[50]

The assumption that women would vote for women for no other reason than their gender is insulting to all women's intelli-gence, as is the insinuation that women candidates who focus on "women's issues" are not also concerned about economic or health care issues. In this statement also lies the quieter yet just as harm-ful assumption that white men only vote for candidates that center their own white male interests.

This dismissive and condescending attitude toward issues of race and gender may have rubbed many women and people of color like me the wrong way, but it was exactly what young white men who were threatened by an increasing political focus on the needs of minorities and marginalized people wanted to hear.

Jordan, a twenty-nine-year-old self-described Bernie Bro, talked with Ruth Graham at *Slate* in 2019 about Sanders's appeal to him in a diversifying political climate where "identity politics" seemed to reign:

I'm not even going to say "identity politics" but identity crisis, where people feel the need to defend their identity more than their politics. . . . I can't tell you how many times I've heard that with this new Congress. It bothers me being a white man who honestly has gotten schlonged most of his life. I didn't have the privilege of having my parents go to a great school. When you hear that this Congress needs to be more brown, or the future is female, I'm not even sure what it means. To a dude, it's like, "No men on the earth."[51]

This claim that the focus on identity distracts from "real" politics—while simultaneously centering how "identity politics" affect white men and claiming not to be engaging in identity politics—is a tightrope of hypocrisy that Sanders himself likes to walk. Let's be clear: centering the needs of progressive, working-class, white men *is* identity politics. It is just as steeped in individual identity as movements focusing on women and people of color. But it comes with a level of privilege built in that allows it to escape wider scrutiny. Here is an excerpt from an interview that Sanders gave *GQ* magazine in 2019:

There are people who are very big into diversity but whose views end up being not particularly sympathetic to working people, whether they're white or black or Latino. . . . My main belief is that we need to bring together a coalition of people—of black and white and Latino and Asian-American and Native-American—around a progressive agenda which is prepared to take on an extraordinarily powerful ruling class in this country. That is my view. Many of my opponents do not hold that view, and they think that all that we need is people who are candidates who are black or white, who are black or Latino or woman or gay, regardless of what they stand for, that the end result is diversity.[52]

When Sanders has engaged on race, he's quickly scurried away from it, in a way that isolates race issues from the issues of "ordinary" white Americans. When he was asked about how to keep voters focused on the issues in the midst of Trump scandals, he replied, "I mean, I think we've got to work in two ways. Number one, we have got to take on Trump's attacks against the environment, against women, against Latinos and blacks and people in the gay community, we've got to fight back every day on those issues. But equally important, or more important: We have got to focus on bread-and-butter issues that mean so much to ordinary Americans."[53]

Oh man, fuck this. Seriously? Who exactly are these "ordinary Americans" whose issues are more important than the destruction of our environment and the systemic racism and sexism that are literally crushing women and people of color in this country? Hint: they don't look like me.

In 2016 Sanders was asked by a Black woman at a campaign town hall, "Can you please talk about specifically Black people and reparations?" The case for reparations is based not only on wealth inequality, but also on the specific history of systemic economic exploitation of Black Americans for over four hundred years—starting with slavery and moving through Jim Crow and mass incarceration—by a white supremacist government. Sanders (who had previously dismissed the idea of reparations as "divisive"), however, insisted on bringing the issue back to whiteness: "It's not just black, it is Latino, there are areas in poor rural America, where it's white." Sanders then focused his talk on helping "all" poor communities, refusing to actually touch the issue of reparations for the Black community.[54]

This line that Sanders insisted on walking had a special appeal to "progressive" white men who held more left-leaning and socialist views but were deeply afraid of being decentered politically by women and people of color. In Sanders, they had a candidate they could support who would allow them to appear "good"—he spoke of equality, of economic justice, of ending wars, of universal health care—while not having to engage with or challenge their own place in exploitative systems of racial and gender inequality.

The white male supremacy of the Sanders campaign and its followers is not the violent, overt white supremacy and sexism of the Trump administration. The Sanders campaign wants to ignore women and people of color. The Trump administration and its supporters want the removal of rights and privileges of women and people of color, and they want vengeance against women and people of color for the rights that they view were gained at white male expense. The Trump administration's white supremacist patriarchy is not white supremacy and patriarchy by the laziness of unexamined privilege—it is the deliberate quest to increase cis, straight, abled, white male power over women, people of color, trans people, queer people, and disabled people.

But the unchecked white male privilege of Sanders and many of his followers will guarantee that privilege and oppression are baked into the policies they create and support. A political movement that focuses on class and ignores the specific ways in which race determines financial health and well-being for people of color in this country will be a movement that maintains white supremacy, because it will not be able to identify or address the specific, race-based systems that are the main causes of inequality for people of color. Health care discrimination, job discrimination, the school-to-prison pipeline, educational bias, mass incarceration, police brutality, community trauma—none of these issues are addressed in a class-only approach. A class-only approach will lift only poor whites out of poverty and will therefore maintain white supremacy.

A political movement that focuses on class and ignores the specific ways in which gender determines the financial health and well-being of women in this country will be a movement that maintains the patriarchy. Reproductive justice, job discrimination, health care discrimination, educational bias, gendered violence, sexual harassment—none of these issues are addressed in a class-only approach. A class-only approach will help some women financially, but not much beyond the degree that their economic status is tied to white supremacy. It will not help women of color much at all.

When Sanders failed to win the 2016 Democratic nomination, a large reason why was his stubborn resistance to centering important issues that impact many women, Black, and Latinx voters. Whereas exit polls showed that younger women, Black, and Latinx voters were more excited about Sanders, Clinton was overwhelmingly more popular with Black voters in the South, and with women, Black, and Latinx voters over age thirty-five across the country. Although appealing to the white male vote can carry an election on the right (even with white women voters), it cannot win national elections on the left. And it is easy to argue that the bile spewed during the primaries—with many Sanders supporters talking about Clinton with the same hate-filled, derogatory comments that Trump supporters did, and others insisting that there was no difference between Clinton and Trump—did serious damage to Clinton's national campaign once she became the nominee. Sanders backed Clinton after the primary and asked his supporters to do the same, but many of those supporters had just spent a year talking about Clinton as a criminal warmonger who was no different than Trump, with very little effort from the Sanders campaign to curtail such vitriol until well past the primaries. Those riled-up voters were reluctant to throw any support her way.

After Clinton lost the general election, supporters of both Clinton and Sanders were angry. Many Clinton supporters blamed Sanders supporters, who they believed were so opposed to a woman in the White House that they had voted for either Trump or Green Party candidate Jill Stein. Many Sanders supporters blamed Clinton supporters and the DNC for "stealing" the Democratic nomination from Sanders, whom they viewed as much more electable than Clinton. The hashtag #BernieWouldHaveWon became popular on social media as many argued that the "identity politics" of the Clinton campaign made her unelectable and drove voters to Trump. They maintained that Sanders was right to refuse to engage on issues of race and gender.

Looking at the role that gender played in the 2016 election, the Center of Southern Politics and Society found that, even though sexism was more common in white Republican men, "roughly 11 million white male Independents and Democrats feel enough animosity towards working women and feminists to make them unlikely to vote for one of them."[55] In the end, 12 percent of Sanders supporters ended up supporting Trump in the general election. When surveyed, almost half of those Sanders supporters turned Trump voters said they disagreed that white people have advantages in the United States, whereas only about 5 percent of Clinton voters disagreed that white people have advantages.[56]

Defection after a tough primary isn't unusual. In the 2008 election, 15 percent of Clinton primary voters ended up voting for McCain in the general election, and many remember the racial tensions in that primary almost as vividly as they do the ones from the 2016 election.[57] But the combination of the charged rhetoric of the 2016 election, the blatant sexism, ableism, and white supremacy of the Trump campaign, and the large policy differences between Trump and Sanders led many to expect that the number of voters who were willing to cross over to support the Republican candidate would be much lower than it had been in the 2008 election.

Looking at the election of 2016, when there was so much at risk, we can ask why so many people would shift their support from a Democratic Socialist candidate to an openly bigoted, highly conservative, and wildly incompetent Republican. Why did Sanders appeal in particular to this subgroup that defected? The answer is that he prioritized issues affecting white men over those affecting women and people of color.

The "why" matters because as a nation where every president but one has been a white man; where, in 2019, only 24 percent of our congressional representatives and only 18 percent of our governors were women; where only 22 percent of our congressional representatives and 8 percent of our governors were people of color—as that nation, we must be able to politically empower women and people of color without it causing a backlash among liberal white men. A backlash that further endangers political representation for minority groups. The next white male candidate that angry white men rally behind may not be Trump or Sanders, and the next female candidate they turn against is unlikely to be Hillary Clinton. But as long as we refuse to address the ways in which white men cling to political power, even to their own detriment, there will always be a white male politician to take advantage of this white male anxiety over the rise of women and people of color.

The answer is not to let go of "identity politics"—we don't magically get to a system that addresses issues affecting minority groups by ignoring issues affecting minority groups. The current numbers are testament to that. If we are going to continue to make progress on issues of race and gender, and if liberal white men want to be on the right side of history, they have to address their personal issues with race and gender.

I asked Robin DiAngelo, author of *White Fragility*, what she thought about the role of white men in racial and gender equality. She agreed that we have to find a way forward with white men: "We absolutely need them. It frustrates the hell out of me that there are very few white men in this work and in this field. And yet it"—the idea of including them—"also makes me nervous because it's so easy for them to then slip into dominance and taking over."[58]

Many women of color saw that slip into dominance in the white men who lectured us about Sanders, telling us that we were too ignorant to realize that Sanders was the best choice for women and people of color. These men may have truly believed that they were allies to women and people of color, unaware of how their white male supremacy was taking precedence over their desire for a more just world—even as they resorted to condescension, insults, and outright slurs.

In this discussion, white maleness is still centered. What happened to white men? What motivated them? What can we do to make sure we don't lose their support in the next election? This matters, because we need a coalition in order to have the numbers to get representatives into office who will address issues affecting minority communities. But even in this discussion, it is important to realize that the real loss is not in the support of white men, but in the safety, freedom, and political voice of women and people of color.

For many women and people of color who engaged in social media during the 2016 presidential election, it will be remembered not only as the time a sexist white supremacist was voted into our highest office; it will also be remembered as the time when they were harassed by white men in their own party for daring to have a political opinion that differed from the men's. This phenomenon has had a cooling effect on many people of color on social media—even some who once supported Sanders.

Imani Gandy has chosen to stay silent in the 2020 election season. "During this cycle, I am keeping my mouth shut," she told me. "All I did in 2015 and 2016 was fight, and it took a really bad toll on me mentally—mental-health-wise. . . . It's just not worth it."

Not only have women, people of color, disabled people, and the LGBTQ+ community been increasingly endangered by the election of Donald Trump; they have been harmed and disenfranchised by the reactionary, anti–"identity politics" factions on the left. Many have learned that speaking out on issues impacting them may leave them further isolated and endangered than before, and they have learned this from people who claim to be friends and allies of marginalized people.

## "I THINK HE FOCUSED TOO MUCH ON BLACK PEOPLE"

My partner and I were in a Lyft on our way to a dinner event when our white male driver asked me the question that I hate being asked more than just about any question: What do you do for a living?

I hate this question most when it's asked by a man who is tasked with getting me safely from one place to another, who asks it when I'm stuck in a confined space with him. It's a forward question to ask any stranger, but the answer is especially uncomfortable when you are a Black woman who writes about race in America. I know that the easy—and more fun—solution would be to make something up. I have never been a deep-sea diver, and every time I'm asked this question, I'm given the opportunity to be one—even if just for a few minutes—and every time, I let that opportunity slip by. The truth is, what I do for a living is document the world as I see it. I'm not a good liar. So this conversation began begrudgingly (on my part) the way it usually does: he asked, and I answered that I was a writer. He asked what kind of writing I did. I told him I wrote about social issues. He pressed: "What kind of social issues?" I took a deep breath and told him. "Race and gender."

We started on more neutral ground—how unbearable Trump is. This is a pretty safe place to start a political conversation with a Black woman who just told you she writes on race and gender in America. I gave plenty of *ohs* and *yeps* as he talked about how much he disliked Trump's racist and sexist rhetoric. He was a friendly driver and obviously wasn't trying to be confrontational. But after that safe introduction, he decided to jump into the deep end.

"Why do you think Hillary lost?" he asked me.

If the driver had been looking at my face instead of responsibly looking at the road, he would have seen every regret I'd ever had in my life flash through my eyes—including my decision to get up that day, put on a dress, and order a ride to my event instead of staying in my hotel room and eating ice cream.

"Oh . . . uh," I stuttered. "I—"

"I just don't think people liked her," he interjected before I could answer. He started listing all the reasons why he thought people didn't like Hillary Clinton. "She wasn't very likeable. She seemed like a typical politician." Equally popular and equally meaningless statements.

My monosyllabic replies must have sounded far more enthusiastic than I had intended them to, because the driver became even more bold.

"So, uh . . . race in America," he started. "That's really interesting. I am a white man and I like Obama, but one thing I'll tell you about him is that I think he focused too much on Black people and ignored white men. I felt like, who was looking out for me? I know some people who voted for Trump were racist, but I think that if Obama had focused on white people more, Trump wouldn't have won."

My partner reflexively gripped my hand.

The car stopped. We were at our destination. My partner opened his door to exit, and I just sat there. I decided, even though my opinion hadn't been asked, to take a page out of this dude's playbook and give it anyway. "Obama didn't focus too much on Black issues," I said. I continued:

If he did, we would have been able to make a lot more progress on issues facing the Black community during his presidency than we did. Obama's presidency meant a lot to me and other Black people, but he was a centrist who would have been impeached if he for one moment had tried to lead as a Black president dedicated to Black interests. Try to think of how many "Black" policies he put forth, and you'll have trouble finding them. Try to find how many "Black" speeches he gave outside of February, and you'll find a few very carefully worded and deliberately inclusive speeches given during times of increased unrest over issues of police brutality. Obama's crowning achievement was health care reform, which benefitted everyone, including millions of white Americans. And nobody voted against Obama because he focused too much on Black people. It was because after hundreds of years of white presidents primarily looking after the interests of white people, white Americans couldn't imagine that a Black president was capable of looking out for the interests of everyone. But if you care about addressing racial oppression in this country, you should want a president who will give far more focus to issues facing communities of color than our past presidents have.

I thanked the driver for the ride and got out of the car as he thanked me for the "great conversation." I took a few deep breaths as we walked from the car to the dining hall, and my partner said softly to me, "You know, love, you didn't need to give all that education for free."

"I know," I sighed. "But I just couldn't leave 'Trump won because Obama ignored white people' hanging out there like that."

And I still can't leave that harmful, racist assumption alone. None of us should. The reflexive narrative on the left after the election of Donald Trump is that years of focusing too much on Black people, on gay people, on transgender people, on women was why Trump won. Black Lives Matter was why Trump won. Transgender bathrooms were why Trump won. Barack Obama was too focused on all of that to pay attention to what was really important: the suffering of working- and middle-class white men.

We had been in a time when the economy was growing steadily, when millions of people who had lacked health insurance were finally able to afford it, when the housing market was recovering steadily from earlier crashes, when the average white American was more prosperous and secure than they had been in the previous few decades. What "special focus" did the queer community get? The same right to marriage that straight couples had enjoyed for hundreds of years. White House Pride celebrations that were free of open hostility. The ability to debate with cisgender strangers over their right to safely use public restrooms. What "special focus" did the Hispanic community get? The first Hispanic and Latina Supreme Court justice in the history of the country. Record deportation numbers. And what "special focus" did the Black community get? We got news headlines and speeches rife with respectability politics when we were murdered by cops. We got the same concentration of poverty. We got the same school discrimination. We got the same mass incarceration. We got rising infant and maternal mortality rates.

Oh, and for eight years we got to know that someone who looked like us could be president of the United States.

And for that, we've had to pay with the most ignorant, hateful, and incompetent president in this country's history.

Along with many other people from marginalized groups, I strive for a day when we will see more people from our communities in leadership and more of the issues impacting our communities addressed by those in power. But I have never had the luxury of shunning everything in our society that does not appear to be built 100 percent for me.

I have had to find a way to enjoy movies and television even when the script is not written for me and the only characters that look like me are peripheral to the main action because I would like to see more than a few movies in my lifetime.

I have had to find a way to work in offices that don't see me as management material while still believing that there is a chance I can get a promotion anyway.

I've had to study history that erased my culture from its pages and know that it did not actually erase me.

I've had to learn laws that weren't written to serve me.

I've had to learn to write and appreciate words in a language that was forced on my ancestors.

Not only have things in America not been built for me; they have *never* been built for me. And although that has been physically, financially, politically, and psychologically disastrous for my community, I have come to see that it is also damaging to be led to believe that *everything* should be built for you and that anything built with the consideration of others is inherently harmful to you. It is harmful to the individual who believes it, and it is harmful to every system they interact with that is supposed to be built on coalition.

In the lead-up to the 2020 election, as with the 2016 election, we were drowning in talk of how we were going to make working- and middle-class white men feel included in order to defeat conservative forces. But I must honestly ask: What exactly do people who aren't white men *have* that could be more inclusive of white men? We do not have control of our local governments, our national governments, our school boards, our universities, our police forces, our militaries, our workplaces. All we have is our struggle. And yet we are told that our struggle for inclusion and equity—and our celebration of even symbolic steps toward them—is divisive and threatening to those who have far greater access to everything else than we can dream of. If white men are finding that the overwhelmingly white-male-controlled system isn't meeting their needs, how did *we* end up being the problem?

In an increasingly diverse country, white men can only demand to be the exclusive focus of our political systems for so long. Looking at how unfavorably some liberal white men view our small, occasional shifts in focus away from white maleness, I am afraid this will be a painful transition. But it doesn't have to be. It is possible to have a different expectation for effective government besides one in which everyone in it looks like you and centers your needs above all else. I know this because my community has always had different expectations of government. Politics that does not always center white men is something that white men can get used to—and they must.

# CHAPTER 3

# THE IVY LEAGUE AND THE TAX EATERS

## *White Men's Assault on Higher Education*

Back in the day, when I was in college, when Facebook was still mostly a chat room for college students, when we were still picking out background colors for our Myspace pages, and before anybody had integrated "tweeting" into their lexicon, we still had fake news. The war of ideas and information was being fought over what was taught in American classrooms, and the internet was being used to sow misinformation about the "dangers" of higher education. I clearly remember the one Black teacher in our entire political science department who let any students who had signed up for his class under false pretenses know that he was aware he was being monitored by conservative groups for his "un-American" teachings on race and politics, and that he was not going to be intimidated. No misleading headlines about his "reverse racism" or "anticonservative bigotry" had yet cost him his job, but student operatives were welcome to do their worst, so long as they turned in their assignments on time and didn't disrupt class.

I remember being as shocked by the gall of the misinformation campaigns as my professor seemed resigned to them. College was not supposed to be like this. Higher education was supposed to be the place where the strength of your work and ideas triumphed over race, gender, class, and political party. Yes, as a poor Black woman, college was still my best—if not only—chance at achieving the financial security for myself and my family that I desperately sought. But I had yet to learn how much smaller that chance was for people like me than it was for white men. And although when lost in my books, or in the middle of a class debate, I was able to see glimpses of the intellectual utopia I had been promised, I had yet to fully see the racist, sexist, and classist system I was deeply immersed in.

After graduating, I forgot much of what I had learned. I didn't really utilize my political science degree in my jobs in tech and advertising. Along with arguments on the pros and cons of Keynesian economics, my memory of the monitoring and intimidation of college professors by conservative operatives was largely forgotten.

It wasn't until I watched the state legislature punish Missouri State University for not cracking down on the protests of Black students and football players that I began to see the clear line of assault on American higher education by the political right that had spanned decades. Jokes have long existed about the supposed "stupidity" of conservatives. Plenty of articles are eager to point out that you are more likely to watch Fox News and vote Republican if you lack a college degree. Plenty of observers on the left have lamented the "dumbing down" of America that many feel is represented by the political right. In these arguments, higher education is often held up as a paragon of American intelligence and virtue. The college campus is allegedly the place where the pure love of knowledge is king, where people succeed based on their talents and efforts alone. A place where racism and sexism wither under the gaze of academic scrutiny.

But the history of American education is far more complicated than that. Our institutions of higher education not only contain the same basic bigotries as the rest of society; they have also been the place where many of those prejudices were legitimized through deliberately biased study. Our college campuses may not have been terribly concerned with elevating the poor white man over the poor Black woman, but they were definitely obsessed with preserving white male elite power at the top of the social and political ladders.

And in light of that history of elitism and bigotry, those who want to undermine the value of a college degree in order to preserve broader white male power are given plenty of justification for their disdain for higher education.

While conservative Republicans and the Trump administration have cornered the market on the political attack on higher ed, they are certainly not the only groups who see political benefit in attacking college campus environments and claiming that such places are harmful to white men. In recent years, in campuses around the country, left-leaning white male students and professors have decried efforts to teach racial sensitivity, to be inclusive of transgender students and staff, and to prevent sexual harassment and assault as attacks on all white men and as examples of progressivism gone "too far." And as angry white male professors from schools like Evergreen State College find themselves the darlings of Fox News when they warn of PC culture run amok on college campuses, while their most vulnerable students feel betrayed and even more vulnerable, we see the danger of not recognizing where the attack on American higher education originates from.

The truth is, those behind the attacks on higher education *came* from higher education. The vast majority of the politicians and pundits who appear on your television screens trying to convince you that a college education will brainwash your children into hating America have a very good college education themselves. They wouldn't for a minute dream of allowing their kids to skip college. It is on those campuses where they first learned how our political systems and our political identities work. And it's on campuses where they learn that those systems and identities can be used to consolidate political power for those who are willing to play on the base racist and sexist fears of white men and of those who benefit from their proximity to white men.

The campuses that many white men are made to fear as a direct threat to masculinity and white supremacy are the same places where white men learn to ascend to the throne of white male political power. The right's political attacks on higher education, and the failures of higher education that open it up to such attacks, are based in the same compulsion to retain white male status above everyone else. Lost in this debate are the people of color and women who depend on college degrees for any chance at financial security. If we fail to understand how white male supremacy has been woven through the entire fabric of higher education, then our colleges and universities—and the debate over the value of higher education itself—will continue to place marginalized people at risk.

## ELITE RACISM IN EARLY HIGHER EDUCATION

*[It] is altogether inadvisable for a colored*
*man to enter Princeton.*

—Woodrow Wilson, president of Princeton University,
to a Black man inquiring about admission, 1909[1]

In 2015 a group of Princeton students were afraid to leave Nassau Hall. They had occupied the hall earlier in the day and were planning to stay.

Nassau Hall was home to the university president's office, and school officials had locked the doors shortly after students occupied it. "We are concerned that once we leave, we will not be able to re-enter in the morning. Thus, we are not planning to leave," student organizer Wilglory Tanjong told the *Washington Post* from the phone of the school president's office. The students stayed for thirty-six hours in the hopes that the university would meet their demands.

Their principal requests? They wanted all teachers and staff to undergo cultural competency training, they wanted required classes on marginalized groups and cultures, and they wanted Woodrow Wilson's name removed from the Woodrow Wilson School of Public Policy and International Affairs.[2]

Before he became president of the United States, Woodrow Wilson was president of Princeton University. He is credited to a large extent for the university's status as one of the top institutions of higher learning in the world. But until recently, Princeton didn't talk much about the less savory aspects of Wilson's legacy. The fact is that Wilson was a racist. He refused to allow a single Black student into Princeton during his tenure. Wilson was open about his segregationist views, even directly discouraging Black students who inquired about admission from applying, and he would go on to become a segregationist US president as well. Wilson personally oversaw the destruction of integration efforts made during the post–Civil War Reconstruction, resegregating federal departments after white department heads complained of having to share workspaces with Black employees. Wilson also fired a majority of Black supervisors, and many Black workers were subsequently let go from federal jobs across the country and replaced with white workers. Wilson was strongly against Black suffrage, and he was a defender of the Klan. His words about the Klan even made it into the infamously racist film *Birth of a Nation*: "The white men were roused by a mere instinct of self-preservation . . . until at last there had sprung into existence a great Ku Klux Klan, a veritable empire of the South, to protect the Southern Country."[3]

Wilson was widely recognized as racist even in his time. While it isn't a surprise that popular culture wouldn't want to draw attention to a US president's racist past, universities are where history— accurate history—is supposed to matter.

When students took their concerns to university officials in 2015, they were effectively told that "everyone was racist" back then—as if it were a popular dance craze and not the violent oppression of people of color. Princeton refused to meet the students' demands, and memorials and departments named for Wilson remain unchanged.

If by "everyone" they meant "most of our elite educational institutions"—they were right.

Universities in America began as religious colleges in the colonies whose purpose was to train wealthy young white men to enter the ministry. This was not necessarily the quiet, humble calling we might think of today. Colonial America was a very religious place, and joining the clergy was the fastest track to social and political power. Although the liberal arts were always an important part of early American religious education (because a well-rounded training supposedly bred true "gentlemen" who would be more fit to lead the common people), after the American Revolution, the religious colleges broadened their fields of study to include areas like medicine and law.

Fewer students overall were entering colleges to join the clergy, but the vast majority of students were still white men from elite families. Universities were seen more as finishing schools for wealthy white men on their path to inheriting leadership than places for practical education. In fact, early degrees were often

awarded in graduation ceremonies that recognized the students
not by order of achievement or even field of study but by family rank.[4] These students were indeed learning how to lead. Their
studies of philosophy and politics, as well as the strong connections they made with other elite and powerful families, prepared
the young men to take their place at the helm of American society.

As colleges expanded beyond religious education and began
to standardize their admissions processes, wealthy and ambitious
families who had previously been denied access to the religious
universities began to send their kids through the doors of institutions like Harvard, Yale, and Princeton. This burgeoning diversity created a problem for elite universities: many of the new
students were Jewish. By the early 1920s, approximately 21 percent of Harvard's students and 40 percent of Columbia's were
Jewish.[5] This was particularly distressing to Harvard president A.
Lawrence Lowell. It was hard enough for Harvard to accommodate the lower-income white students they were now allowing in,
he argued. The school didn't need all these Jewish and Black students scaring away the wealthy white Christian students who paid
Harvard's bills.

Lowell got to work on fixing the problem. First, he banned
Black students from dormitories and dining halls, so wealthy
white parents would no longer have to worry about their children
fraternizing with Black ones.[6] Next, he made it a priority to stop
the smart Jewish kids from getting in.

Lowell went through student rolls from the previous two decades and classified students as J1 (Jewish), J2 (probably Jewish),
J3 (maybe Jewish), and "other." Just as Lowell suspected, he found
an alarming rise in the percentage of Jewish students—from 7
percent to 21 percent of the overall student body in just twenty
years. Lowell took these numbers to the board of trustees in 1922
in hopes of convincing them to implement a quota system to cap
the number of Jewish students admitted.[7]

Lowell claimed that he was not antisemitic or racist; he just be-lieved that the increasing number of Jewish students would drive away students who *were* antisemitic. Lowell explained this ratio-nale to a philosophy professor: "The summer hotel that is ruined by admitting Jews meets its fate, not because the Jews it admits are of bad character, but because they drive away the Gentiles, and then after the Gentiles have left, they leave also."[8]

Once the bigoted white students left, Harvard would obviously lose its appeal to Jewish students, and then who would Harvard have? The few Black students that were being forced to go else-where to eat and sleep? Nobody wanted that.

The Harvard board declined to institute the strict quotas on Jewish enrollment that Lowell wanted. Instead, they changed the admission criteria, opting instead to focus more on things like birthplace and family background. They also looked at subjective qualities: athletic ability and the vague "personality."[9] While Har-vard touted these changes as steps to increase diversity, they really gave the school a way to quietly prioritize non-Jewish students by emphasizing traits and criteria, like athleticism, that they assumed Jewish students were less likely to have. They were able to hide big-oted admissions decisions behind a so-called broadening of their enrollment initiatives. (This debate continues today, as similar cri-teria have been shown to be disadvantageous to Asian American students at Harvard, leading many to believe that Asian Ameri-can students are being discriminated against in the same way that Jewish students were. But the current debate is complicated by the fact that those criteria are advantageous to Black and Hispanic stu-dents, who have been and continue to be severely underrepresented at the college.)

Lowell's legacy is still felt today on Harvard's campus. In a 2019 discussion on whether or not to remove Lowell's portrait from one of the school's dining halls, student Richard Yarrow said, "The portrait of A. Lawrence Lowell doesn't need to be peering down at students in the middle of lunchtime or breakfast. I'm a Jewish student. A. Lawrence Lowell was a notorious anti-Semite. He kept out my grandfather."[10]

It was not just elite universities that were concerned with the impact that increased diversity might have on American colleges and universities. In the age of eugenics (the now widely denounced "science" of improving society through the controlled breeding of people with desired characteristics), many well-off white people were concerned about the effect that regular contact—and even, gasp, *intermarriage*—with poor people, Black people, Jewish people, and disabled people might have on the aptitude of their future generations.[11]

One person who was particularly concerned was Princeton psychology professor Carl Brigham. Brigham's career started in World War I in the Sanitary Corps, where he worked in the psychological service. Concerned with the overall mental fitness of its soldiers, the US military had Brigham run psychological tests on soldiers to screen for intelligence and mental health. After the war, Brigham joined Princeton and became more heavily involved in the eugenics movement, even sitting on the Eugenics Advisory Council. He used his testing on soldiers to justify his calls for anti-immigration and racial segregation to preserve the intelligence of "European national groups." In 1923 Brigham published his landmark book, *A Study of American Intelligence*, in which he warned white society of the dangers of rising racial and ethnic diversity. Brigham's book was used to justify everything from anti-immigration legislation to forced sterilization of people deemed "unfit" to procreate: "The decline of American intelligence will be more rapid than the decline of the intelligence of European national groups, owing to the presence here of the negro. These are the plain, if somewhat ugly, facts that our study shows. The deterioration of American intelligence is not inevitable, however, if public action can be aroused to prevent it."[12]

The book was highly influential in American society and academia, and shortly after, Brigham was asked by the College Board to help develop a new test to screen college applicants for academic ability: the Scholastic Aptitude Test, or SAT.[13]

Brigham's test was quickly rolled out to high schools and by 1926 was used by many colleges and universities across the country to help them select students most likely to find academic success in their halls. But by 1930, Brigham had rejected his own eugenics-based tests. He'd found some fundamental flaws in his methodology. In particular, he had come to realize that what his tests showed, instead of intelligence, was the test-taker's ability to speak English, attend good primary schools, and demonstrate a strong familiarity with white culture. He wrote a refutation of his earlier army research in a paper titled "Intelligence Tests of Immigrant Groups" and later denounced the SAT tests that he had based on that research, but by then it was too late.[14] The SAT persists as the primary test of student readiness used by colleges and universities throughout the United States.[15]

It should come as no surprise, then, given the SAT's racist origins, that since its inception, poor students, Black students, Hispanic students, and Indigenous students have consistently received scores on the test that are double-digit percentages lower than white students. And that SAT scores have long been recognized as poor indicators of actual college readiness. Given what we know about society's biases and how the scales are always tilted toward people in power, it was inevitable that a test that so clearly showed favor to wealthier white students would be eagerly adopted by schools seeking ways to keep their percentages of wealthy white students high, and their percentages of poor students and students of color low. In disadvantaging poor students and students of color, and in advantaging white students more for their race than for their actual college aptitude or readiness, the SAT test has always worked as designed.

## COLLEGE FOR EVERYONE

Higher education would not, as we know, remain the exclusive bastion of rich white men forever. By the late 1800s, the federal government, in its recent expansion across the continent, had acquired (mostly through violence against Indigenous peoples) more land than it knew what to do with. In order to fund economic expansion to go with territorial expansion, Representative Justin Smith Morrill of Vermont proposed a national education scheme. With Morrill's plan, the federal government would give large pieces of land to states. The states could sell the land under the condition that they would use the proceeds to fund higher education focused around agriculture, engineering, or veterinary sciences. These were not the high-minded liberal-arts studies of wealthy white children. The goal of these new colleges was to provide, say, a layer of "middle management" to the American economy. Across the country, sixty-nine new colleges and universities sprang up to give practical education to middle-class Americans that would prepare them to help drive economic growth in their states. Some of our most highly respected universities (including Cornell University, Purdue University, and the Massachusetts Institute of Technology) are land-grant schools.[16]

In 1890, Morrill sponsored a bill to increase funding to land-grant colleges. The bill specified that states would be denied the money for their institutions if they discriminated against African Americans in their admissions. In order to make this provision a little more palatable in the post–Civil War South, states were also given the option of educating Black Americans in separate institutions, provided that funding was "equitably divided" between Black and white institutions. While "equitably divided" was a term vague enough to allow Southern states to give a disproportionate percentage of funds to white schools, the funding did lead to the establishment of sixteen Black land-grant institutions.

These HBCUs were denied the needed funding to invest in agriculture and mechanical sciences, the way white land-grant colleges had been able to, so they focused primarily on teaching future educators. The lack of investment in mechanical and scientific programs would hurt the reputations of HBCUs for decades to come and would cut them off from valuable sources of research funding through today.[17] And although HBCUs suffered from unequal funding and support in the land-grant program, they still fared better than colleges serving other communities of color. There are only two Hispanic-serving land-grant colleges, and American Indian colleges were denied land-grant status and funding until 1994.[18]

Over the next few decades, the US government would significantly increase the funding to land-grant colleges and universities, allowing them not only to serve more students but also to offer broader fields of study. The massive increase in college facilities came at a perfect time, as the United States was about to see unprecedented growth in college attendance. World War II was ending, and the federal government was concerned about the futures of returning soldiers. Expecting unemployment rates of up to 25 percent, the government came up with benefit packages for veterans that would prepare them for employment in the new businesses created by wartime industrial expansion. The GI Bill was a large program of various benefits, all designed to help returning soldiers land on their feet, but one of the most utilized and successful was the education benefit.

With new facilities and funding, for the first time in US history higher education was now easily attainable for working- and middle-class white men. The GI Bill (and military service in general) hadn't been made widely available to women yet, and the majority of colleges enrolled few, if any, Black students.

The increase in well-paid, skilled positions after WWII brought higher wages to workers who were able to get higher educations. A college education quickly became the best path to success for working- and middle-class white men in America. In 1964, fewer than 10 percent of college-aged Black and Hispanic Americans attended college. By 1971, the mostly white men with college degrees were earning 22 percent more than men of the same age who only held a high school diploma.[19] This difference was more than worth the cost of what was then still a relatively affordable education. As a college education moved from a luxury to a requirement for millions of Americans looking for financial security, federal and state governments increased their investments in higher education, and the number of colleges and universities across the country grew rapidly, from 1,851 to 3,535 in the forty years between 1950 and 1990.

But by the 1970s the American establishment's enthusiasm for higher education had started to dwindle. Why? Maybe because it wasn't all about white men anymore.

The benefits of higher education could not be the exclusive privilege of white men forever. As schools integrated under affirmative action programs and funding opportunities opened up to women and people of color, campuses across the country rapidly diversified. Along with that diversification of the student body came demands for diversification in fields of study. The first women's studies department was established in 1970 at San Diego State University, and other, similar programs began opening shortly thereafter. In the late 1960s and early 1970s, multiracial and multiethnic student coalitions at West Coast schools like San Francisco State University and University of California, Berkeley, held protests and strikes demanding the creation of ethnic studies departments, leading to the first such program in the country at San Francisco State University in 1969.[20]

With higher education more widely available, the extreme financial benefits of holding a college degree started to level. There were now more qualified workers than ever before. As women and people of color found that their new degrees offered them great financial benefits that they had previously been denied, white men found that for them, the return on investment of their higher education, although still significant (and still leading to income that was much higher than what women and people of color earned), was not increasing at the same pace.[21]

Even though a college education was lifting white men, people of color, and women out of poverty at a reliable rate, the attitude toward higher education began to shift. As white men saw that their degrees no longer put them as far ahead of women and people of color as the degrees once did, they began to question whether a diploma was worth the cost.

To add insult to injury for white men, suddenly women and people of color were demanding that college courses represent their interests as well. Students began agitating for social and political change on campus. Even white students were coming home filled with new ideas about peace and equality, which caused white parents across the country to think that a degree might not be as good for their children as they had once thought.[22]

The growing doubts about the value of a college education were not entirely based on resentment over the rising status of women and people of color. Starting in the 1980s, costs for education rose rapidly. Although a college education in the 1980s and '90s was more valuable than ever, as employers increasingly insisted on college degrees, the sticker shock of the upfront cost—especially compared to what earlier generations had paid—left many feeling as though college was once again a rich man's game. But even with the increasing outcry over tuition prices and the seemingly lackluster returns on that investment (cries that came most notably from conservative circles), college enrollment levels kept rising—especially for women and people of color.[23]

Riding the wave of economic and educational dissatisfaction in white America, President Ronald Reagan's administration began to argue that perhaps the government funding of higher education was little more than a drain on revenue to support jobless young people on the taxpayer's dime. They were, the Reagan administration said, "tax eaters."[24] Like Reagan's infamous invoking of the "welfare queen," his rhetoric on higher-education assistance fell in line with his stories about how supposedly undeserving groups were taking advantage of the hardworking American.

Reagan's disdain for higher education—especially government funding for higher education—was both political and personal in nature. In his run for governor of California in 1966, Reagan successfully campaigned in part on a pledge to "clean up" UC Berkeley. Outraged at 1960s protests against the Vietnam War, Reagan painted a picture of spoiled hippie kids learning to be ungrateful while living on taxpayer money. Once elected governor, Reagan had UC president Clark Kerr fired, violently cracked down on student protests (in 1969, the police response to one such protest—at the People's Park in Berkeley—left one student dead and dozens of students wounded), and immediately began undermining the UC system's programs to keep college financially attainable to any student who wished to attend.[25]

Having practiced on the University of California system, Reagan, once he became president of the United States, took his educational reforms national. He passed sweeping tax and spending cuts that slashed funding for students, making college more expensive and inaccessible to those who needed it the most. Due to the racial economic disparities in America, students of color were often more likely to need the financial assistance and educational programs that the US government had previously funded and were therefore some of the most greatly impacted by Reagan's funding cuts. But at a time when middle- and working-class white America was dissatisfied with slower economic growth and increased competition at home (from women workers and workers of color) and abroad (from the rise in foreign manufacturing), Reagan was not punished politically for cutting the feet out from under underprivileged students. He was rewarded with reelection and the highest approval ratings since Franklin Roosevelt.[26]

## THEY'LL TEACH YOU TO HATE AMERICA

*We'll take $200,000 of your money; in exchange,*
*we'll train your children to hate our country. . . .*
*We'll make them unemployable by teaching them*
*courses in zombie studies, underwater basket weaving*
*and, my personal favorite, tree climbing.*

—*Donald Trump Jr.*[27]

In July 2017 the Pew Research Center found that a whopping 58 percent of Republicans and right-leaning Independents thought that colleges and universities were having a negative impact on our country. That number had increased from 37 percent in just two years. "Why does a kid go to a major university these days? A lot of Republicans would say they go there to get brainwashed and learn how to become activists and basically go out in the world and cause trouble," Trump supporter Frank Antenori explained to the *Chicago Tribune*. More right-leaning Americans appear to agree with Antenori every day. While the majority of parents in America know that their kids must attend college to have a chance at a financially secure future, the university is no longer a place that many conservative white families look forward to sending their kids.[28]

In March 2019, President Trump proposed an $8.5 billion cut—an astounding 12 percent—to our nation's overall education budget. On the chopping block were after-school programs, funding for textbooks and school counselors, teacher-development programs, college work-study programs, college-preparation programs for disadvantaged youth, some federal student-aid programs, and subsidy programs that delay the accrual of interest on student loans while recipients remain in school.[29] In addition, Trump proposed lower limits on student loans with the justification that it would force colleges and universities to lower costs.[30] Juxtaposed against the massive budget cuts were enormous increases in private-school vouchers, high school vocational programs, and funding for trade schools, community colleges, and apprenticeship programs.[31] These changes are unlikely to get past a Democratic House, and his previous attempts at gutting higher education were so drastic that they were unable to get past a Republican House either. But chances are, he'll keep trying.

Trump has not been the only Republican determined to undermine the American higher-education system, and this trend will likely continue long after Trump leaves political life. "Wasteful," "greedy," "elite" colleges have been a target of Republican politicians and officials since the Reagan years. Tuition had long risen faster than inflation, and the returns on that increased spending seemed to be decreasing. For the working-class white male who missed the days when a man could get a good-paying job at a factory with no need for a college degree, a politician willing to blame it all on a liberal college system getting rich off taxpayer money so that it could turn your children into hippies and position women and people of color above you was almost guaranteed to gain conservative support.

In looking at right-wing political rhetoric around higher education, we see a pattern of complaints. Some are based in real problems, others in bigotry and resentment:

- **Colleges are turning your children into ungrateful liberals who hate America.** A college campus, especially at a liberal-arts institution, is a place where many young people first discover the power of civic engagement. As students learn more about injustices in our systems and are empowered by new adulthood, they are perhaps more likely to voice their opinions and work for change. There are, of course, many different ideologies on any given campus, but college activism has been an easy target of conservatives since the 1960s.

• **Obama went to college.** It might sound like I'm making this up, but I'm not. As part of the anti-Obama backlash that white conservatives embraced after his election and re-election, his Ivy-league degree became one of the strongest symbols of his "out-of-touch elitism" (or, if you are listening closely, his "uppityness"). Obama's elite-college experience became a stand-in for what an Obama presidency would force on Americans: a bloated, expensive system that turned your children into communists and threatened traditional American values on the taxpayer dime. Conservatives wanted a president who could relate to the everyday man, not a bourgeois Kenyan from Harvard.

• **College has gotten far too expensive because colleges tried to maximize profits while your children got degrees in rhythmic screaming and cultural studies.** The cost of a college education has indeed risen dramatically, especially in the last decade. In 2016, the average yearly cost of an education at a four-year public university was almost 52 percent of the median man's yearly income and 81 percent of the median woman's, versus 20 percent and 52 percent in 1980.[32] But this rise is by Republican design. In response to growing discontent with higher education, Republican-controlled state governments across the country started reducing their spending on public colleges and universities. When the Great Recession hit, higher-education budgets were among the first items to be cut as state budgets plummeted; overall, states collectively reduced their annual education funding by $9 billion in the years 2008–2017. Colleges responded by passing a sizeable amount of their expense burden on to students. Even though the recession is years behind us, most states have not increased their education funding to even prerecession levels. Adjusting for inflation, states still paid on average 10 percent *less* on education per student in 2017 than they did in 2007.[33]

- **Compared to possessing only a high school diploma, obtaining a four-year degree from any not-for-profit college or university is likely to financially benefit a student.**[34] This fact defies claims that students today get degrees in wildly impractical fields that are a waste of money. Bring on the rhythmic screaming.

In the midst of all this anger and discontentment, what is the reality of the value of a college education? Yes, higher education is too expensive; many state colleges and universities are far more focused on increasing revenues than they were a decade ago. But there is still no surer path to financial security in America than getting a college degree. Today's college graduate can expect to make over $1 million more on average over their lifetime than someone with only a high school diploma. Even as the average student debt rises above $30,000 per student, college is still a pretty good deal in the long run.[35]

If there is one person in the post-Obama years who values an elite college education, it's Donald Trump. He proudly attended the Ivy League's Wharton School of Finance at University of Pennsylvania. Trump was pleased to send three of his children—Don Jr.,

Ivanka, and Tiffany—to Wharton as well. For all his attacks on higher education and the "elites" who go to fancy schools, Trump has managed to brag quite frequently about his own elite education and how intelligent it obviously means he is. He has mentioned it so often that it caught the attention of the *Daily Pennsylvanian*, who decided to count how many times he discussed his Ivy League education. The paper found that, from May 2015 through January 2018, Trump discussed his degree an impressive ninety-three separate times in interviews, speeches, tweets, and other public commentary. Trump flaunted his education with statements like: "So I went to the Wharton School of Finance, which is considered the best business school, okay? Gotta be very smart to get into that school, very smart. The Rubios of the world cannot get into that school, believe me," and "Hey, look—I went to the hardest school to get in, the best school, the Wharton School—it's like super-genius stuff."[36]

If self-avowed "super-genius" Donald Trump values his college education so much that he would mention it publicly almost a hundred times in under three years, why is he working so hard to undermine higher education for the people he represents? The 2016 election numbers offer some strong clues. In 2016, 66 percent of white voters without a college degree voted for Trump. For white men without a college degree, the number jumps to 71 percent.[37] On the flip side, Clinton took college-educated voters by nine percentage points, and she received a larger share of the votes from white college-educated voters than Romney did in 2012.[38]

In short: people with college degrees are far less likely to vote Republican.

A few people on the left like to extrapolate and say these numbers mean that people who vote Democratic are smarter than people who vote Republican. That is an unkind and untrue assumption. It also ignores many of the reasons why people do or do not go to college (or even have access to it) and erases the various ways in which we can define knowledge or talent outside of academia.

There are, I believe, a few reasons why white people with college degrees are more likely to vote Democratic than white people without a college degree:

- **College puts you in closer contact with more marginalized people than life outside of college is likely to.** White people, as part of the majority of this very racially divided country, rarely have to spend a lot of time with people who are not white. The ability to live in a racially and culturally homogenous society is not a luxury that minority populations have. This racial separation is by design. For generations, white communities have placed barriers to access before people of color in order to ensure that their neighborhoods, primary schools, and workplaces stay as white as possible. And it has worked. The average white person in America has less than one friend of color.[39] Getting to know people of different backgrounds and identities is one of the best ways to build empathy and community with them. Issues impacting communities of color will not seem like your issues if you do not consider any people of color a part of your community. It is far easier to see the interests of marginalized communities as competing with yours instead of a part of yours. A white American perspective will seem to be the "normal" one, and everything else will be "other." Accommodations will feel like sacrifices—or even worse, theft. When the majority of people from communities of color and LGBTQ+ communities vote Democratic because they believe it is the party that gives some concern to their needs, the Democratic party will seem more like the party of "them" not "you"—so long as you see marginalized people as "them."

- **College teaches you the basics of how our political and economic systems work.** Any sort of liberal-arts degree—the kind most targeted by Republicans and the Trump administration—will require some basic classes on history, politics, or sociology, no matter what major you end up declaring. One of the fundamental charges of a liberal-arts education institution is to create an informed, active citizenry. Regardless of party, people who understand how our political systems work are less likely to fall for (without being entirely immune to) reactionary populists who want to blame the failures of complex socioeconomic systems on "the Blacks," "the illegals," "the gays," or "the elite media."

- **Having a college degree makes women and people of color less of a socioeconomic threat to you.** This may sound highly cynical, but it is perhaps the most important factor in why whites who have a college degree are less likely to vote Republican. White workers with college degrees are pretty much at the top of the economic ladder in the pool of average Americans. For white households where the head of household has at least a bachelor's degree, the average net worth is almost $400,000. For Hispanic households with a college degree, it is $74,000. For Black households, it is only $68,000.[40] The only demographic group that earns more than college-educated white men is college-educated Asian men, but at less than 3 percent of the US population, Asian-American men are less of a threat to white workers than other workers of color. (That said, Asian Americans regularly face employment discrimination and are less likely to be promoted above middle management than their white peers, which indicates that they are indeed seen as a threat to their white coworkers.) Generally speaking, fewer white workers will end up working with—and therefore having to worry about competing with—Asian Americans than with other racial and ethnic minority groups.

- **If you are a white man with a college degree, you are far less likely to have to worry about watching anyone that you feel might be undeserving move past you on the socioeconomic ladder.** By contrast, if you are a white man without a college degree, although your household is still likely to hold more net worth than a Black or Hispanic household headed by someone *with* a college degree ($100,000 versus $74,000 and $68,000 respectively), and you will still likely earn higher wages than a Black or Hispanic woman *with* a college degree, yours is the white demographic most likely to compete directly with people of color for jobs, income, and status. As more people of color enter college, and the percentage of jobs requiring a college degree increases, the perceived threat to the socioeconomic status of white men who lack college degrees goes up. You don't have to have a single person of color in your office to believe that women and other people of color are passing you by. Just log on to social media or turn on your television to see increasing numbers of images of successful minorities. You are being outpaced. If you are a white man without a college degree, Trump's promises to bring back high-paying factory jobs and to lessen the importance of elite education will appeal to you in a way that it cannot to white people with college degrees.

In demonizing higher education—the same education that Trump ensured all his children received—Trump can maintain popularity among white voters who feel left behind by calls for increasingly skilled labor and who feel threatened by the seemingly rising socioeconomic status of women and people of color.

Further, by undermining higher education, he can ensure future voters for himself and the Republican party.

At the root of all this we have a consolidation of power and knowledge by the elite, with the intention of keeping the working classes divided and disenfranchised. In Trump's (and many other conservative politicians') ideal world, the average American seeks only enough knowledge to fulfill his or her part of a capitalist system, while those born to privilege will learn the ways of world leadership at elite institutions.

This was Lowell's aim when he goaded Harvard into setting Jewish quotas. It's what Brigham was designing when he wrote the SAT. And it is a future that right-wing populists, those who have spent decades demonizing higher education in order to feed into white male fears of their own mediocrity, are actively creating.

## I REALLY HATE DEFENDING HIGHER EDUCATION

I've spent a lot of time these last few years on college campuses. After the publication of *So You Want to Talk About Race*, I was invited to many colleges and universities that did, indeed, want to get better at talking about race.

These visits were never easy. More often than not I would meet with reluctant white professors who thought that race had nothing to do with the classes they taught, and with burned-out professors of color who were trying to teach their classes, advocate for students of color, and deal with white colleagues who refused to address racial issues in their work. At every college I went to— every single one—at least one teacher of color broke down in tears describing their struggle to advocate for their students of color in such a hostile environment.

Higher education is not the racial utopia that Republicans are scared of. It is not some bizarro world where students of color wield power over white students and faculty. It is a white supremacist system at its core, like all our other systems are. That is shown in the numbers. Black students, Hispanic students, Indigenous students, and Pacific Islander students all fare far worse on college campuses than white students—they are less likely to be admitted, and when they are admitted, they are far less likely to graduate than white students.[41]

I remember sitting with Black social work students on a campus in Illinois. They told me they had chosen social work because of all the ways in which they had been failed in their own lives by social workers and others who held similar positions of authority in local government. They wanted to be able to support people whom traditional social work had left behind, like them. The students shared their struggles to make it out of areas like Ferguson, Missouri, and into college when so many people had told them it wasn't possible. Some students were homeless during their first years of college. They talked about how all their professors were white, and how in every class their professors pathologized people who looked like them and who came from the communities they grew up in. They talked about how they struggled to make good grades in classes that wanted to teach them that people who looked like them were fundamentally broken. They put up with these insults and hurdles so they would have a chance to be social workers who could tell their community members that they weren't flawed.

I say all of this to make the point that I really hate defending higher education. It is a broken system that can do a lot of harm to marginalized people. Yet it's the best place in America for our young people to formulate their social and political consciousnesses. How very sad.

I loved my days at Western Washington University. I loved them even though I had to take specific classes on race and politics if I wanted to hear any discussion about race in any of my political science classes. I loved them even though I only had one Black professor and one Asian American professor in a sea of white male professors. Even though I was the only Black person in every one of my classes. Even then, I loved college. I think I fundamentally knew that the occasional research paper written by a scholar of color, the chapter discussing queer activism in 1970s politics, the brief introduction to intersectionality and the work of Kimberlé Crenshaw—I knew that those few instances in which the scholarship of women, people of color, disabled people, and LGBTQ+ people were treated as valid and worthy of respect were the closest I would get to an America that respected and appreciated people who weren't white and male. And when I looked at my classmates bent over the words of Black women and queer women, studying them intently and discussing them respectfully—I knew that this was the closest many of them would come to respecting the opinions and perspectives of people who weren't white and male. If we lost that, then where would we be?

I am not defending higher education because I love, or even like, the institution. I am defending it because without it, we are lost. And because I have seen, in my own academic history and in the countless hours I've spent on campuses across the country, what higher education *could* be.

It could truly be the place that angry white men hate and fear if it put in the effort. It could be a place that dares to believe that the world does not revolve around white men. It could be a place that promotes the idea that people who aren't white men have just as much right and ability to shape our future in their image as white men have. It could be a place where we learn to respect consent and pronouns, where we learn about intersectionality, where we learn the truth about our corrupt systems and begin to demand change, where we learn to respect and appreciate people who are different from us, where we start demanding justice for the oppressed, where we investigate our histories of bias and bigotry. Higher education could be all of that, and the world would be better for it.

The war on higher education is coming from both the outside and the inside. As Trump and others on the right try to delegitimize higher education, conservative professors and administrators have long tried to delegitimize teachers and faculty who are dedicated to social justice in their fields. As funding is cut for higher education in states across the country, conservative think tanks are reaching out to the institutions and offering funds—but only for conservative teachers and courses.[42] Across the country, race- and gender-studies professors are seeing their budgets slashed and their deans removed so their departments can be swallowed up by more "respectable" ones in science, technology, and business.

Trump and others on the right want to make sure that working-class white men don't want to go to college and distrust those who do, and conservative educators want to make sure that people from marginalized communities don't want to go either. All of this works by design. It is to ensure that enough of us keep our heads down, focus on surviving our nine-to-five jobs, don't ask questions, and don't demand more from a system that owes us a lot. The death of American higher education will harm the most vulnerable of us first, but its goal is not to harm or oppress only us—that work is fully implanted in all our systems. Its goal is to continue to oppress and exploit white supremacy's most powerful tool: the angry white working-class man.

# CHAPTER 4

# WE HAVE FAR TOO MANY NEGROES

*White America's Bitter Dependency on People of Color*

Even the most virulent American racist has to wrestle with the fact that the United States would not exist were it not for people of color. The blood that soaked this soil so it could be called America came from Native people. The earliest agricultural techniques were taught to white colonizers by Native people. The farms were worked by people of color. The buildings, roads, and railroads were built by Black Americans, Asian Americans, and Hispanic Americans. Every white supremacist who claims that the United States is a white country knows that white settlers would have frozen to death faster than you can say Pocahontas if it weren't for Native people.

And a white man who loves the rock music Black musicians invented, who quotes Dave Chappelle at the watercooler even though he never understood the jokes' nuances, who grabs Chinese takeout on his way home to watch football every Monday night will still fix his mouth to say that he would be better off without us.

The white man who emails me to tell me that my people are a drain on society wouldn't have a computer without Black and Asian people—not the machine, the electrical components, or the math in its programming. Mathematics itself would not exist without the Middle East. The rubber on the bottom of his tennis shoes wouldn't exist without Native people. His grandma would have died without the pacemaker invented by Black people. And when he emerges from his mom's basement after a day of playing video games—on a system that wouldn't exist without Asian people—to make himself a peanut butter sandwich, the fact that the spread wouldn't exist without a Black man sticks in his throat a little.

I do not seek out these angry white men. I don't know any people of color who do. Yet they find us. They send us online messages out of the blue letting us know that they think they are better than us. They scream from cars telling us to go back to where we came from. Most white Americans have exclusively white friendship circles; three-quarters of white Americans have less than one friend of color.[1] In this racially segregated society, some white people seem more than eager to emerge from their normal circles to find people of color to yell at. I'm surprised at how those who claim they would be better off without us can't seem to leave us alone.

White America does not need us merely for what we contribute to culture, science, or the arts. It needs us as an outlet for its rage. I have found that a segment of white men absolutely needs to be angry at me and others who look like me: men who cling to their identity of being both better than me and aggrieved by my existence. Why do these white men need to be angry at us? People of color—especially Black people, Hispanic people, Indigenous people, and people of Middle Eastern descent—are convenient scapegoats for white people who are disappointed by life's outcomes. We are also the distraction that those in power point to when they want to avoid the blame for this country's vast wealth and opportunity gaps.

The fear of Americans of color is almost wholly manufactured by the imaginations of white America. The average white American has always been more likely to be physically harmed by another white person than by a person of color. The average white American has always been more likely to lose their job to another white person than to a person of color. The average white American is more likely to lose a spot at their dream college to a white person than to a person of color. The messaging that claims the opposite has not been created by people like me.

In the internet age, this resentment is more easily manufactured and distributed through social media and disreputable news sources. A story of Black crime that may have riled up one white neighborhood can now be used as a warning against integration and diversity across the country. While these sensationalized news stories keep many white people in fear, they also reinforce an aggrieved identity that gives a sense of community and belonging. White supremacy is just good business. Manufactured fear is a cheaper and more reliable driver of clicks and media market share than nuanced and deeply reported news stories.

Many of us shake our heads at how quickly hate and misinformation are spread in this new digital world, but none of it is new. White American identity was built on its opposition to people of color, especially Black people. Long before the country's first blockbuster movie, the 1915 film *Birth of a Nation*; before the infamous "Willie Horton ad," which used the story of a Black murderer to scare white voters out of voting for a liberal candidate who would be "soft on crime"; before the demonization of Black people on cable news; before today's racist memes and fake-news stories aimed at stoking anti-Black racism on social media—long before all these phenomena, the fictionalized story of Black brutality has for centuries provided many white Americans with terror, rage, entertainment, community, and profit. Even though stoking white Americans' fear of Black Americans caused them anxiety, they wanted more. Even though this myth distracted white Americans from addressing issues that were actually harming them, they wanted more.

Due to the legacy of slavery and its continuation in the form of the prison-industrial complex, white America's relationship with Blackness is unique. It is an active form of violent racism that started when white Americans began to depend on the forced, free labor of Black people to work their plantations and raise their kids, and it continues in the forced, free prison labor that earns white men and their investors healthy profits.

And thus whiteness in the United States has always been bitterly and unhealthily bonded to Blackness.

## THE SOUTH'S SELF-DEFEAT

*Politically speaking, there are far too many negroes, but from an industrial standpoint there is room for many more.*

—Southern politician interviewed about the
exodus of Black Southerners, early 1900s[2]

What happens when you are terrified of living alongside your neighbors, yet even more terrified of living without them? That was a dilemma white Southerners faced at the close of the Civil War.

Determined to help the devastated South recover as quickly and peacefully as possible, the US government invested heavily in rebuilding Southern infrastructure after the war. But along with the investment came efforts to ensure the enfranchisement of newly emancipated Black Americans. It was Southern whites' worst nightmare and shame come true. "Nigger voting, holding office, and sitting in the jury box are all wrong," declared the *Columbus Democrat*, a Mississippi paper.[3] But it was a humiliation they would not have to endure for long. As the federal government quickly ran low on money, it also depleted its will to oversee the Reconstruction of the South, and so Washington handed over the reins to the states themselves.

And the states burned it all to the ground.

In what is now known as the post-Reconstruction South, whites went on a murderous rampage in order to restore the racial hierarchy they had previously enjoyed. Over twenty-four hundred Blacks were murdered by Southern whites between 1882 and 1930.[4] Most Black Southerners had no connections in the North and no means to get there. As before, Black Americans were trapped. Until one day they weren't.

> *Dear Sir: Now I am writing you to oblige me to put my application in the papers for me please. I am a body servant or nice house maid. My hair is Black and my eyes are Black and smooth skin and clear and brown, good teeth and strong and good health and my weight is 136 lb.*
>
> —Letter from a Black woman in Natchez, Mississippi, to the Chicago Defender, *inquiring about work in the North, 1917*[5]

The nation found itself at war again, this time overseas. With millions of Americans away fighting in World War I and a slow-down of European immigration, the industrial North found itself short on labor when it needed it the most. The few Blacks who

had fled to the North earlier out of desperation now found themselves in coveted factory positions, making six times the wages
they could earn working the fields down South. They sent word to
friends and family back home that there was a way out of the terror, devastation, and extreme poverty that they had felt trapped in.

Black Southerners left in droves. Recruiters from the North
accelerated the departures with promises of living wages, access
to education, and an environment free of the racial terror of the
post-Reconstruction South. Southern white community leaders
panicked. Agriculture at the turn of the twentieth century was still
very labor-intensive. The industry couldn't survive without large
numbers of cheap workers. And although the abolition of slavery
meant that the labor of Black workers was no longer free, as the
only financially and logistically viable option open to white planta-
tion owners, they were still grossly underpaid.

Southern whites tried multiple tactics to get Blacks to stay.
They cut the wages of Black workers so they couldn't afford trans-
portation north. They refused to cash paychecks for Black workers
if they had a suspicion that the money would be used to finance
travel north. Lawmakers made the recruitment of Black workers to
the North illegal and started jailing recruiters who showed up in
Southern cities. They printed horror stories of Black Northern life
in local papers. They refused to sell bus and train tickets to Black
travelers. They arrested Black people at bus stations on vagrancy
charges. They started beating Blacks whom they caught leaving.[6]

None of this, unsurprisingly, was effective in convincing Blacks
that they should stay in the South. They fled in record numbers.
Between 1916 and 1930, more than one million Blacks moved
north in the hopes of finding jobs, education, and safety. By the
time Southern leaders changed tactics and decided to improve
working and living conditions for Blacks instead of antagonizing
them, it was too late. The Southern cotton industry was in sham-
bles. Because the Southern elites had tied all their financial hopes

to that single industry and had driven away the workforce that could have helped the region transition into new industries, the South would never be the model of prosperity it had once considered itself. And by the end of the Great Migration, more than six million people had left the South, which would be forever changed.

At the beginning of the Great Migration, 90 percent of Blacks in the United States lived in the rural South. By 1970, only 47 percent of Blacks lived in the South. Today, the legacy of slavery in the South is seen not only in the remaining plantations and Confederate flags. The South, with its insistence on avoiding most political or economic progress that would threaten white supremacist power by benefitting Blacks as well as whites, has cursed itself. Of the ten poorest states in America, eight of them—West Virginia, Kentucky, Arkansas, Louisiana, Mississippi, Alabama, Georgia, and South Carolina—are in the South.[7] Of the ten states with the worst food insecurity and the most hunger in America, eight of them—West Virginia, Kentucky, Oklahoma, Arkansas, Louisiana, Mississippi, Alabama, and North Carolina—are in the South.[8]

Slavery and violent white supremacy are the story of the South's past, its present, and, likely, its future. In 2017, when researchers from Harvard Business School looked at the socioeconomic histories of various regions of the United States to determine which factors supported economic growth and innovation, they found a lot of interesting patterns. They found that places that were more economically and socially open to diversity were more conducive to innovation in business and technology. They also found that having once been a slaveholding state was a good predictor of stagnant economic growth, based on past growth patterns.[9]

An overwhelmingly popular narrative states that the South's great wound is the Civil War and the aggression of the North. Even recently, as I traveled through Southern states, I was struck by how wed we are to the idea that if it weren't for the war, the South would have been so much more. But the system of slavery could not have been maintained forever—even the most racist white Southerner admits that it was untenable and couldn't have survived much longer than it did. Still, if the South had managed to cling to chattel slavery until it could transition to some other industry, the region would have faced an impossible battle. The North was already far ahead in industrializing, and the moment a place existed that offered even slightly better conditions than the horrors of slavery, Blacks would have left. In the end, the Great Migration sealed the South's fate more than the Lost Cause that it has glorified.

The South fought the Civil War because it could not envision life without Black labor. It was a cause worth sacrificing hundreds of thousands of white Southern lives to. There is irony in the fact that while the South could not envision itself *without* Black labor, it would suffer a second defeat—at its own hand—because it couldn't imagine living *with* Black people.

## THE OTHER MIGRATION

*White men have an equality resulting from a presence*
*of a lower caste, which cannot exist where white men*
*fill the position here occupied by the servile race.*

—*Jefferson Davis, president of the Confederate States of America*[10]

If you engage in debate with a proud white Southerner about racism and slavery in the South, there is a good chance they will point out that the majority of white Southerners were not slaveholders. They may say that many were poor and treated as second-class citizens by white elites, and that all white Southerners were looked down on by Northerners, regardless of class or slaveholding status. These points are often made to argue that perhaps there is no real history of deep-seated racism in the South, and perhaps even that the Civil War was not about slavery.

The initial points of the argument are true. The great majority of Southern whites did not own slaves. Black people, as slaves, were property. We were wealth. And like any other form of wealth in a capitalist system, we were hoarded by the elite few. Only 25 percent of Southern white households owned slaves (man, it is so weird to type that "only" 25 percent of a group of people owned another group of people), and the majority of slaves were held by the wealthiest 7 percent of white households.[11]

The average white Southerner was not a slaveholder. The average white Southerner was not rich, and the average white Southerner was often exploited by the same elites who enslaved Blacks. But just because all of this is true does not mean that the average poor white Southerner was against slavery. Quite the opposite. Yes, poor Southern whites were low on the socioeconomic ladder, exploited by elite whites as the underpaid muscle holding the whip. But it was a ladder they intended to climb, and the top rung always stretched just out of reach.

White supremacy is, and has always been, a pyramid scheme.

> *Among us the poor white laborer is respected as an equal. His family is treated with kindness, consideration and respect. He does not belong to the menial class. The negro is in no sense of the term his equal. He feels and knows this. He belongs to the only true aristocracy, the race of white men.*
>
> —*James Henry Hammond, slaveholder, former governor, US senator, and US representative for South Carolina*[12]

The poor, ignorant white Southern field managers for rich white slaveholders *were* looked upon by many in the North with contempt. Even Black slaves reserved for them a particular disgust and malice. In *Stamped from the Beginning*, Ibram Kendi reports that the term "white trash" may actually have been coined by enslaved Blacks to describe the poor whites doing the dirty work of wealthy slaveowners.[13]

Poor Southern whites had sold their souls for their sense of racial superiority, and for many, it was all they had. They would not let go easily.

> *The South fought to preserve race integrity. Did we lose that?*
> *We fought to maintain free white dominion. Did we lose that?*
>
> —*Florida senator Duncan Fletcher, 1931*[14]

While much has been written about the Great Migration of Black Southerners to the North and West, it is important to note that it was not only Blacks who fled. Poor white Southerners had little reason to stay in an economically devastated South and every reason to leave for the same opportunities in Northern factories that Blacks were leaving for. The Great Migration changed the landscape of the United States in immediately visible ways as Black communities became established across the country for the first time in history, but the migration of Southern whites shaped the American landscape in ways that we are perhaps only beginning to understand. In the end, twice as many Southern whites left as Blacks.

As poor whites left the South, they took their anger and bitterness with them. Defeated, embarrassed, and forced to leave their homes, poor Southern whites were further victimized by the cool welcome they often received from established Northern and Western whites. Many early reports of white migration show that Southern whites had difficulty adjusting to city life, their kids had trouble in more rigorous schools, and they felt mistreated by their new bosses. To add insult to injury, they often had to compete against Blacks for jobs and sometimes even had to work alongside them. The trials of the white Southern migrant were canonized in books like *The Grapes of Wrath.* The story of the suffering and abuse of Southern white men became part of the identity not only of those who stayed in the South but also of those who left.

But the story of the broken Okie was more often found in the imaginations of writers like Steinbeck than in real life. Yes, there were some greedy and unscrupulous farm and factory owners who sought to take advantage of desperate migrants. Yes, white Southerners did struggle to fit in with Northern and Western social norms. Initially. Yet studies show that white migrants integrated into their new communities rather quickly. Financially, the average white migrant almost immediately saw better wages and opportunities than they had in the South. Within a generation they were making wages that were practically the same as those earned by Northern- and Western-born whites; they were consistently chosen for higher-paid labor over Blacks.[15]

Southern or not, these migrants were, after all, white.

> *And in the eyes of the people there is the failure; and in the eyes of the hungry there is a growing wrath. In the souls of the people the grapes of wrath are filling and growing heavy, growing heavy for the vintage.*
>
> —The Grapes of Wrath, *1939*

In the plants and factories of the North and the West, racial strife did not begin with the influx of white Southerners. Neither did it begin with the influx of Black workers from the Great Migration. Black labor, Asian labor, and Mexican labor had always been a flash point for white workers. From the beginning of the US expansion west through the industrial age, the United States needed more manpower than the white citizens of a still relatively young country could provide. And if businesses could get that dirty and dangerous work done for as little money as possible, all the better.

Wherever white workers encountered nonwhite workers vying for similar jobs, there was trouble. Strikes, riots, even murder were not unusual in areas where white men believed they might be in danger of being replaced by workers of color—even though the companies that paid their wages would not have been viable without the cheap labor of workers of color.

But although white Northerners had long resented the presence of workers of color, white migrants from the South endured the added insult of having to put up with people they were supposed to own. Furthermore, they were being regarded as lowly as Black workers. Their entire world had been turned upside down—they had gone from masters-in-training to everyday working nobodies. How was a white man supposed to be a man in a world that seemed to be functioning to disempower him?

## THE NORTH'S RAGE

Many white people like to think that racism is really just a Southern problem. Sure, there are ignorant people everywhere, and yes—occasionally—racist incidents happen in California or New York, but those are exceptions. The South was the place that *wanted* slavery, and the rest of the country fought to end it, right? So how bad can it be once you leave the South?

The answer is very bad. Rodney King was not beaten in the South; he was beaten in Los Angeles. Eric Garner was not choked to death in the South; he was choked in New York. Laquan Mc-Donald was not shot sixteen times while walking away from police officers in the South; he was shot in Chicago. I could, to my great despair, go on for quite some time.

Although white people in our progressive cities and towns may pat themselves on the backs for having never called anyone a nigger, many of them also hope that we will not notice the strict racial segregation of neighborhoods and schools, the overpolicing of Black and brown neighborhoods, the job discrimination, or the persistent racial wealth gaps. The concept of race in America was created for the subjugation of Black and brown bodies for the seeming benefit of white Americans. There are no pockets of America that are exempt from this. There is no liberal utopia that got a different memo.

The story of the hardships that people of color have faced in this country does not end when Black people left the South, and the story of violent white male supremacy doesn't stop at the Mason-Dixon line.

> *The lot, nor any part thereof, shall not be sold to any*
> *person either of whole or part blood, of the Mongolian,*
> *Malay, or Ethiopian races, nor shall the same nor any*
> *part thereof be rented to persons of such races.*
>
> —*From the deed of a property in Seattle, Washington, added 1929*[16]

During the Great Migration, Blacks relocated in a steady stream from the South to Washington, D.C., Baltimore, Philadelphia, New York City, Boston, St. Louis, Chicago, Cleveland, Detroit, Los Angeles, and Oakland. Black workers, Black families, came in search of work, school, and dignity.

The letters that Black migrants sent home reporting their successes encouraged more flight from the South. "I should have been here twenty years ago. I just begin to feel like a man. It's a great deal of pleasure in knowing that you have got some privilege. My children are going to the same school with the whites and I don't have to be humble to no one," crowed one migrant to a friend back south.[17] Some of the country's most iconic artists, athletes, and leaders—including James Earl Jones, Zora Neal Hurston, Malcolm X, and Ella Baker—were Southern migrants or came from Southern-migrant families.[18]

But this honeymoon was short-lived. While many businesses and cities thrived economically with the influx of much-needed labor, local whites were unprepared for such rapid changes to their communities. Between 1910 and 1930, the Black population of Chicago grew by 600 percent. In that same time period, the Black population of Detroit grew by an astronomical 2,000 percent, from a population of 6,000 to 120,000.[19] As soldiers began returning from World War I in greater number, many white men were coming home to find themselves in direct competition with Black laborers for the first time in their lives. Black migrants found themselves facing hostility that felt a lot like what they had faced in the South. Suddenly, they weren't allowed to shop in white stores, they were rarely hired for jobs white men wanted, and employers who did hire them often faced the fury of white workers.

White anger exploded in the summer of 1919, known as Red Summer. Across the country, anti-Black riots broke out in cities including East St. Louis, Chicago, Omaha, and Houston. Whites in approximately twenty-five cities enacted widespread violence on Black residents.[20]

In the Chicago riots, the first victim of racist violence was a Black child. Seventeen-year-old Eugene Williams was playing in Lake Michigan on a hot summer day when his raft wandered over the unofficial border between the white and Black sides of the beach. Enraged by Williams's transgression, George Stauber, a twenty-four-year-old white man, threw rocks at him until he drowned.[21] When police officers arrived and Black witnesses identified Stauber as the man responsible for Williams's death, officers refused to arrest him.[22] Black and white crowds clashed on the beach, and the local violence soon spread into the city, igniting the long-standing white resentment over having to compete with Blacks for jobs in the meat-packing industry. Violence broke out throughout South Chicago, terrorizing Black neighborhoods. Eight-year-old Juanita Mitchell, her sister, and her mother had just made their journey north from New Orleans to Juanita's uncle's home in Chicago when she witnessed Red Summer. Nearly a hundred years later, at 107 years old, she still remembered it well: "We were in the living room. That's when I saw my uncle at the window, and I heard him in a gruff voice say, 'Here they come!' I didn't know what he meant. I said, 'What's going on?' My uncle said, 'The race riot. The white people are coming down 35th Street with loaded guns.'"[23]

After five days of violence, 23 Black and 15 white Chicagoans were dead, and 520 Chicagoans (most of them Black) were injured. One thousand Black families were left homeless. A burgeoning Black community was psychologically and economically scarred.

Red Summer continued, moving west. In East St. Louis, tensions had long been brewing over jobs at Aluminum Ore Company. When workers went on strike, Black workers, who were already barred from union membership, were brought in as strike breakers. This unenviable position was one that many Black factory workers across the country found themselves in.[24] The backlash against Black strike breakers was swift. Local papers published false stories of a crime wave being perpetrated by Black migrants against white people. White people drove through Black neighborhoods at night, shooting at Black-owned businesses and homes. Black residents armed themselves for protection.

On the evening of July 1, 1919, Black residents shot at a vehicle that looked like one that had driven through their neighborhood earlier that evening, whose occupants had fired at their homes. The two men inside the vehicle were killed. They were not among the feared local terrorists; they were undercover police officers.[25]

The next day, white residents of East St. Louis went on a murderous rampage. Black residents were beaten, shot, raped, lynched. For three days, East St. Louis was in flames as homes were burned to the ground. W. E. B. Du Bois and Martha Gruening traveled to East St. Louis to interview survivors for *The Crisis* and gave a grim account of what had happened there: "from noonday until midnight; they killed and beat and murdered; they dashed out the brains of children and stripped off the clothes of women; they drove victims into the flames and hanged the helpless to the lighting poles."[26] Historians estimate that over one hundred Blacks were murdered and seven thousand terrified Blacks fled to neighboring cities.

Violence against Black migrants went beyond physical endangerment. One of the most widespread ways in which Black communities were harmed—and are still harmed today—was through the use of racist housing covenants. When outright bans of minority groups in white neighborhoods through the use of zoning was deemed unconstitutional in 1917, white communities and developers banded together to form housing covenants, which they wrote into their deeds and community charters. These covenants typically banned property owners from selling or renting property to anybody who was nonwhite.

Across the Northern and Western United States, people of color seeking a better life for themselves and their families were pushed into smaller, less desirable, and more crowded areas. The use of covenants was so widespread that by 1940, 80 percent of the property in Los Angeles and Chicago banned Blacks.[27] Housing projects that were built to provide shelter in Black neighborhoods were soon dangerously overcrowded, filled with families who had nowhere else to go. Schools serving these segregated Black communities quickly became overcrowded as well. The housing fell into disrepair, creating pockets of crumbling infrastructure and poverty concentrated within cities.

In 1965 Dr. Martin Luther King Jr. went to Chicago at the invitation of the Chicago Freedom Movement, a coalition of civil rights organizations dedicated to fair housing for Blacks in the city. When King and his family moved into a dilapidated west-side apartment, a typical example of the housing available to Blacks, the news coverage brought national attention to the issue of housing discrimination in Chicago. King marched with members of the Chicago Freedom Movement through all-white neighborhoods in a push for open housing in the city. The marchers were met with violence. Angry white residents hurled racial slurs and rocks at the protesters. One rock hit Dr. King on the back of the head hard enough to knock him to the ground.

King was shocked at the extreme violence and vitriol he saw in Chicago—in a region that was supposed to be so much less racist than the South. "I have seen many demonstrations in the South," King commented. "But I have never seen anything so hostile and so hateful as I've seen here today."[28]

Just about anywhere that Blacks pushed for greater integration into the broader community and for more open housing, they were met with violent resistance from Northern whites. Northern whites have taken pride in being on the right side of history regarding slavery, which they saw as a Southern problem. It was a Southern problem, however, because Northern whites had apparently expected that freed Blacks would stay chained to the South. When Black people migrated North, whites forced them into areas of concentrated poverty and misery. Then they pointed at the conditions Black Americans were living in—pointed at their desperation—and harnessed it to justify further discrimination.

But just as Black labor was needed to maintain Southern agriculture, Black labor was now needed to support Northern industrial economies. The North's need for Black labor, and its hatred of Black people, was nothing new, and neither was Black survival while fighting against it.

## SEGREGATION FOREVER

*George [Wallace] doesn't give us some mealy-mouth*
*"on the one hand and on the other" spiel. He tells it*
*like it is and if it offends some government bureaucrats*

> *and loudmouth civil rights agitators, so what? He's*
> *standing up and fighting for real Americans.*
>
> —*Wallace supporter, 1968*[29]

> *When George Wallace is elected president, he's going*
> *to line up all these niggers and shoot them.*
>
> —*Wallace supporter, 1968*[30]

The thing about anger is that it needs a home. When you are angry because you are a white man stalled in your career—uncomfortable with a changing world and uncertain of your financial future—it is very hard to find a concrete target for your anger. When society is constantly telling you that you are not supposed to be facing any of these problems, because you are a white man, your anger will convince you that *somebody* has stolen what should be yours. The danger with this type of anger becomes most apparent when a savvy populist decides to name that target for you. In the 1960s, the opportunist who exploited white male fear and anger was George Wallace.

Wallace had made a name for himself as governor of Alabama with his theatrical, fire-breathing anti-integration stance. While his brazen antics, like standing in front of the University of Alabama to prevent Black students from entering, had made him popular with Southern whites, many pundits and politicians were sure that somebody so controversial would have no chance on a national stage. That sort of virulent racism didn't play well in the North and the West. Their gross underestimation of George Wallace and the power of blatant racism would change American politics forever.

It is important to understand that although Wallace had gained notoriety for shouting racist slogans like "Segregation now, segregation tomorrow, segregation forever," he likely wasn't much more racist than the average white politician—especially in the South. Above all, Wallace was an opportunist.

When Wallace first ran for governor of Alabama in 1958, he conducted a relatively progressive campaign. He was outspoken against the KKK and was even endorsed by the NAACP. And he got his ass handed to him in the primary by an openly racist candidate, John Malcolm Patterson. In defeat, Wallace learned that his path to electoral victory did not lie in peace and love. After the election, Wallace was quoted as saying to his friend Seymore Trammell, "I was outniggered by John Patterson. And I'll tell you here and now, I will never be outniggered again."[31]

When Wallace ran for governor again in 1962, he was able to outnigger his way to a landslide victory on a campaign of "segregation forever"—aided by the mass disenfranchisement of Black voters in Alabama. When setting out for a national run in 1968, Wallace recognized that the same anger that had motivated Alabama voters was widespread among white working-class men across the country—especially in places that were adjusting to an influx of Black industrial workers, and especially among white Southern migrants up north. Wallace revised his language to broaden his audience, but if you listened closely the message was still the same. "The dangers of integration" was replaced with more respectable stand-ins like "a need for law and order" and "fighting school busing." "Evil commies and civil rights activists" became "evil commies and hippies." "Northern aggressors" became "Washington elites" and "the liberal, know-nothing press."

There wasn't a lot of policy talk; even Wallace's campaign team acknowledged that they had no real plan for what Wallace would actually do if elected to office. Chances are, even setting his bigotry aside, he would have made a very bad president. Wallace's campaign lacked any substantial policy positions and was abundant in promoting hatred of Black people, hippies, and the political elite. Even one of Wallace's campaign workers said she didn't think Wallace had "really thought about being president, in the sense of presiding over the country."[32] But Wallace didn't need a strong, thorough policy platform. He promised with gusto to take

on the hippies and commies and activists and establishment politicians. That was enough for the white men who had been looking
for someone to punch. Wallace's campaign slogan promised that
he would "Stand up for America"—and it was clear whose America he would stand up for and whom he would stand against.

Pundits were surprised when Wallace garnered support in cities
like Akron, Ohio, but this was probably not a surprise for Wallace
and his team. Wallace's initial base was strongest in places where
Southern white migrants had ended up. Wallace spoke their language, and their early enthusiasm helped legitimize his campaign
and introduce him to larger audiences. And Wallace's barely veiled
racism wasn't a hard sell for working- and middle-class white men
in general. As Wallace, running as an Independent, saw his support rise into the double-digit percentages, his Republican opponent, Richard Nixon, began to panic. Large portions of his support
were being siphoned by this upstart, and Nixon's campaign feared
that Wallace would steal enough of his votes to lead to a victory
for Democrat Hubert Humphrey.

In response to Wallace's appeal to white, working-class voters,
the Nixon campaign decided to outnigger Wallace with a so-called
Southern Strategy. Shifting the focus of the campaign to one of
law and order, protecting state's rights, and promises of returning America to the average workingman, the campaign employed
clearly recognized codes (which are still used to this day) for "we
will restore your position of superiority over Black people."

Nixon's move toward a white supremacist campaign, coupled
with the power of the Republican Party, was enough to defeat both
Wallace and Humphrey and win him the presidential election. A
strong message was sent from Nixon's victory: if you want to mobilize the white American working class, you must at least allude
to reinforcing its economic and political power over communities
of color. Several future presidents—from Reagan to Clinton to
Trump—took the lesson to heart.

## "MAYBE WE'RE ILLEGALLY OCCUPYING YOUR HOUSE RIGHT NOW"

My family is the only Black family within three blocks. That has been the case for the entire five years that we've lived in this working-class neighborhood. And I moved here for the diversity. This is Seattle—and in Seattle, diversity is relative. Yes, our suburb is only about 6 percent Black, but with only two high schools in our district, they can't racially segregate the schools the way many other Seattle-area schools do. So . . . diversity, Seattle style. I do not think I would have the writing career I have today if I had not grown up in the Seattle area. This city has forced me to understand all that is unsaid about race and racism in America.

Seattle is in a beautiful location, with water, mountains, and trees just about everywhere you look. It is a city where everyone recycles and everyone votes Democratic. It's a city that has ridden multiple tech booms to many consecutive decades of prosperity and security.

The only thing Seattleites love more than recycling is coming up with new ways to avoid talking about race and the city's issues with racism.

I am, even now as I near forty, followed by security staff in stores. I am followed by cops while driving. I am stared at when I attend social or work gatherings. I hear the reliable "click" of people's car doors locking as I walk past their vehicles in a grocery store parking lot.

My entire life in Seattle has required that I navigate how whiteness refuses to acknowledge itself and yet insists on asserting itself whenever it encounters people of color.

When I discuss these everyday issues with my white neighbors, I'm met with either angry denial or overblown shock and dismay. If I express that I would like to be able to walk through a grocery store parking lot in broad daylight without hearing car doors lock as I approach, I am flooded with explanations as to why those doors were likely locked—surprise, none of them have to do with the color of my skin. Or I have to listen to excessive virtue signaling from whites declaring Seattle the worst place in the world and sympathizing that I have to put up with living in a place like this.

But the little slights live on the surface of a much deeper racist violence, one that white Seattle does not want to address.

When Charleena Lyles was killed in 2017 by police officers, in her own Seattle home while surrounded by her four children and pregnant with a fifth, I was absolutely gutted. Lyles and her children had been living in a housing complex for families trying to move out of long-term homelessness. Many of the residents in the area carry deep trauma from their hardships. Many are people of color.

I had been a longtime financial supporter of the organization that owned the housing development. While attending a "giving day" at my fancy tech job, I watched a presentation given by one of the heads of the organization. When they showed a photo of the apartment complex, I recognized my childhood. Before the area had been developed into housing for formerly homeless people, it was old military barracks that had served as low-income housing for Seattle families in the 1980s and '90's. I had lived there as a child.

I remembered playing at the beach down the hill and buying Now and Laters at the corner store. I remembered the community garden where we supplemented our diets when we couldn't afford or find fresh produce at the local grocery store.

As I read the articles about Charleena and listened to police recordings of officers quickly deciding to end her life and endanger the lives of her children, I saw the anguish of her family on the news. I saw all of it and knew that liberal, self-identified "antiracist" white Seattle would share a few upset Facebook posts and that would be the end of it. There would be no marches that looked anything like the ones that took place in Ferguson. There would be no widespread cries for justice. And when it was determined that no charges would be filed against the two officers who shot Lyles seven times, there would be little outrage in the streets.

Black people in Seattle would be outraged. Black people in Seattle would demand justice. But there were not enough of us to be heard. And that was by design.

Growing up on the north end of Seattle, I was the only Black kid in all my primary-school years except for the year that we lived in the low-income apartments in Lyles's neighborhood. I did not have a single Black friend outside of that year until sixth grade. I did not have a single Black teacher until college, and then only one.

My partner, who grew up in the city's now rapidly disappearing historically Black neighborhood, knew only Black friends and friends of color. He had Black teachers. He also attended chronically underfunded schools and was regularly harassed by police officers.

He grew up in the invisibility of the "Black neighborhood" in a white Northern city: the social and structural erasure of an entire community that occurs once all the Black residents have been corralled into a small corner, away from everyone else. I grew up in the hypervisibility of the "Black family" in a white Northern city, as the token Black household whose presence allowed the neighborhood to call itself diverse.

The racial segregation of my city and of so many other cities across the Northern and Western United States is not by accident. Think of the covenants. White residents have banded together to keep people of color out of their neighborhoods, and those efforts have often been supported—and even initiated—by local and federal governments. Our government built segregated, low-income housing projects where integrated ones once stood, keeping poor whites and Blacks apart. And many of the neighborhoods where we find those racist homeowners' covenants initially had homes that qualified for FHA loans and so were in part financed by our federal government. Yet not only did the housing discrimination keep Black and white families separated, it also prevented many Blacks from buying homes at all. During the postwar era, when the government actively worked to increase homeownership, loan programs like the FHA and the GI Bill were of much less use to Blacks. Banks wouldn't work with them, and Blacks were banned by covenants from living in neighborhoods with the most affordable new homes. The intergenerational wealth lost to Black families who were kept from buying homes during the postwar housing boom was the foundation for the vast wealth gap between white and Black families today.[33]

Today, decades after racist covenants were banned, many white neighborhoods maintain their segregation in less explicit ways, but with the same overall effect. Vigorous fights against affordable housing in wealthier, and even middle-class, neighborhoods have kept people with lower incomes out of white neighborhoods. While the discussion has shifted away from race and toward class, the impetus behind the fight against affordable housing often gives the racist intent away. When *ProPublica* spoke with residents in wealthy white towns in Connecticut about why they were fighting the construction of mixed-income housing developments in their neighborhoods, the dog whistles abounded.

"The challenge to our community is not just to the character of neighborhoods, but also to firefighting and police response, potentially to educational capacity, to human services support and to our tradition as a single-family-home community," said Jim Marpe, Westport's First Selectman.

"The drug addicts are going to be here, believe me," said local resident William Woermer. "There will be a lot of riffraff. Then we go on to, with a project like this, you need security guards in the area."

"I'm sure they could have their little parking spaces, but somebody throws a party, or it's Cinco de Mayo or something else, and pretty soon you can't park there," said George Temple, concerned about the impact an affordable-housing complex would have on neighborhood parking.[34]

There was more familiar, coded language: Adding affordable housing would bring loud music and crime to their city. It would threaten school test scores.

This sort of resistance to low-income housing is found all across the country, even in liberal Seattle. It has kept Black and brown people from moving into neighborhoods that might be closer to their work. It has concentrated the poverty in neighborhoods of color, leaving schools that rely on property taxes underfunded. It has kept businesses that are concerned about their ability to recruit white workers out of Black and brown neighborhoods. It has, along with other deliberately designed systemic oppressions, helped trap generations of Black and brown families in poverty.

The pattern has taken a toll on entire states as well. Pockets of poverty compound themselves, concentrating crime in neighborhoods with high poverty and reduced resources, and increasing the drain on public health and safety resources in areas with reduced tax revenue. When I discuss race and poverty, it is a common tactic of white trolls to ask me, "What about Chicago? That's Black people shooting each other. There's no white people in those neighborhoods keeping them poor. How do you explain that?" I hear them, and I envision Dr. King being knocked to the ground by a rock flung by white Chicagoans who were angry that he would dare fight for the ability for Black Chicagoans to move out of ghettos and try to improve their lives. I think of Black neighborhoods burned to the ground in East St. Louis. I think about anti-Black violence and terror in Black neighborhoods in Omaha, Houston, Indianapolis, Washington, D.C., and dozens of other cities across the country. I think of the massacre of Black Wall Street in Tulsa. I think of the MOVE bombing in Philadelphia. I think of all the times that Black Americans had to struggle to build communities and to build an economic foothold for those communities, only to have to start all over again.

When I was scanning historical homeowners' covenants from the Seattle area that had banned people of color from integrating white neighborhoods, I was not at all surprised to see some in the neighborhood where I live. My partner suggested that I go to the records office and get a copy of my deed to see if there was a covenant written into it.

"Maybe we're illegally occupying your house right now," he said with a twinkle in his eye.

There's a good chance that if my particular parcel of land had ever been in one of the many communities in the neighborhood that banned people of color, the covenant would still be there, written on my deed. It would not have been removed. It would have been passed down generation after generation, long after Seattle had claimed to have moved past what it considered its small ventures into systemic racism. Only since January of 2019 have homeowners been able to request that the racist covenants be removed from their deeds.

But I don't need paperwork to tell me that I'm illegally occupying my neighborhood—every person of color in this city has been considered an illegal occupant for well over a hundred years.

# CHAPTER 5

# FIRE THE WOMEN

## *The Convenient Use and Abuse of Women in the Workplace*

"While you were away we managed to make a few changes."

In the 1980 comedy film *9 to 5*, Doralee Rhodes (played by Dolly Parton) and Judy Bernly (Jane Fonda) are describing the improvements that they and their coworker Violet Newstead (Lily Tomlin) made in the office while their abusive and sexist boss, Franklin Hart (Dabney Coleman), was . . . away. The women had kept Hart tied up in a bedroom for six weeks so they could implement the changes.

They enter a bustling workplace that has a decidedly "feminine" energy. The room is bright and buzzing. The women at work are visibly happy and relaxed. As they walk by walls freshly painted in cheerful colors, they discuss the new programs they have introduced, like job sharing, flexible hours, and an onsite daycare facility.

Hart is outraged by the changes and vows to return everything to the way it was, until Russell Tinsworthy, the chairman of the board, shows up unexpectedly to congratulate Hart on his division's 20 percent increase in productivity in just six weeks.

Hart nervously takes credit for the improvements implemented by Doralee, Judy, and Violet, which have brought such success to the company. As Tinsworthy congratulates Hart again, he leans in and says conspiratorially, "But that equal pay thing—that's got to go."

Hart is rewarded for his success with a new assignment in Brazil, where he is kidnapped by Amazonian people and never seen again, leaving Doralee, Judy, and Violet free to enjoy their new, more worker-friendly environment without Hart's abuse. Normally I'd be mad at such a weird, racist characterization as people of color kidnapping white people, but I'm going to be generous and assume that the Indigenous people of Brazil had just had enough bullshit from rich white men like Hart and did what we all should have done a long time ago.

9 to 5 received a lukewarm reception from many male critics. Roger Ebert, for the Chicago Sun-Times, gave the film one of the more generous reviews at three stars and called it "only a fairly successful comedy." He reserved most of his positive comments for Dolly Parton and her portrayal of Doralee. Ebert was careful to point out that he was not praising Parton for her famous bustline, even writing that "she hardly seems to exist as a sexual being in this movie"—before stating that he needed to regain his composure to be able to finish his review.[1]

Vincent Canby, writing for the New York Times, only doles out praise for the male star of the film, saying, "Considering the

militancy of *Nine to Five*, it may be fitting that the funniest performance in the film is given by Dabney Coleman, who plays
Franklin Hart Jr." He describes as hilarious all the horrible ways
in which Hart harasses and abuses the women in his employ.
Canby apparently found that his enjoyment of the parts of the
film that caused the majority of women in the audience to cringe
with uncomfortable familiarity was cause for deeper reflection.
For women. He closed his review by saying, "There's some sort of
lesson to be learned from the fact that the biggest laughs in *Nine
to Five*, as well as in several other feminist comedies, depend on
enthusiastic, unabashed sexism."[2]

Despite the grumbling of critics, *9 to 5* was a success. The comedy resonated with many women. In workplaces across the country they had experienced their own version of a Franklin Hart—an
incompetent male boss who treated the women in the office like
shit while also depending on their competence to make him look
better. *9 to 5* was a revenge fantasy wrapped in the safety of absurd
comedy. Many women had likely wished that they, too, could exact payback for the sexual harassment they had endured at work.
I don't doubt that many women also recognized themselves in the
underutilized talents of Doralee, Judy, and Violet and knew that
if anybody had thought to ask them, they could make some great
improvements to their workplaces.

While the improvements that Doralee, Judy, and Violet brought
to Consolidated Companies were very much based on the workplace changes that many real-life women had been requesting for
decades, the movie was a comedy—and a fantastical one at that.
*9 to 5* was absurd not only because three women kidnapped a rich
and powerful white man and held him prisoner for days without spending a moment in jail, but also because they got to run
a company. Women—successfully running a company! Listening
to employees! Establishing corporate daycare programs! What will
Hollywood think of next?

Although *9 to 5* was released eleven days before I was born, it still resonated with me when I first watched it as a young adult, new to the professional world. Yes, the fashion and cars were outdated, but I had already been subjected to years of sexual harassment and other abuses in the workplace, beginning with my first job at sixteen. I had already seen the way that women were spoken over and overlooked. And as I had children and became a working mother, I grew even more aware of how far we still were from the workplace improvements that had brought so much contentment and productivity to the employees at the fictional Consolidated Companies.

For centuries, Western society has tried to keep women out of the workplace. Men have ruled over government, offices, mills, plants, cubicles, and more—the domains of power—while women worked at home. The definition of success for a middle-class family was a man who earned enough money outside the home to support the wife, who raised his children.

Of course, situations have always existed in which women had to work in order to earn their own living or because one income was not enough for their family to live on. Even in those cases, strict gender segregation of work was usually enforced. Domestic work, caretaking, teaching, and eventually secretarial work were "pink collar": women's work. Just about everything else was for men. With that segregation came a distinct difference in the value and compensation afforded such work. Women were paid less, and their jobs were considered less skilled, less essential, less physically demanding, and less intellectual than men's work.

These classifications were always a white working- and middle-class ideal, and they never quite fit poor households and households of color. Poor women and women of color have always engaged in physically demanding—and often very dangerous—jobs. Women and girls worked long, grueling hours as maids and cooks. There were the laundresses who suffered regular injury (including burns) and illness from their working conditions, the radium girls who lost their lives or were permanently disfigured from working in watch factories. Women and girls died in factory fires and building collapses. Sex workers often faced abuse and disease. In all these occupations, women regularly withstood sexual abuse and exploitation from their male bosses, coworkers, and other men, who took the women's socioeconomic status as an open invitation to indulge their violent whims. Women and girls who had to take on demanding work—especially those who were unable to quit after marrying—were pitied or ignored. They didn't fit with society's ideal of itself. And because they were invisible, they were exploitable. They often labored in conditions that many men would balk at, and at a fraction of the pay.

But women have always shown their intellectual and leadership skills. Since before the time of the pharaohs, women have been fierce leaders, savvy politicians, and skilled teachers. Women have created masterpieces since the first cave dwellers were drawing on walls. Women have invented some of our most important devices, have led some of our most important scientific advancements, have written classic novels. They have healed the sick and philosophized about the world's biggest questions. Women's work has greatly benefitted society throughout history—even in the face of dismissal, derision, and hostility from male colleagues.

The idea that women were not made for work is only true to the extent that men have ensured that work was not made for women. Men have designed offices that don't suit women's needs, have established work hours that compete with child-rearing, have developed education and training programs that regularly discourage women's aspirations in male-dominated fields, have formed mentoring and networking relationships on golf courses and in clubs, places where women are not welcome or comfortable—or sometimes even allowed.

Men have used these deliberately structured environments to prove why women are naturally "not a fit" for the workplace.

Nursing mothers who cannot work in spaces that don't accommodate breast pumps are "obviously not that interested in the job."
Women who need flexible hours to care for children, in a society
that still expects women to do the majority of child-rearing regardless of employment status, "lack the work ethic necessary to
put in the hours needed for the job." Women who have always
loved math but were told from primary school on that they would
be better at English and art than science and engineering "must
not be interested in STEM." And men who make all their business
connections at the country club or through their old fraternity
buddies "just haven't come across any women who are as qualified
for a job at their company as men."

As promotion after promotion goes to men, as men are encouraged to start businesses and women aren't, as men flow into fields
that are more open to them, the definition of an ideal worker and
leader becomes even more stereotypically male—even if those
"ideal" traits and skills are not the most beneficial.

The ways in which women have been undercut in the workplace
don't harm only women. When women are denied fair wages,
the entire household that depends on their money is harmed.
Workplaces that fail to mentor women or build networking environments that are inclusive of women miss out on the talents
women offer. Workplaces that refuse to address issues of sexism
and sexual harassment suffer not only higher turnover in their female employees but also lower productivity in all employees, regardless of gender. Workplaces that don't promote women or fully
support women in their leadership ranks miss out on the diversity of thought, skill, and approach that having more women in
management can provide. Workplaces that devalue traits and skills
like empathy, communication, and cooperation, which women are
more likely to be socialized to have, almost always overvalue traits
like hypercompetitiveness, aggression, and impulsiveness, which

men are more likely to be socialized to have, even when those characteristics harm a work environment.

Although consistently shown to be counterproductive, a pattern emerges in how men treat women in the workplace. Women have to fight to enter the workforce. Then when men need women—whether it's to help keep families afloat during economic hardship, to fill labor shortages, or to lead a new business strategy when traditionally masculine approaches have failed—women are denied the necessary tools and support to achieve their full potential. In many cases, the more a woman is needed in the workplace, the more hostile men seem to act toward her—even if that hostility puts their own livelihoods at risk.

At the root of this seemingly nonsensical behavior we can observe the almost pathological need for many men to see their identities as wholly distinct from, and superior to, women's—especially in the workplace, which has long been a primary source of ego for men in America and is a place that women aren't even supposed to be. Separation from and degradation of the feminine in the workplace have been reinforced by our popular culture, replicating themselves generation after generation to our collective detriment.

This power structure is built and maintained primarily by white men. Not because men of color are naturally less driven to control women than white men are—but because white men view their superiority over people of color as equally important to their identity as their power over women. In the public sphere white men rule over people of color, and in the home they rule over women. The extent to which they can do so defines their success as white men. The presence of women in the workplace not only undermines white male authority there; it also lessens men's opportunity to dominate women at home. The power and ego of entitled white men—who maintain firm control of the vast majority of government offices, manager's offices, corporate boards, and other realms of leadership—remain the biggest obstacles that most women face in their careers.

## THE GREAT DEPRESSION AND THE SUPPRESSION OF FEMALE LABOR

*Simply fire the women, who shouldn't be working anyway, and hire the men. Presto!*

—*Norman Cousins, 1939*[3]

The Great Depression was one of the most devastating economic events in our nation's history. An entire generation was shaped by the trauma of rapid economic decline and uncertainty. My great-grandmother Inez, until her death in 2019 at the age of 104, insisted on washing and reusing the red plastic disposable plates you buy for picnics and parties because "once you've lived through the Depression, you don't let anything go to waste."

She lived in the same small house she had bought with her husband eighty years earlier. She covered all her furniture in plastic and only replaced items when they were literally falling apart. She purchased only one new car in her entire life, when she was well into her eighties. I have many friends who have similar stories of their grandparents' and great-grandparents' amazing frugality that grew from living through the Depression.

Not only were members of that generation shaped by the Great Depression; many of our current economic theories and policies were developed in response to the Depression. It is the crisis against which all other American crises are measured. Did the fuel shortages of the 1970s signal an upcoming Great Depression? No, perhaps not. What about the burst of the tech bubble in the 1990s? No, too limited in scale. How about the housing crisis and Great Recession of the early 2000s? Closer, but still no.

To this day, economists disagree about what caused the Great Depression. Some say it was the decline in exports to Europe after World War I, when the massive production of food in the United States to meet the needs of wartime Europe decreased sharply and suddenly, leading to a huge surplus that devastated the agricultural industry and other peripheral trades.[4] Some claim it was the growing economic disparity in American society and the vast hoarding of wealth by those at the very top. In 1929, the top 0.1 percent of American households held as much money as the bottom 42 percent. With such a huge amount of available income removed from circulation, and with so little remaining for the lower classes to spread around, there was not enough surplus wealth in the average American household to maintain the consumption needed for a healthy economy.[5] Many point, too, to the unregulated, Wild West environment of Wall Street at the time. It was a place where everybody believed they could make their fortunes in the stock market, and people (as well as businesses and banks) speculated and short-sold stocks with abandon, regardless of their financial knowledge or whether they had the income to back up the risks they were taking.

Many more theories have emerged, from environmental devastation of resources to overseas trade wars. But no matter what economic school you come from, no matter which cause you choose—if there's one thing we should all be able to agree on, it's that the Great Depression was man-made.

Man-made as in caused by dudes. More specifically, white dudes. The socioeconomic exclusion of women and people of color in political decision making, stock trading, and business running means that no matter where you place your blame, there are likely some white men.

And in the midst of the Great Depression, there was plenty of blame to go around. People pointed fingers at ungrateful Europeans, at greedy and incompetent business owners and CEOs, at irresponsible and selfish stock-market pillagers like General Motors founder William Durant. But a lot of blame and anger were also focused on one group that contributed in absolutely *no way* to the Great Depression: women.

At the beginning of the Depression, 24.3 percent of all workers in the United States were women. At the end of the Depression, 25.1 percent of workers were women.[6] At a time of rising male unemployment, an increase in the percentage of women workers, even an increase of less than 1 percent, made it seem as though women were taking jobs from men. Men grew angry, scared, and desperate as the idea took hold that women workers were, if not the primary cause of the Great Depression, at least exacerbating the problem.

"There are approximately 10,000,000 people out of work in the United States today; there are also 10,000,000 or more women, married and single, who are jobholders. Simply fire the women, who shouldn't be working anyway, and hire the men. Presto! No unemployment. No relief rolls. No depression."[7] Those were the words of Norman Cousins in 1939, and they summed up the feelings of a lot of white Americans. Cousins, recognized widely as an intelligent and informed political journalist, certainly should have known that his logic was, well, nonexistent. The simple fact was, during that time in American history, women and men were not going after the same jobs. Women were not filling industrial plants and factories. They were not in trade. Those areas were where the majority of job and income losses were felt. Women were working as housekeepers, teachers, seamstresses, and laundresses. This was "women's work," and not even financial desperation could send men to their nearest school or hotel to compete with women for low-paid and less-respected employment.

The percentage of women workers increased because as men were losing jobs and income, more women needed to enter the workforce to help provide for their households. If a husband or father lost his job or was forced to take a large pay cut, then the additional income from a wife's or daughter's job might just help a family scrape by. (That said, the wages of women were not nearly enough to replace the incomes of men—especially when incomes were reduced by businesses that took advantage of a desperate job market to slash the wages of male workers.)

Ironically, employment that was considered "women's work" or "colored work" (primarily service and domestic work) was far less impacted by the Great Depression. The one exception was in the urban North, where low Black population numbers prevented the necessity of a classification of "colored work," which meant that Black people—in particular, Black women—lost jobs en masse to white workers the moment jobs became scarce.[8] It would have been smart for young white men to seek work in those fields. But white men would not dare lower themselves to do the jobs that women or Black people were doing. They also could have encouraged their wives and daughters to enter those industries to supplement the family income, but many would not countenance watching more women enter the workplace while so many men looked for "suitable" work. (And they say *we're* the irrational ones.)

Resentment toward working women during the Great Depression was a uniquely white problem. In many Black households, women had always worked to supplement the discriminatorily low wages paid to Black men and to help balance the effects of widespread hiring discrimination that kept Black workers out of many fields of employment. Black women were not expected to stop working due to any misguided efforts to preserve jobs for Black men.

"The Negro was born in depression. It didn't mean too much to him, the Great American Depression, as you call it. There was no such thing," recounted Clifford Burke in *Hard Times: An Oral History of the Great Depression*. "The best he could be is a janitor or a porter or shoeshine boy. It only became official when it hit the white man. If you can tell me the difference between the depression today and the Depression of 1932 for a Black man, I'd like to know it."[9]

In reality, it didn't make any more sense for white men to force women out of the workforce during the Great Depression than it would have made for Black men to do so, but they did it anyway. As anti-woman-worker rhetoric heated up, employers increased their hiring discrimination against married women (who, in sexist theory, shouldn't have had to work because they were married— and were therefore only working selfishly, for personal gain). In 1932, federal economic recovery efforts required that if both husband and wife held a government job, one would have to leave or be fired. We can guess which spouse in this equation was usually out of a job.

Before the Great Depression, only nine states had laws on the books restricting the employment of married women. By 1940, twenty-six states did.[10] The argument against married women working was both economic and moral. One 1935 Wisconsin resolution against the employment of married women stated, "The large number of husbands and wives working for the state raises a serious moral question, as this committee feels that the practice of birth control is encouraged, and the selfishness that arises from the income of employment of husband and wife bids fair to break down civilization and a healthy atmosphere."[11]

In the 1930s, 77 percent of school districts in the nation had a policy against hiring married women as teachers, and 50 percent had a policy of firing women teachers once they got married.[12] Working mothers were blamed for young people's truancy and other bad behavior and for the general decline of good society. Women's magazines like *True Story* published lurid tales of working women whose selfish ways led them down disastrous paths of sexual promiscuity, divorce, and infertility.[13]

Married women who did not work participated in the social shaming of married women who did work. Frances Perkins, the

New York Commissioner of Labor, gave a speech in 1930, just as the economy was beginning its downturn, attacking married women who worked as selfish and interested in their own personal pleasure at the expense of those in need of employment: "The woman 'pin-money worker' who competes with the necessity worker is a menace to society, a selfish, shortsighted creature, who ought to be ashamed of herself."[14]

Many women continued to work because, regardless of public opinion and societal abuse, they had to in order to feed their families. But a lot of women were kept out of much-needed jobs because of social pressure: the wrongheaded idea that a woman in the workplace would mean the loss of a job for a man.

Women were not the only scapegoats during the Great Depression. Although Black unemployment overall during the Great Depression didn't rise nearly as much as it did for white workers (due to the fact that Black workers in the South had long been kept out of the industries hardest hit), Black factory and service workers in the North faced immediate and widespread layoffs as their jobs were taken from them and given to white workers. In the western United States, economic anxieties gave xenophobic politicians and locals the fodder they needed to push out Mexican American workers. As was the case with Black and women workers, the few jobs that were open to Mexican Americans in states like California were not regularly sought after by white workers, even during the Great Depression. Still, there was a rising fear that Mexican American workers were taking "American" jobs, and that an "indigent" Mexican American population would suck up the few resources available to white Americans during hard economic times. Government officials, including Labor Secretary James Doak, pushed the idea that deporting Mexican Americans would solve job woes in the West. In his hunt for undocumented Mexican American immigrants, Doak authorized raids of private homes, businesses, and churches, and the deportation of thousands of people without proper hearings.[15]

Even more devastating than Doak's deportation efforts was the massive "repatriation" of Mexican Americans to Mexico. Between 1931 and 1934, over three hundred thousand Mexican Americans were coerced, threatened, or forced to leave the United States for Mexico—an estimated one-third of the national Mexican American population. Let's pause to let that sink in: *one-third* of Mexican Americans were driven from the country against their will because white men, unable to fix the mess they had made of the economy, decided to take their frustration out on brown workers in a fit of xenophobia. Sixty percent of those repatriated were American-born.[16] Entire Mexican American communities were decimated by this widespread and often violent discrimination and removal and did not recover in numbers for decades.

Jose Lopez, a US citizen who was forcibly removed to Mexico with his family as a child, later testified at a hearing before the California legislature about the devastation the deportation brought to his family and community. "I was five years old when we were forced to relocate," he said. "I . . . bec[a]me very sick with whooping cough, and suffered very much, and it was difficult to breathe. . . . Living conditions in Mexico were horrible, we lived in utter poverty. My family ate only tortillas and beans for a long time. Sometimes only one meal a day." Both of Lopez's parents and one of his brothers died in Mexico before he and his surviving siblings were able to make their way back to the United States in 1945.[17]

The mistreatment of women workers and workers of color did not end when the Great Depression ended. Women and people of color were excluded from the bulk of job-creation efforts during the New Deal. Black sharecroppers, tenant farmers, and domestic workers were by and large omitted from federal relief efforts, jobs programs, and minimum-wage enforcement. Many youth and young-adult job programs refused to admit Blacks.[18] Many employment opportunities, such as those with the Civilian Conservation Corps, were open only to men, cutting young women out of steady work with federal agencies like the National Park Service.[19] Other programs, like the Works Progress Administration (WPA), hired millions of Americans across the country for various public-works infrastructure projects. Black and brown Americans found that prime placement in those jobs went to whites, and many of the jobs were deemed unsuitable for women. There was also a limit of one WPA job per household, effectively eliminating women if a man in the family needed work.[20]

Hostility toward women workers and workers of color did not start during the Great Depression, but even during that white-man-made disaster, white men diverted a sizeable amount of time and resources to ensuring that women and people of color understood that the American workplace—whether it be factories, plants, or offices—was only for white men.

## WORLD WAR II AND THE NEED FOR QUITE A FEW GOOD WOMEN

Patriarchy is oppressive, cruel, destructive, inefficient, and—sometimes—quite absurd. A few years after the Great Depression, the editors of *True Story* magazine faced a bit of a conundrum. How could a magazine that had spent years villainizing women workers in scandalous "true" (but really fictional) stories help get women *into* the workplace? *True Story* and other "confessional" magazines had made their money by weaving lurid tales of women who went seeking adventure or a career (two things decidedly reserved for men) and were met with infertility, miscarriage, divorce—even sexual assault. Brought to the brink of absolute ruin, the women would repent for their misdeeds of ambition or audacity, and then were shown grace and mercy with the opportunity to embrace the life they were meant to have—that of a happy, docile, and grateful wife and mother.

This formula worked quite well for providing women readers with scandal and excitement during their often long and predictable days caring for home and children, while also helping to make sure that they appreciated the fact that this was their only thrill. But it did not work for the Magazine Bureau, a government office created in 1942 to help coordinate war coverage and propaganda in mostly women's magazines like *Women's Day, Ladies' Home Journal,* and *True Story.*[21]

More than eleven million men went overseas from the United States to fight in World War II, leaving a severe deficit in manpower for noncombat military-support positions, jobs in munitions factories, and many other occupations throughout the war industry, just when the need for manufacturing production increased. Desperate to fill these vacancies, companies targeted people they were not used to recruiting: women and people of color. It wasn't difficult to get Black and Latinx workers to line up for jobs. Their communities had long been excluded from the higher pay and employment security of skilled factory work, and many leapt at the chance. The harder part was convincing factory owners, managers, and employees to work alongside people of color. Many white workers protested, and riots broke out over the new workplace diversity.[22]

But there were not enough workers of color to fill all the open positions. Even if there had been, people of color would probably have wanted to keep their jobs after the war ended and the white soldiers returned home and looked for work. The US government needed a workforce that would happily give up their employment once the war was over. Officials found those potential employees in their own homes: women. In particular, married white women. Married women, demonized for working during the Great Depression because they obviously didn't *have* to work, became the ideal candidates for wartime employment for the very same reason—they didn't have to work! Not motivated by personal need or ambition, married women would work both because doing so was their patriotic duty and also to support their husbands' efforts overseas. Furthermore, they would, it was assumed, happily give up their jobs once their men returned home. And women did go to work: 6.5 million women entered the workforce during the war years, with nearly one in four married women working outside the home. Not only were women working—they were working in roles that had been closed to them before the war. According to Maureen Honey in *Creating Rosie the Riveter,* "By the end of 1943, women comprised 34.2 percent of all ammunition workers, 10.6 percent of those in steel production, 10 percent of all personnel in shipping, 8 percent of railroad workers, and 40 percent of people employed in the aircraft industry."[23] Women were an essential force in the domestic war effort.

So how do you encourage women to work after having spent the last decade encouraging them not to work—while also making sure they won't want to work for any longer than the government needs them to? Well, getting magazines like *True Story* to stop telling women that employment would only lead to divorce, infertility, and sexual assault was a start.

The Magazine Bureau started reaching out to publishers to coordinate stories. It used its *Magazine War Guide* to help shape war coverage and to provide tips to popular women's magazines on how to help improve social opinions about women workers. First to go was the idea that women who were engaged in war work would meet the scandalous fate that many women workers had met in past *True Story* confessionals. Officials at the bureau wrote, "May we suggest that care be observed not to create the impression that women engaged in any phase of war work, whether with the military services, in civilian war agencies or in war industry, are more tempted or more susceptible to extra-marital dalliance than others?"[24]

The confessional magazines were asked to tweak their formulas to inspire women workers to find excitement in doing their patriotic duty as well as deeper and more satisfying love in supporting their men overseas—instead of the death and destruction they had foretold in past stories. Loathe to completely give up their reliable model of sin-ruin-redemption, however, *True Story* created two new story types: the selfless woman who would find satisfaction, joy, and love in working to help bring men home sooner, and the selfish woman who worked only for personal advancement and was met with the usual heartbreak, miscarriage, and assault.

Here's an example: in "Make Believe Marriage," published in 1944, a wife struggles with balancing the needs of her marriage and her work supporting the war effort. But she takes pride in knowing she's supporting soldiers and strength in the knowledge that as soon as the war is over, she can go back to being a house-wife. By contrast, the selfish woman working as a surgical nurse in "A Solemn Promise," published that same year, seeks only to fulfil her ambitions, stating, "At 23, I had no life beyond the great walls of mercy—desired none. My work was meat and drink to my soul." She falls in love with and marries a patient, but her commitment to her career causes her marriage to fall apart, and she miscarries their baby. She is left lamenting, "We might have prolonged the rapture of our honeymoon indefinitely had I stayed in the shining little rooms and devoted my time to making a real home."[25]

Many of the government's attempts to recruit and keep women workers for the war effort enforced this same dichotomy. Women who had never expected to work had to be recruited and kept happy while working. But they also had to leave their jobs as soon as men returned. To that end, working conditions for many women suddenly became much better than they had been before the war. Recognizing that women would still be expected to care for their families and homes while working, factory owners started adding daycare centers. Facilities were adjusted for women's comfort, and training programs were created just for them. To protect women's supposed sensibilities and purity, they were primarily hired at facilities that had few or no male coworkers (outside of supervisors and managers, who were still predominantly male). Fearful that the low wages typically paid to women would keep employers from firing them when the war ended, unions pressed for competitive wages for women. These gains were often denied, and most women still earned a good deal less than men—but their wages did increase once unions got involved. Women were living a workplace dream they had never seen before—and wouldn't see again.

To stave off massive unemployment once the war concluded, government officials began preparing for the millions of soldiers who would need work when they returned, mapping out a plan as early as the beginning of the war. All studies, surveys, and strategy meetings conducted to work on the issue of postwar unemployment were based on the idea that the only workers who counted were men—in particular, white men. No strategies were put in place to deal with the future of women workers, beyond how to most quickly and easily transition them out of work to make room for men.[26] The US government commissioned studies on existing attitudes toward women workers and what should be done with them when the war ended.

Not content to just gauge public opinion, government officials aimed to shape it. Propaganda was targeted to women (like that developed by the Magazine Bureau), but pamphlets and short films were also produced to mold male opinions on working women. One pamphlet commissioned from the American Historical Association (AHA) by the War Department, titled *Do You Want Your Wife to Work After the War?*, was a discussion guide of sorts that endeavored to get GIs thinking about how they would handle the presence of women workers when they returned home. Covering historical opinions, the pamphlet highlighted flaws in past hostility toward women workers (while reaffirming how understandable those attitudes were) in order to soften men's views toward women's employment. It featured a fictionalized discussion between two soldiers on the pros and cons of women workers. One soldier argued that while most women were happy to be wives and mothers, many also needed the excitement and purpose of outside employment. He talked about the financial benefits and security of having a wife who was also bringing in income. The second soldier argued that women workers would be in direct competition with returning soldiers for employment, and that they would abandon their wifely and motherly duties in order to keep a job that should go to a man. "How about competition from these women that are staying on the job to support guys like you?" the second soldier argued. "They're going to make it harder for me to do it my way."

The debate on the surface seemed to evenly represent the issue—if we ignore the fact that the entire debate is situated within the needs, desires, and opinions of men. The final section of the pamphlet—titled "Some Attempts to Solve the Women Problem"—lists possible ways to deal with women workers after the war, including those who wanted to keep working. Possible solutions include treating housework and child-rearing more like "a profession" and establishing training programs on household management. Another is to pay women *not* to work. The prospect of women staying in the workplace so long as men helped them with household chores in order to lighten their burden is briefly floated but immediately dismissed as too upsetting to the "traditional scheme of things."[27] While the pamphlet was initially framed as an impartial document in support of the war effort, the American History Association now acknowledges that it and other organizations like it were a part of the war machine intended to shape public opinion instead of merely gauging or reflecting it. The AHA admits that it "tailored its pamphlets to paint an idealized image of a postwar world that was essentially free of minorities, where women happily moved out of the factories and back into the kitchen, and where America would largely dominate the world stage."[28]

I'm sure that many in the War Office congratulated themselves on the success of their propaganda campaigns (and celebrated them as proof of the suggestible nature of women). But it is likely that a large percentage of the 6.5 million women who worked did so because they needed to support themselves and their families. Perhaps they had always wanted to work but had previously been denied decent-paying jobs.[29] Regardless of why they started, once the war was over many women wanted to keep working. The efforts of the US government may have helped cement public opinion overall against women working after the war; studies showed that when asked what to do with women workers postwar, 48 percent of respondents said "fire them" and an additional 36 percent said "fire them, unless they have dependents, or are war widows, or there are plenty of jobs." The government was far less successful in getting the women who were doing the work to eagerly give it up.[30] Studies and polls conducted in 1944 of working women showed that 75–80 percent of them wanted to keep their jobs after the war ended.[31] Apparently, they decided to risk the possibility of divorce, infertility, and death that *True Story* had warned them of for daring to want to work for any other reason than to bring soldiers home.

Regardless of how vital the work of women had been to the war effort, the only jobs that the US government and factory owners cared about saving after the war were the jobs of men—even if a large percentage of the men returning had never worked in plants or factories. A million women were fired as the war ended, two million more left the workplace, and many were funneled into lower-paying "women's" roles. White women were steered toward clerical work and lower-paying, low-skilled manufacture work, and Black women were placed in domestic service and laundries.[32] Women who tried to stay in other fields and were not immediately fired found that the daycare services and welcoming work environments disappeared, unions weren't interested in protecting their wages, and they were stripped of the promotions they had worked for. Often they were demoted to the lowest-paying and lowest-skilled positions in their plants and factories. As women were shoved out of higher-paid positions, many of which hadn't existed prewar (especially in factories and plants built for the war effort and those utilizing newly developed wartime technologies), men quickly moved into them—and up the employment ladders that women had helped build.

Returning soldiers who failed to land these promising positions were not left out to dry. The GI Bill provided education, training, financial relief, home loans, small business loans, and more. Between those benefits and the new skills and businesses that had been opened up by wartime production, and with the financial support of the US government, many men found themselves on the path to financial security—even prosperity. Enrollment in college, which prior to the war had been a place still mostly reserved for wealthy and socially connected sons, skyrocketed, as did home ownership. Almost half of all veterans started their own businesses.[33]

Women were almost completely cut out of GI benefits. Of the eight million WWII veterans who used the GI Bill, only about sixty-five thousand were women.[34] That's 0.008 percent. Meanwhile, the average Black veteran found that the GI Bill simply returned him to his lower economic caste. College aid was offered to Black veterans, but it was moot; the vast majority of US colleges and universities refused to accept Black students, and those that did accepted so small a number that most Black veterans were unable to use the tuition benefits. Homeowner's assistance was of even less use to Black vets, since banks refused to work with Black buyers, and cities redlined Black families into neighborhoods designed to keep the return on their investments as low as possible. The GI Bill was legislation designed to benefit only white men.

Even unemployment assistance worked against Black veterans. When they returned home to find that among the new, promising jobs, the only positions offered to them were the most dangerous, the lowest skilled, and the lowest paid, they were forced to accept them. If they turned down these hazardous and poorly compensated jobs, they were reported to the Department of Veterans Affairs, and their benefits were cut, leaving them with nothing.[35]

In nearly every instance of notable social progress and opportunity for women and people of color, we see immense efforts put forth by white men to build further guarantees of their power into those advances. Many still view WWII as a turning point for working women because it was an era when more women worked than ever before. And it's true that many women continued to work after the war, helping to normalize the idea of women in the workplace. But when we look at the huge effort and expense the government expended on developing propaganda, as well as at legislation like the GI Bill—still so celebrated today—we can also see that it was a time when sexist and racist norms were modernized and cemented into the postwar economy. Due to the combined efforts of the federal government and business owners, the rigid definition of "women's work" was scaled up to ensure that it could accommodate rising numbers of female employees—even if those low-paid and low-skilled jobs were not the ones they sought. People of color were once again forced into jobs and neighborhoods that continued to guarantee the conditions of poverty they had always known. And white men were given more opportunities than ever before to access highly skilled and well-paying work, education, secure housing, and entrepreneurial opportunity—simply because they were white men.

## WOMEN ONLY AS A LAST RESORT, AND THEN NOT REALLY: PUSHED OFF THE GLASS CLIFF

When the *New York Times* announced in the summer of 2011 that Jill Abramson would become the next executive editor of the nation's paper of record, few people were surprised. She had been established as the heir apparent in her previous role as its managing editor, and after scandals involving white male executive editors and struggles to adapt to a digital news world, Abramson represented both the change and the stability that the *Times* needed. Usually, when the person that everyone knows is going to get the job gets the job, it doesn't make headlines. But Abramson's promotion was widely talked about and celebrated.

Why? Because the Gray Lady had managed to operate for over 150 years without a single woman at its helm.

You'd think the *New York Times* would be embarrassed that it took so long to place one of its many talented women in charge. You'd think the paper would have gotten to it at some point in the thirty-five-and-counting years since it was sued by multiple women employees for harassment and discrimination. But instead of the promotion being viewed as underscoring the sexist legacy of the paper, the *Times* was celebrated for taking only sixteen decades to decide that a woman could lead it. And when you look back over the last few hundred years at how other companies have treated women, it makes sense that Abramson was regarded as a unicorn instead of as a hardworking, competent, and highly qualified employee earning a well-deserved promotion.

Although no American company in this era can be openly against women workers without facing customer backlash and major lawsuits, women in general haven't enjoyed the extraordinary gains in the workplace that those who were fighting for the right to work in the 1940s hoped for. Women are still paid significantly less than white men; Black, Indigenous, and Hispanic women barely earn half of what white men make. Surveys show that between 30 and 80 percent of women report having been sexually harassed in the workplace. Most women still work at companies that don't provide daycare assistance or adequate family leave to care for sick children. This country's average maternity-leave programs are an embarrassment when compared to those of most European countries. In Washington, my home state, new parents are guaranteed only twelve weeks of paid leave following the birth or adoption of a child.[36] In Sweden, new parents are given sixteen *months* of paid leave.[37]

I know these truths personally. I remember tearfully leaving my son at daycare for nine hours a day just four weeks after he was born because I couldn't live on the 50 percent maternity pay my company offered. I remember pumping breast milk in a supply closet in the women's restroom because there were no sanitary or private accommodations offered. Outside of one brief stint at a women's clothing store in my early twenties, I have not worked at a company where I wasn't sexually harassed by a manager or coworker. I have been groped, kissed, propositioned—all without invitation or consent. I've been passed over for promotions because I wasn't "strong enough to lead" and uninvited from meetings because I was "too opinionated." And I've watched the same things and much worse happen to countless women friends and colleagues over the decades.

Even though there are more women in the workplace than ever before, even though women are now more likely than men to get a college degree, and even though we can look up just about any corporate values statement and see something about "gender equality" written there—workplaces across the country are still, by and large, antiwoman. American business today is still a world run by and for white men. Women are ignored at best, treated like hostile intruders or sex objects at worst. After many decades of struggle, we are still so far away from gender equity that we can't even see it.

In 2019, women made up just 5 percent of Fortune 500 CEOs. Five percent. And yet women make up a little more than half the overall population. We find more dudes named John at the heads of top companies than women.[38]

So when Jill Abramson was promoted to executive editor of the *New York Times*, it was, sadly, a big deal. Many, myself included, took Abramson's promotion as a sign of positive change in the publishing world. And when she was publicly and abruptly fired just two years later, many of us realized that maybe she—and the rest of us—had been set up.

When you can't keep women out anymore, and you can't force them all to become secretaries or teachers because modern social politics demand that you at least pretend to support gender equality in the workplace, what can you do to keep women out of powerful positions in business? You can set them up to fail—or, to be more accurate, you set them up to fall.

It's called the glass cliff, and it's a phrase that was first coined in 2005 by University of Exeter researchers Michelle K. Ryan and S. Alexander Haslam. Their research was inspired by an article in the *Times* (of London, not New York) that suggested women leaders have a negative impact on stock performance. Perhaps Ryan and Haslam smelled the whiff of bullshit coming from the page. They wondered if it was actually true that women brought doom and gloom to the businesses they led, or if there was some other reason why women were more likely to be found in leadership positions at troubled businesses. They found that women were indeed more likely than men to be in leadership positions at distressed companies, but they also found that the problems were not the women's fault. In researching the one hundred companies listed on the London Stock Exchange that the *Times* had reviewed for its article, they found that although women were vastly underrepresented on the boards overall, they were most likely to be added to the boards of companies that were in serious trouble. These firms had shown months of decline and seemed at risk of failure *prior* to adding women to their boards.[39]

When Alison Cook and Christy Glass at Utah State University followed up on this research by looking at US companies, they also discovered disturbing patterns impacting women and people of color in business: women and people of color were most likely to be placed at the head of a company when it was already at risk of failure; white men were less likely to accept leadership positions when companies were at risk of failure; and when women or people of color failed to quickly turn around the struggling company, they were most likely replaced with white men. Women and people of color are often only given the opportunity to steer ships that white men have already rammed into icebergs. Then, when the ship sinks, the media reports that women make bad captains.

When Marissa Mayer was chosen to steer Yahoo, many argued that the ship had already sunk. After years of making bad business decisions and suffering increasing irrelevancy in the ever-changing digital world, the one-time internet giant appeared to be beyond saving. And yet many celebrated Mayer's hiring as a step forward for women in the industry while acknowledging that her chances of success were slim at best. Ellen Pao's appointment as interim CEO of Reddit surprised just about everyone—even her. But following the abrupt departure of their former CEO, the social media platform needed to change if it was going to expand beyond its reputation as a dark, smelly place for dudes to talk about video games and how mad they are that women won't give them blow jobs.

If you are seeing a pattern here, that's because there is one. After everything else has been tried ("everything" being multiple mediocre white dudes) and time is running out, I imagine people start saying crazy things like "What if we tried a woman?" or "What if a brown person gave it a shot?" or, even crazier, "What if we put a *brown woman* in charge?" Women and people of color are often seen as Hail Marys for businesses in desperate need of change. They are tossed, eyes closed, fingers crossed, across the field with little direction other than a prayer that they will land the team somewhere better than it is now.

Why do women and people of color take on these roles that seem doomed to failure? Are we not paying attention? Are we too prone to risk? Are we not smart enough to see the disaster in front of us? I think it's pretty obvious: it's because we don't think we have a choice. We are never more likely to be given an opportunity to lead than when we will probably fail. We know that we will probably be denied that chance when the company is on sure footing. So we say a prayer and risk it all in the hopes that maybe it will pay off for us and for the company.

But then, a funny thing happens when a woman or a person of color is promoted to the head of the company. White male managers stop collaborating with their coworkers—especially their women coworkers and coworkers of color. Why do white men decrease their level of performance when a woman or person of color becomes CEO? Because suddenly they feel less connected to the company.[40] If this little fact has you thinking of the collective white male response to the presidency of Barack Obama and the rhetoric of the 2016 presidential election—yeah, I hear you.

This is not all that happens when women reach the top. Often, they find themselves criticized for the "feminine" traits that were a symbol of the "change" that companies wanted when they decided that change was necessary. Many journalists and tech commentators criticized Marissa Mayer's youth and fashionable wardrobe, even though Yahoo was desperate to appeal to a young, fashionable, internet-savvy audience. When she gave interviews requested by news outlets, she was critiqued by the press for seeking the limelight (similar critiques were aimed at Abramson). Even Mayer's voice wasn't beyond appraisal.

Women who lead with a more "male" style do not fare any better. Women are often punished for the same personality traits that men are praised for. Less than a year into Abramson's role as the head of the *New York Times*, Dylan Byers published a scathing exposé in Politico on her leadership style, titled "Turbulence at the

*Times.*" The piece alleged that Abramson was widely disliked at the paper for her "brusque" and "difficult" manner. The article started by detailing an alleged confrontation between Abramson and her second in command, Dean Baquet, that ended with Baquet storming out of her office and punching a wall. This altercation was used as the first example of Abramson's apparent provocation, with anonymous employees telling Byers, "If Baquet had burst out of the office in a huff . . . it was likely because Abramson had been unreasonable."[41] Yet she wasn't the one who punched a wall. "Unreasonable" behavior by women apparently justifies violent behavior by men.

Marissa Mayer faced similar critiques. She was too brusque and not collaborative enough. She was a perfectionist and a micromanager. The traits that Abramson and Mayer were criticized for are traits that make men into legends in their industries. Imagine complaining that a male editor in chief at a bustling newspaper is "too brusque." That has literally been the stereotype of newspaper editors from the moment newspapers were invented. Who would Steve Jobs have been without his singularity, his perfectionism, his uncompromising management style, and his personal attention to detail?

When women try to create the change they are hired for, they are often met with open revolt. This was the case for Ellen Pao at Reddit. "Everything was a push uphill. We didn't have mobile. I was like, 'Who doesn't believe in mobile?' But the whole team didn't believe in mobile," Pao explained to me.[42] We were discussing how she had worked to increase Reddit's mainstream appeal and ease of use through important changes like making the site accessible to people who want to use their cell phones for social media.

As Reddit struggled to diversify its employee and user demographics, Pao started making practical changes in recruitment, hiring more women and people of color and changing long-held

practices like only recruiting from the Reddit site. She also eliminated salary negotiations, instead offering prospective employees
a choice of compensation packages since research has shown that
women are often at disadvantages in salary negotiations, which
can contribute to gender pay gaps. As the demographics in the
office began to shift, some employees saw the changes as a threat
to Reddit's culture: "There was a strain of, like, 'We only want
longtime Redditors to work at Reddit,'" Pao told me. "And those
longtime Redditors were mostly white men, mostly introverted,
mostly had this point of view of, 'We can say whatever we want,
we can do whatever we want, and we don't have to be inclusive,
and we only like people who are like us.'" Reddit was the white
man's domain.

It can be argued that the biggest factors preventing diversification of Reddit's user base were the rampant racism, sexism,
homophobia, transphobia, and ableism found in the platform's
threads. Conversations on Reddit are grouped by subject matter
called "subreddits," and when Pao decided to shut down the openly
abusive subreddits charmingly named "r/FatPeopleHate," "r/Ham-
PlanetHatred," "r/ShitNiggersSay," and "r/Transfags," many of the
white men who visited the platform just to be able to bathe in
their hatred of others were outraged. They considered themselves
victimized, unfairly silenced. The closed subreddits were quickly
replaced by ones with names like "r/EllenPaoIsACunt."

The response to Pao's attempts to change office culture, while
extreme, is probably unsurprising to any women who have tried
to increase equity or inclusion in their offices—especially women
of color. The truth is, even though many women believe that they
must work to increase inclusion in their workplaces, for their own
survival and for the survival of their women peers, they are almost
always punished for it. Women and people of color who advocate
for diversity and equity are often punished for their efforts in peer,
team, and management evaluations. Ironically, the people who are

not penalized in their evaluations for their diversity and equity efforts are—say it with me—white men.[43]

The career trajectory of women who make it to the top is marked with battle scars. They often have to battle high school teachers and college instructors who steer them away from STEM fields or business and toward the arts (I'm not knocking the arts here—my liberal-arts degree has served me quite well), and they have to fight for attention that is given more generously to the young men in the room. Then they have to battle sexist work environments where they may be vastly outnumbered by men and isolated on their teams. They have to overcome reduced access to the internships, mentorships, and office friendships that many men use to secure opportunities. They have to fight upper managers and subordinates who don't see them as "management material." And they do this for less pay than their male counterparts.

After all that struggle, women have to jump at fraught and risk-filled leadership positions at failing companies because they know those are likely the only chances they'll get. Once at the top, they have to battle a team of white male managers who suddenly don't feel like working as hard as they used to. They have to find a way to be a "strong leader" while also not seeming like a "bitch." They have to battle to push forward every change they were brought in to make, no matter how incremental. And through it all the news articles documenting their efforts will focus on their appearance, their voice, their age.

When we look at the treatment of women in business and in business leadership, how Abramson, Pao, and Mayer fared in their jobs will probably not come as a surprise. When Abramson was very publicly fired with little respect for her years at the *Times* (even though past executive editors at the *Times* who had been involved in serious misconduct and scandal had been eased out of their roles with much more grace), women in the journalism world clearly saw hands pushing Abramson off the glass cliff. She had,

by many measures, done a superb job. Prior to Abramson taking
the helm, the paper had, like many older newspapers, struggled to
engage readers online as the popularity and profitability of print
publishing continued to decline industry-wide. Under Abramson's
leadership, experiments with interactive, multimedia stories helped
establish the *Times* as a leader in the digital news sphere, and the
paper took home an astonishing four Pulitzer Prizes, for Investiga-
tive Reporting, Explanatory Reporting, International Reporting,
and Feature Writing.[44] In the end, *New York Times* publisher Ar-
thur Sulzberger Jr. stated that Abramson was fired for a "series of
issues" including "arbitrary decision-making," "inadequate communication," and "public mistreatment of colleagues." Abramson
was replaced by Dean Baquet, the man who had punched an office
wall during a disagreement with her.

Mayer's downfall seemed predestined before she even took on
the role at Yahoo, but it was accelerated by activist investors. Just
days after Mayer gave birth to twins, Eric Jackson of Asset Management threw a metaphorical brick through her window in the
form of a ninety-nine-page presentation sent to Yahoo shareholders
lambasting the company and Mayer's leadership. Jackson hoped to
convince other shareholders to join him in demanding that Mayer
be fired. Mayer survived Jackson's attempts to oust her, only to be
brought down by another activist investor simultaneously working toward her demise. Jeffrey Smith of Starboard Value decided
that Mayer couldn't save Yahoo—nobody could—and he used his
influence to pressure Yahoo to break itself apart and sell off its
profitable holdings.

To have two separate activist investors targeting you at once
might seem extreme—unless you are a woman running a company. A study by the University of Missouri found that, even
though women make up only 5 percent of Fortune 500 CEOs,
activist investors are more likely to target companies helmed by
women with the intent of directing their management decisions,

even when controlling for company performance. This means that activist investors are seeking out companies that are led by women with the goal of taking that leadership from them—because they are women.[45] Mayer was ultimately forced to oversee the scrapping of Yahoo and the end of her job.

Ellen Pao was brought down in a storm of fit-throwing Redditors. The moderators of the most popular subreddits took their pages private in protest of Pao's leadership decisions, effectively shutting down the site for a majority of users. In the midst of the crisis, Reddit's board surprised Pao with new and unrealistic goals for the company, demanding that it grow from 135 million monthly users to 350–500 million monthly users by the end of the year. To Pao, the writing was on the wall. Reddit wanted her out.

When Pao resigned she was replaced by Reddit cofounder Steve Huffman. He didn't roll back the changes that Pao had implemented—the ones that apparently had caused so much outrage with Redditors—and yet, for some mysterious reason, the outrage ended. The protests stopped; the popular subreddits were taken out of their private settings. There wasn't an influx of new subreddits titled "r/SteveHuffmanIsACunt." Soon Facebook and Twitter would also take steps to remove abusive accounts from their platforms, and yet the widespread uprising against their male CEOs that Pao had faced never materialized. And even though the ambitious user goals Reddit had set were apparently so important that failure to meet them would have forced Pao to resign, it took Reddit over three years after she left to reach the half-billion monthly-user goal they set for her in 2015.

I'm not trying to paint a picture of perfect women being taken down by awful men. Abramson, Mayer, and Pao were far from perfect. Abramson herself admits that she wasn't the best editor. She made that admission in an autobiography that showed serious lapses of judgment and even breaches of ethics on her part when it became clear that she likely plagiarized parts of the book. But

Abramson wasn't fired for lapses of judgment or plagiarism—she was fired for being . . . difficult. And despite a record that was widely praised within and outside Yahoo, Mayer also made a lot of decisions that many people thought were unwise, especially with regard to the rapid acquisitions that she oversaw of more than fifty companies by Yahoo in just four years. I'm not saying that if all CEOs were women, every company would be improved. But it's not as if white dudes have been doing all that great. So why aren't women given an honest chance?

The hard truth is, the characteristics that most companies, including boards, shareholders, managers, and employees, correlate with people who are viewed as "leadership material"—traits most often associated with white male leaders—are actually bad for business. The aggression and overconfidence that are seen as "strength and leadership" can cause leaders to take their companies down treacherous paths, and the attendant encounters with disaster could be avoided by exercising caution or by accepting input from others. These same qualities also mask shortfalls in skills, knowledge, or experience and may keep leaders from acknowledging mistakes and changing course when needed. They prevent healthy business partnerships and collaborative work environments. These traits can and do spell disaster for many businesses.

And yet many of the white men who embody these characteristics are held up as masters of business, even when they fail in front of our eyes. Yes, Trump's multiple bankruptcies and business fiascos are good examples, but so are the public failures of Martin Shkreli, who is still running companies from prison and is thought of by many young businessmen as a bit of a rock star, even after his scams ruined lives; of Elon Musk, who seems to be too busy tweeting insults at people and giving away submarines to effectively run Tesla; and of John Schnatter, who finally left Papa John's Pizza after blaming poor performance on the NFL and using racial slurs in company conference calls.

What is lost is not just the potential for new and different leadership, but the general practice of valuing women leaders—or at least seeing them as equally likely to lead a business to success or failure as white men—and what being valued would mean to the millions of women in American workplaces. Many people never want those women to be CEOs, but women are not devalued only as CEOs; they are devalued in every part of the American workplace. Women are demeaned, dismissed, abused, and underpaid in nearly every industry. These insults hurt individual women, their families, and the businesses they work for.

Many of the hardships women face in the workplace are due to the overvaluing of white men. How many times in recent years have you heard the argument that a white man shouldn't be fired for sexual harassment or other gross misconduct because it would "jeopardize his future" or "waste his potential"? Every white man in business is pure potential. Every white man from unpaid intern to CEO could be our next great leader, our next great innovator. To harm the trajectory of any white man—no matter how incompetent, no matter how many women or people of color he stepped on or groped along the way—would be a risk too large to take.

But what are women worth? What would it look like to value us and our potential? What is the risk of destroying our careers before they even start?

Industries and institutions—and larger societies—that believe in women's leadership potential, even if it looks different from what tradition dictates, will invest in the careers of women from beginning to end. They will care about how girls are taught in school; they will create internship opportunities that help women along their path; they will look for and nourish the strengths of individual women. They will create family leave and child care programs that allow women to grow their careers without sacrificing their families; they will adopt strong and proactive policies to address sexual harassment and assault in the workplace so that women feel safe and don't have to split their energies between focusing on their jobs and avoiding being groped by a supervisor. When we believe that women can and should lead, we value their skills, talents, and potential in the boardroom and the executive offices, but also in product development, finance, advertising, engineering, and everywhere else. When we believe that women can and should lead, we unleash the potential of half the American workforce. Even if we can't guarantee that every woman promoted to CEO will outperform her male counterpart in company growth or profitability, the important benefits for workplaces and the broader society of elevating women to positions of power will always be worth the risk.

CHAPTER 6

# SOCIALISTS AND QUOTA QUEENS

## When Women of Color Challenge the Political Status Quo

"What's your major?"

That's a question every college student is asked more times than they can count. When I was in college and would answer "political science," the follow-up question was almost always: "Are you going to run for office one day?"

My answer was always a swift no. I was studying political science because I was a politics nerd who looked at electoral processes with the same fascination that science nerds looked at chemical reactions. I would answer that I hoped to maybe be a political analyst for a few years and then maybe a teacher. The behind-the-scenes work suited me better.

But also, I would joke, I would never pass any personal vetting during an election cycle.

I was keenly aware that I was a Black woman. I was a Black, single mother with shitty credit, a few questionable romantic decisions in my past (and future), and some pretty liberal political views that I didn't seem to be able to shut up about. Some of my earlier political memories were watching Anita Hill and Lani Guinier getting torn apart by mainstream media. I saw their political ideas twisted and used to discredit them. I saw their personal lives put on display. I saw how friends and colleagues turned against them. I did not want that for myself or my children.

Instead of becoming a political analyst or professor, I eventually became a writer. And even though I don't write about the inside-baseball of politics like I once thought I might, I write about political issues. My education has served me well in this career, even if it was not what I originally imagined for myself. It also, like a job as an analyst likely would have, fits my introverted yet very opinionated personality. I spend a lot of time observing, thinking, commenting. I do not have to compromise my principles or soften my message to make friends or keep a job (I have certainly lost a gig or two, but the beauty of freelancing is that editors have short memories and you do your best to move on to the next one). And I do a lot of it in the privacy of my own home—sans pants.

The personal insults and slurs started fairly quickly. In the comments sections of my articles I'd be called a "dumb bitch" or an "ugly nigger." People soon started dropping my personal information into comments as well—information about my children or past jobs. The death threats came pretty quickly too, if not as frequently.

To my knowledge, 2017 was the first time I was doxed. Doxing is when someone posts your home address, email, phone numbers, financial information—pretty much anything they can find on you—online for people to do with what they wish.

In 2019, my home was swatted. Swatting is when somebody calls the police from a phone number in your neighborhood and states that there is some violence or threat of violence happening in your home in order to have an armed SWAT team sent to your house. In 2017, a swatting led to the death of a Kansas man, who made the mistake of lowering his arms when a SWAT team showed up at his home out of the blue. In my case, a caller pretending to be my son phoned the police and said that he had shot his parents to death. Six officers holding rifles pulled my son out of our home at six a.m. and searched our house.

If I hadn't become aware before the swatting that my personal information had been placed online, the situation could have been much worse. But I had received notice that my address (and my mom's address, and my sister's and brother's addresses) had been placed on a website that specifically encourages swatting. I had called my local police department and let them know that they might be called to my house on a swatting attempt. So even though they still sent an armed response to my house, they did so knowing it was unlikely that they were going to find two dead bodies inside. It meant that when my sleepy teenage son opened the door and saw police and then quickly shut the door so he could put his shoes on, they didn't open fire. I cannot tell you how often I've played out worse, alternate scenarios in my head since that happened.

The website that posted my personal information had listed me as an "antiwhite" writer and had included links to my articles on racial justice and to my previous book, *So You Want to Talk About Race*, in order to incite harassment and even violence against me.

A few days after the police showed up at my door, my mom started receiving harassment at home. A few more days later, somebody tweeted out my social security number.

In my career as a writer, I have been able to speak more openly on social and political issues than any other Black woman I know. I do not have to worry about being fired from my job; speaking out is literally my job. I do not have to worry about losing friends—I lost all the ones who were going to leave a few hundred articles ago.

But my children and I have had to spend quite a few nights away from our home for our safety. I have had my email hacked, my financial information compromised. My sons' schools have reached out to make sure there are safety plans in place for them there. I've received so many death threats via email that they have their own folder (which I've titled "fan mail"). Armed police have been sent to my house looking for my dead body.

And still, that is nothing compared to what many of the women of color in political office—women like Ilhan Omar, Rashida Tlaib, Alexandria Ocasio-Cortez, and Ayanna Pressley—face every day. They face threats, insult, and harassment on a level that I can't imagine. All for being women of color who dare represent their populations and therefore challenge the status quo.

Twelve years after finishing college, and I can still confidently say that there is no way I'd ever run for office.

As I write this, we have white men holding major political office who believe that global warming is a hoax. We have white men holding major political office who believe that racial integration is bad for America. We have white men holding major political office who believe that women can't get pregnant from rape. We have white men holding major political office who believe that there's nothing wrong with being a white supremacist. We have white men holding major political office who have been accused of sexual assault. We have white men holding major political office who have publicly used racial slurs. We have white men holding major political office who believe that Muslims should not be allowed into the country. We have white men holding major political office who have physically assaulted reporters.

These white men can say and do those things with little worry for their careers. In fact, for some of these men, it *is* their careers. Even openly defending white supremacy will get you little more than a slap on the wrist. To be a white man—a straight, abled, cisgender white man—in public office means never having to say you're sorry and still getting reelected.

This freedom means that a full range of white male concerns and viewpoints are centered in our government. Those vying for the white male vote can appeal to either the white male environmentalist or the white male climate-science denier. They can represent the socially liberal white male or the fiscally conservative white male. They can stand for the white male socialist or the white male sexist. White men can run for office on their deeply held, most daring beliefs—or they can run on the most jaded of party lines. Either way, they are unlikely to see the entirety of their personal life used against them; they are unlikely to face an endless barrage of threats for daring to believe they should be heard. They will be able to be the most radical without being branded as too radical. They can be the most violent without being branded as violent. The most racist without being branded as racist. They can focus almost exclusively on the needs of white men without being branded exclusionary or divisive.

Women, people of color, disabled people, LGBTQ+ people— they are afforded no such grace. Those of us who wish to hold office must have personal lives beyond reproach; we must be sure to moderate our political views. We must hold degrees from traditionally white institutions, or be able to prove that our education at schools of color did not radicalize us. We cannot appear to ever be angry. We must always prove that we are willing to prioritize the concerns of white men in our work no matter how few are in our constituency.

So while just about every flavor of white man in America is going to have at least a few representatives in their government, the rest of us are lucky if we have any. One Latinx person in office is supposed to represent the needs of all Latinx, Black, Asian American, Indigenous, and Pacific Islander constituents. One woman in office is supposed to represent all women of varying races and ethnicities, sexualities, classes, and political ideologies.

It is psychologically damaging to never see yourself reflected in positions of leadership in your own country. It limits our feeling of citizenship, and it limits the possibilities we see for ourselves and our children. It creates a feeling of unsafety. Growing up, I can count on one hand the number of friends of color I knew who thought that holding political office was a possibility, let alone a goal.

Even more damaging than the psychological toll is how this exclusion limits the ideas that make it into government. The diversity of problems discussed, solutions offered, and priorities debated in our government often fails to reach beyond those of white men—usually the most privileged of white men. The political and social failings of our society are most likely to hit marginalized populations first and hardest. Our communities have, in lieu of social and political assistance, developed our own mechanisms for identifying and addressing these issues. Our solutions are often, by nature of our political exclusion, outside the box. Our work and creativity have kept us alive and helped us thrive when the odds were stacked against us.

Those of us who have been systemically marginalized in the American political process are certainly not the only people who are frustrated with our current government. We are not the only people who think that our government is out of touch, out of date, sluggish, and uncreative. The system was set up to *appear* to serve the average white American man while simultaneously working against the best interests of the majority of Americans, regardless of race or gender. But even the pretense of representing the "average white man" holds more appeal than political ideas offered up by those who aren't white men, even when those ideas could better serve white men.

When a cause for public concern centers issues impacting communities of color or poor communities—even if the same issues also affect white communities or more affluent ones—it's considered fringe. The crumbling infrastructure that affects the drinking water of the residents of Flint, Michigan, is a national issue that affects many poor communities—poor white communities and poor communities of color. It is likely to impact middle-class communities as our infrastructure ages and we continue to avoid paying for its upkeep. But when the community most injured has a majority Black population, then it becomes a problem that is easily written off as a "Black" issue until it grows too large to ignore or fix.

Likewise, police brutality devastates all communities and families of all racial and ethnic groups. Black and Indigenous people are approximately three to four times more likely to die in an encounter with police than white people—but in 2015 and 2016, 1,158 white Americans were killed by police officers.[1] Over half of all people killed by police are disabled. Even though many hundreds of people are killed by officers every year, between the years 2005 and 2018, only thirty-five officers were convicted of a crime connected to the deaths of civilians; only three of those convictions were for murder.[2] We should all be concerned about the lack of true oversight and accountability in our police forces. It makes us less safe and undermines our democracy. But because the people most likely to be killed by police are Black and brown, and the people most likely to be police are white, and the police have long been known to serve white America's interests, many white Americans have decided that to stand for police accountability is to be antiwhite, and that those who offer real solutions to end police brutality are the enemy.

Then there's political gerrymandering, which has been undermining our democracy for centuries. If political control of a state changes parties in between the US Censuses that take place every ten years, state representatives scramble to redraw voting districts to maximize the impact of their voters and marginalize voters most likely to vote for the other party. Across the country, large pockets of populations are silenced in the electoral process because of this process. People of every political party and every racial demographic reside in districts that are subject to gerrymandering, and it impacts how services and dollars are distributed as well as who gets elected into office, local through national. Gerrymandering also enables elected representatives to effectively write off large portions of their constituency to focus on those who they think will most benefit them and their party. Because gerrymandering has been used most effectively by the Republican party to undermine Black and Latinx votes, and because those who most loudly raise the alarm about the devastating costs of gerrymandering are often people of color, it is an issue that many white Americans have felt safe to ignore, even those who identify strongly with American values of democracy.

I have seen this phenomenon in my own work. I am not someone who thought that racism was defeated when Barack Obama was elected president in 2008. Very few people of color did. I have spent years writing about issues of race and gender in America. I and many other writers on social issues have long raised the alarm on the violent racism and sexism in this country, and the ways in which it is encouraged in various corners of the web and on social media platforms. Yet when the 2016 election put a misogynistic white supremacist in the nation's highest office, I was inundated with messages and emails from liberal white people asking, "How did this happen?" Overnight I went from being someone who wrote about "Black issues" to someone who wrote about their issues. People came to me looking for answers, and all I could do was point them to what I and so many other writers and speakers of color had been saying for literally hundreds of years and ask, "Where have you been?"

I shouldn't have to write any of this. It should be enough that these issues are impacting communities of color. We should care about what is harming our fellow human beings, even if it affects only their communities and not ours. It should be enough that this is hurting us. It is insulting that I have to point out the ways in which these issues also hurt white Americans in the hopes that I might get more people to care.

It is not simply that many white Americans do not care; it is that many white Americans are so invested in the political exclusion of people who are not white men that they will actively work against any political change that would meaningfully enfranchise women, people of color, LGBTQ+ people, and disabled people—even when they are aware of the potential costs to their own well-being. Many have decided that the psychological benefit of looking at government and seeing a room full of white men is worth the very real cost to their financial and physical welfare. Somehow, even though history has shown that it is not the case, many white Americans are still able to convince themselves that listening to the same people they've always listened to will pay off for them in the end.

In the meantime, those who work to represent the voices of marginalized people and to bring new ideas into our government are not only fought every step of the way by their peers and rivals, they often face torrents of threats and abuse as they do so. And they continue to push back against a status quo that does not want them to be heard—not only because they truly believe in what they have to offer, but also because they know that their community desperately needs them to fight.

## SHIRLEY CHISHOLM DECIDES TO GO FIRST

*I do not believe that in 1972 the great majority of Americans will continue to harbor such narrow and petty prejudices. I am convinced that the American people are in a mood to*

*discard the politics and political personalities of the past. I
believe that they will show in 1972, and thereafter, that they
intend to make independent judgments on the merits of a
particular candidate, based on that candidate's intelligence,
character, physical ability, competence, integrity, and honesty.*

—*Shirley Chisholm, from her presidential campaign
announcement speech, January 25, 1972*[3]

Shirley Chisholm ran for president in 1972 and briefly took
the country by storm. If you haven't heard much about Shirley
Chisholm, that's not surprising. Black women who make history
are often written out of it. But Chisholm's campaign, and the response to it, changed American politics while also showing how
our nation's lack of collective faith in the possibility of social progress that doesn't center white men will always hold us back.

In late 1971 and early 1972, Black male political leaders were
getting ready to put forward the first major Black candidate for the
US presidency. The discussion had been in the works for years, but
turmoil after the assassination of Dr. Martin Luther King Jr. in
1968 had made settling on a candidate difficult. As leaders debated
who might be the best choice to run, when he would run, and how,
it began to look like the 1972 election might pass them by. As Black
elites raced to come up with solutions, Shirley Chisholm stunned
them all by announcing that she was running for president.

"They were standing around, peeing on their shoes," a Chisholm
campaign aide told the *New York Times* shortly after Chisholm
announced her candidacy, "and so, Shirley finally said to hell with
it and got a campaign going."[4]

Chisholm ran for president on a platform as bold as her announcement, especially considering the time. She stood for wom-
en's rights, ending the war in Vietnam, campaign finance reform,
environmental protections, congressional term reform, the protection of individual rights against government surveillance, police

reform, veterans' benefits, minimum family income, and more.[5] Her platform would likely still be considered progressive were a candidate to run on it today, because many of the issues that she discussed are still primary concerns of progressive voters. I know I would vote for her.

While the announcement of her candidacy may have shocked the media and political elites, Shirley Chisholm's trailblazing style was probably not much of a surprise to those who had followed her political career. She had already proven herself a competent and confident change-maker. A Quaker-raised teacher with a master's in education who had long advocated for education reform and child welfare, Chisholm had been actively involved in local politics for over a decade. After years of working in political clubs and committees, she was elected to the New York State Assembly in 1965. Three years later, she ran for the House of Representatives and won in a landslide two-to-one victory, becoming the first Black woman elected to the US Congress.[6]

In Congress, Chisholm quickly made a name for herself. She was a vocal opponent of the war in Vietnam and was one of only nineteen representatives willing to hold hearings on the war. She was a founding member of the Black Congressional Caucus and the Congressional Women's Political Caucus.[7] Chisholm's early congressional work included addressing food security and veterans' affairs. At a time when government offices were overwhelmingly white and male (which was all the time, honestly—including today), all of Chisholm's congressional staff were women, and half were Black women.[8]

At the time of Shirley Chisholm's campaign, people of all races and genders had been advocating for change. The unwinnable Vietnam War was increasingly unpopular, and the president, Richard Nixon, widely blamed for deepening US ground involvement in the war, was falling out of favor due to his reputation for corruption and political bullying. An unpopular war, a rise in inflation and unemployment, and the rollback of civil liberties to combat political protesters (exemplified in acts such as controversial "no-knock warrants") left many Americans feeling ignored and abused by the government. Chisholm's platform of progressive reform should have had wide appeal throughout the political left—especially with women, people of color, and the working and middle classes of all races.

Shirley Chisholm herself saw the potential for broad appeal in her campaign. "I stand before you today as a candidate for the Democratic nomination for the presidency of the United States of America," she said in her 1972 announcement speech.

> I am not the candidate of Black America, although I am Black and proud. I am not the candidate of the women's movement of this country, although I am a woman and I'm equally proud of that. I am not the candidate of any political policies or fatcats or special interests. I stand here now, without endorsements from many big-name politicians or celebrities or any other kind of prop; I do not intend to offer you the tired clichés that have too long been an accepted part of our political life. I am the candidate of the people of America.[9]

Mainstream press responded predictably. It decided that Black candidates could only represent "Black" issues and that women candidates could only represent "women's" issues and that therefore Chisholm, being both Black and a woman, could not in any way represent the white majority. The *New York Times*, the paper of Chisholm's own state, published dozens of articles on Chisholm's candidacy. In the majority of them, she was described as a candidate for women voters, Black voters, or both. Only four of the thirty articles about her campaign mentioned her possible appeal to white voters. Three of those four were written by a reporter of color.[10]

Many of the sexist critiques and dismissals thrown at women political candidates today were hurled at Shirley Chisholm in

1972. Chisholm's physical appearance garnered regular comment. Not only was Chisholm Black, but she was dark-skinned, broad-nosed, and she dressed like, well, a Quaker schoolteacher. Beyond her appearance there were the general dismissals by men who believed that women have no place in serious politics. Men interviewed in the *Chicago Defender*, a major Black newspaper in print since 1905, accused Chisholm of playing "vaginal politics."[11] One columnist at the *Beaver County Times* (Pennsylvania) lamented that voters were "doomed to an era of female meddling in the political process" but gave Chisholm credit for being a "realist" about her election chances.[12]

On top of the sexism, Chisholm also faced some of the worst racism of the day in her presidential bid. Almost immediately, the racist tone was set when a campaign worker traveling with boxes of campaign flyers received them back from airport security with the words "Go home nigger" scrawled across them.[13] The threats against Chisholm were so intense that she was offered protection by the Secret Service.[14]

Sadly, as we saw with the *Chicago Defender*, it was not just white men who wrote off Chisholm's presidential bid. Chisholm found out what many Black women find out when we try to lead: we are the only ones who have any faith in us. Even with a strong record of advocating for issues impacting women and the Black community, Chisholm found support from the broader feminist and Black political circles to be sorely lacking. Some believed that only a white man could defeat Nixon. Many Black political leaders decided to support front-runner George McGovern instead of Chisholm. Women also hedged their bets. Chisholm had helped found the National Organization for Women (NOW) in 1968 with Gloria Steinem, and although Steinem gave Chisholm her personal endorsement, the organization itself decided to throw its weight behind McGovern for its official endorsement. It had been so long established in American politics that only white men could hold real political power that even many women and people of color had difficulty imagining a departure as far from the norm as a Black woman president. For others, resentment and personal bigotry likely also kept them from supporting Chisholm. While white feminists may have wanted to see a woman as president, and Black men may have wanted to see a Black president, some of those whose race or gender placed them higher on the sociopolitical ladder than Chisholm probably resented what they saw as the attempts of a Black woman to leapfrog over them into the nation's highest office.

Chisholm was, as the sexist columnist at the *Beaver County Times* had stated, a realist. But within that realism was a vision for radical change. Although she was running a serious campaign, Chisholm did not expect that her efforts would place her in the White House. But nor was her campaign an exercise in pride or protest. She may not have had a chance of becoming president, but there was a real chance that her platform could appeal to enough primary voters to get her a healthy delegate count. If her delegate count was high enough, she could use those delegates as leverage with whichever leading candidate needed her delegates at the national convention. If Chisholm's voters were necessary to secure the Democratic nomination, then her politics would be too, and she'd have an opportunity to include some of her progressive priorities in the Democratic national platform. The possibility that those who had long felt overlooked might have their needs included in the platform of the next presidential nominee offered a real opportunity for meaningful political change. That change could benefit anybody Chisholm's platform was designed to lift up. Her strategy to use her support to pressure the Democratic candidate to adopt policies that would help women, people of color, and the poor and working classes directly countered the idea that a vote for her was unproductive—and even harmful—to progressive causes. And yet that dialogue about "harm" was what prevailed. Little serious discussion was given to the political power that could be gained by sending Shirley Chisholm to the national convention with a strong delegate count.

In the end, Chisholm did not get the delegates she had hoped for, and McGovern's decisive nomination victory meant that he had no reason to listen to any of her requests to make his platform more inclusive or progressive.

Rarely do the white men that we choose over Black women end up leading us safely to the victory that we seek. McGovern did not end up being the strong white man the party thought it needed to defeat Nixon—not by a long shot. His choice of the unvetted Thomas Eagleton as his vice-presidential running mate turned out to be a disaster when Eagleton's long and recent battles with mental health were revealed. Still, McGovern voiced strong support for his VP choice (laudable), only to withdraw that support just days later (not so laudable)—making him seem both unprepared for the presidency and like a disloyal opportunist. As the vice-presidential fiasco dominated news cycles in a society that held, then and now, deeply ableist notions that stigmatized anyone with mental health issues, McGovern's chances at victory tanked. His humiliating defeat was the second worst in US presidential election history. Nixon remained president until resigning from office in 1974 in the midst of the Watergate scandal, still recognized as one of the United States' biggest presidential disasters. Whereas Chisholm's candidacy had been ridiculed and dismissed, the white male candidates ended up making history for their embarrassing levels of incompetence and corruption.

Shirley Chisholm, on the other hand, went back to kicking ass at her job. She returned to Congress and continued to work on the issues that meant the most to her constituents. She was well loved by her peers and her constituency, retiring in 1982 as one of the top-ranking members of Congress. After retirement she went back to teaching, this time at Mount Holyoke College, where she was a popular professor of race and gender issues in politics.

A study at Columbia University showed that people are less likely to remember the faces and words of Black women than they are to remember Black men or white women. That goes a long way toward explaining our amnesia surrounding Shirley Chisholm's political legacy, which was quickly forgotten in much of mainstream media. When Jesse Jackson ran for president in 1984, he was often touted as the first African American to run a serious campaign for president. For years, no biography of Chisholm was available in print from a mainstream publisher.

While Chisholm may have been quickly erased from many history books, her impact on national politics for Black Americans and Black women was real. Chisolm was the first. Someone had to be, and she stepped up to show that a Black American—a Black *woman*—could run a serious campaign for president of the United States and could take that campaign all the way to the national convention. The spirit of Shirley Chisholm was felt when Barack Obama became the first Black president in 2008. In 2015, Shirley Chisholm was posthumously honored with the Presidential Medal of Freedom. "When asked how she'd like to be remembered, she had an answer: 'I'd like them to say that Shirley Chisholm had guts,'" Obama said during the medal ceremony. "And I'm proud to say it: Shirley Chisholm had guts."[15]

When I think of Shirley Chisholm, I think of another quote from her about how she wanted to be remembered: "I want history to remember me not just as the first Black woman to be elected to Congress, not as the first Black woman to have made a bid for the presidency of the United States, but as a Black woman who lived in the twentieth century and dared to be herself."[16]

Chisholm dared to be her full self as a Black woman in America: a strong, talented woman who was passionate about including all Americans in the American dream. For her efforts, she received ridicule and threats, but she also helped create change that improved the lives of countless Americans, through her work in Congress, her work in education, and her example as a Black woman willing to challenge the white male status quo. We still fight for many of the reforms that marked Shirley Chisholm's presidential platform, but perhaps we will one day honor her not with posthumous medals but with the open embrace of the next Black woman who shows up on the steps of Washington, ready to lead the country to a more inclusive and just future.

## LANI GUINIER DARES TO SUPPORT GREATER DEMOCRACY IN OUR ELECTIONS

> *We already have moved a long way toward Guinier's*
> *goal of a nation of grievance groups exploiting the*
> *coveted status as "victims" (of America's wickedness)*
> *to claim special rights and entitlements. . . .*
> *People like Guinier, who affix the label "civil*
> *rights" to every bit of their political agendas, have*
> *made it an empty phrase—a classification that*
> *no longer classifies. This, too, is a consequence*
> *of a "progressive" idea: "critical race theory."*
>
> —George Will, 1993[17]

On January 29, 1993, the Clinton administration announced that it had nominated Lani Guinier to head the Civil Rights Division of the Justice Department. Guinier, forty-three at the time, was a well-respected legal expert on voting rights law and a law professor at the University of Pennsylvania, as well as a personal friend of Bill Clinton. Weeks before the administration announced the nomination, conservative advocacy groups had warned Clinton that if he nominated Guinier they were prepared to vigorously fight her appointment and would make specific issue of her published opinions on the Voting Rights Act. Clinton moved forward with the nomination anyway.

This was the opportunity that Clint Bolick, a conservative legal activist, had been waiting for. The next day Bolick published an op-ed in the *Wall Street Journal* with the headline "Clinton's Quota Queens."

The article launched a media firestorm that would make Guinier the target of hatred, bigotry, and lies for months before it all ended with a betrayal by her onetime friend Bill Clinton.

Bolick would later admit freely to the *Washington Post* that he had no idea who Guinier was and no particular grudge against her before her nomination to the Justice Department. He had been looking for a way to exact revenge on leftists, whom he blamed for dragging his friend Clarence Thomas through brutal confirmation hearings after Anita Hill came forward with allegations of sexual harassment against him.[18] When he was informed that Clinton was planning to nominate an "activist" Black lawyer with controversial views on the electoral process, he created a devastating title for Guinier that would quickly poison her nomination in the opinions of both Congress and American voters.

"Quota Queen" was a title that was impressive in its racist connotations. "Quotas," of course, had been a major source of fear and outrage for white Americans—and especially white American men—since the inception of affirmative action programs in the 1960s. "Queen" was a reference to the highly effective—and highly racist, sexist, and classist—exploitation of the case of Linda Taylor, the woman who had used "80 names, 30 addresses, 15 telephone numbers" to obtain fraudulent welfare benefits. While Taylor does appear to have been a very accomplished scam artist (and possible murderer and kidnapper—google her story sometime, it's fascinating), her exceptional case had been used by Ronald Reagan to paint a picture of widespread fraud being perpetrated across the welfare system in order to bilk taxpayers out of millions of dollars, all under the watch of a bleeding-heart liberal government. Reagan rode his promise of welfare reform to victory.[19]

By referencing two classic, even if untrue, narratives of "minorities stealing from hardworking Americans" in one name, Bolick found a shortcut to white American anger. As a successful Black woman who held challenging political ideas, Guinier made a perfect target. Suddenly, hundreds of articles about Guinier appeared that referenced her advocacy of "racial quotas" in the voting process to give people of color—Black people in particular—power over whites.

"Guinier, who has been a voting rights litigator for the NAACP Legal Defense and Educational Fund, seeks a society in which a minority can impose its will on the majority," wrote Lally Weymouth at the *Washington Post*.[20]

Democratic representative Dave McCurdy felt the need to remind people, in a bizarre analogy that he apparently said without irony, that there was no chance Guinier would be confirmed because: "Majority rule is what this country was built on. This is not South Africa."[21]

There were, of course, a few flaws with the reasoning behind all the outrage over Guinier's nomination. "No one cared that, in fact, I did not believe in quotas," explained Guinier in her memoir.[22]

If Guinier wasn't actually advocating for racial quotas in voting, what was she advocating for?

Guinier was concerned with the impact that the concepts "one man one vote" and "winner take all" voting were having on the political representation of people of color. Unless minorities in an area were especially politically aligned with the majority in the population, they were never going to have elected representatives that actually represented their needs. If a candidate needed more than 50 percent of the votes to win, then it would almost never be a good idea for the candidate to prioritize the needs of a minority group when that group's numbers would not give the candidate enough votes to achieve victory. In winner-take-all elections, an elected official can represent 51 percent of their electorate and *not* represent 49 percent of their electorate, and it would still be considered a representative democracy. Further, because there are often only two choices in systems of simple majority rule, each candidate is forced to establish positions as far away as possible from their opponent's views on select hot-button issues to ensure that they don't lose undecided voters to the other side.

In these scenarios, especially when the victors get to redraw electoral districts to further marginalize minorities, minority groups remain voiceless. This is beyond theory; the overwhelming white maleness of our elected government is testament to how this plays out.

As a possible solution, Guinier proposed a system of "cumulative voting." It is not a new system and is practiced successfully in countries all over the world, as well as in multiple cities and counties across the United States. Cumulative voting is a way to increase minority representation by pooling multiple votes across a larger group of candidates and allocating seats based on the pooled votes.

To nerd out a bit here, let's see a breakdown of how it might work.

Instead of having one small representative district that would give you two final choices to vote on, districts would be combined into much larger districts, and each voter would get a set number of votes. If your larger district has six candidates for three open positions, you might have six votes.

Now, you can do whatever you want with those six votes. Do you feel strongly about one candidate, and are you convinced that if your community banded together, you'd have enough votes to put the candidate in the top three? You may want to put all six of your votes toward that one candidate and try to convince your community members to do the same. Do you really love one candidate, but you know that there's a second candidate you'd be pretty happy with if your first pick doesn't have enough votes? You may want to give your first pick four votes and your second pick two. At the end of the election, the top three vote-getters win.

Instead of an election where you are likely to have large minorities of the population who are the ideological opposite of their representatives, you may have one representative that the majority liked enough to put into office, and another that was able to build a broad enough coalition among minority groups to come in second or third. This would increase the number of people who feel represented by their government. When I say "minorities" I don't just mean racial minorities. This voting process would ensure greater representation for people of all races who feel like their voices haven't been heard because their needs or values differ from the majority's. In addition, it would be less conducive to the extreme division of current two-party politics, because instead of an alternative third candidate spelling potential doom for the candidate they are closer ideologically to, they are instead a viable third option that can secure enough votes from a wider geographic area while not stealing votes from main candidates. Candidates would be rewarded for building coalitions, instead of punished for it, and extreme candidates who aim to "fire up the base" would have a harder time holding voters hostage over hot-button issues when voters know that they have the option to support other viable candidates that are not their opposite ideologically.

Although this system would create a markedly different political environment than we have now, it is not a quota system, it is not "South Africa," and it is still very democratic.

Guinier advocated consideration of these systems as a law scholar and professor, but she had not advocated for implementing such changes in her role as a member of the Justice Department, nor would she have had the power to make such a monumental change. Guinier tried to explain cumulative voting to the press and also tried to assure people that she had no intention or ability to change the US electoral process as an assistant attorney general, but nothing she said mattered.

"'Quota Queen' made any further communications superfluous," Guinier later explained on C-SPAN. "It announced my agenda loud and clear as a Black woman who did not know her place. I would do to whites what centuries of whites had done to Blacks."[23]

Republicans, Independents, and even some Democrats began to ask Clinton to withdraw Guinier's nomination.

Whereas President George H. W. Bush, who had nominated Clarence Thomas to the Supreme Court, remained a stalwart supporter of Thomas against serious sexual harassment charges, in the face of the rising backlash Clinton didn't seem very inclined to defend Guinier when she dared to try to address the suppression of minority voters. His first response to the controversy was a tepid dismissal. "The Senate ought to be able to put up with a little controversy for the cause of civil rights," Clinton told reporters in May.[24] As the backlash continued and Guinier was further caricatured into the image of a white-hating Black supremacist, Clinton remained mostly silent.

Clinton's camp began to pressure Guinier to withdraw her name from consideration, but she refused. Guinier tried to meet with Clinton to discuss the nomination and the controversy, but he wouldn't even extend to her the basic respect of a meeting. He did not speak with her personally until right before he announced that he was withdrawing her nomination. Guinier had tried to convince Clinton that she should at least have the chance to be heard before the Senate Judiciary Committee to give them a chance to decide for themselves on her nomination, but he had refused. Black women weren't worth that much trouble.

On June 3, 1993, Clinton announced that he was withdrawing Guinier's nomination. Even though the two had been friends since they had met at law school, and even though Clinton had been specifically warned about Guinier's "controversial" writing on the electoral process, Clinton claimed that he had not read Guinier's writing until shortly before then, which makes him either dangerously forgetful, wildly irresponsible, or a liar—you choose. Clinton said that once he read Guinier's writing, he found within them "ideas which I myself cannot embrace," and added, "Had I read them before I nominated her, I would not have done so."[25]

Guinier's nomination was over, and so was her long-standing friendship with the Clintons, who would never attempt to repair the severed relationship. When interviewed years later about the nomination and her feelings about Bill Clinton, Guinier was generous but honest. "I respect him. I admire him. But I don't think I want to be in his company—not without some prior conversations."[26]

Guinier went on to a prestigious teaching career at Harvard. In 2018, Harvard held a symposium to honor Guinier's contributions to the university and to the field of law. "She has done nothing short of change the way we think about law," said Harvard Law School dean John Manning. "And she's made us rethink the fundamental connection between race and the distribution of political power in our system. She's been a great scholar, a great teacher, and an unfailingly generous colleague."[27]

Columbia Law School professor and Harvard Law alum Patricia Williams spoke of the time, fifteen years earlier, when she had watched her colleague endure widespread anger and accusations for words that she didn't say: "I remember seeing her on TV, her lips were moving but you never heard her voice. People were speaking over it, talking about how dangerous she was and saying what she was [allegedly] saying—but never saying what she really represented. I thought about this again when I saw Elizabeth Warren being silenced. It showed that honor for some can mean the silencing of others."[28]

## OCASIO-CORTEZ, PRESSLEY, TLAIB, AND OMAR: THE MOST DANGEROUS WOMEN IN CONGRESS

*So far we have not seen that Speaker Pelosi will
exercise any kind of control, or that she knows
how to exercise control over these socialists.*

—*Republican Representative Liz Cheney*[29]

In the fall of 2019 I was speaking at a conference in Idaho that celebrated racial and ethnic diversity in the fight to end violence against women. Attendees were mostly women, and I would guess that about 20 percent of them were women of color. Considering that Idaho itself is 91 percent white, this was a pretty diverse crowd. The speech I gave was about how to decenter whiteness in our racial justice efforts. After my speech, I led a workshop on the same topic.

When the workshop broke out into group activity, I sat at an empty table to prepare for the next segment in the session. As I sat, quietly writing in my notepad, I was approached by a white male attendee. He did not ask if it was a good time to approach me; he did not seem to care that I was obviously working. He just sat next to me and said, "Oh good, now I can talk to you. I have a question."

The man did not wait for my consent to the conversation. He just dove in. He described a few of the political activism groups he's involved in, mostly around environmentalism. He goes to fundraisers and events, he attends meet-up groups and protests. He was going to a fundraiser dinner for environmental causes that very evening. It was, he described, going to be a fancy event, requiring cocktail dress. And he was sure that, just like every other event he had attended, it would be populated exclusively with white people. He would love to see more people of color at these events, he said, but they were nowhere to be found.

"Why," he asked me in conclusion, "don't people of color care more about important political issues?"

Many white men see a political landscape dominated by white men and think it is that way because white men are just more politically minded. They think that the absence of women and people of color from powerful rooms is due to self-selection. They do not question how unwelcoming the room they have built might be. They do not question whether or not the discussions they are having in that room are inclusive and generate productive discussions for women and people of color. They don't ask if there are other, equally important conversations happening in other rooms. And they don't even bother to ask if anyone unlocked the door. They look at the room and say that women and people of color aren't in it because women and people of color aren't interested. Then they cite this supposed disinterest as proof that women and people of color are too unqualified to even be invited in.

I tried to raise the possibility that maybe a room full of white people in one of the whitest states in the country was not the most welcoming to people of color. I tried to assure him not only that people of color cared about the environment, but that Indigenous people actually invented the environmentalism he was claiming as his own. But he didn't want to hear me. He finally shook his head and said, "Well, we don't have to agree on all that."

As he walked away and I went back to teaching the class, I couldn't help but imagine how this man would react if the people of color who had long been fighting to protect the environment and protect people of color from the devastating environmental impacts of white supremacist capitalism were to just show up at his next environmental club meeting. I don't think he'd love it as much as he claims.

While we like to give lip service to the diversity and open opportunity of our political process, the truth is that much of white America completely ignores the political lives of people of color—especially women of color. We are often seen as a reliably Democratic voting bloc, to be pulled out each election cycle to vote for a mediocre white Democratic candidate and then put back in storage until the next election. At least that's how white Democrats see us. Many white Republicans also see us as a reliably Democratic voting bloc, to be prevented from exercising our right to vote at all costs. Sure, one is worse than the other, but both are pretty shitty.

Both the white right and the white left often like to assume that our issues are just "our issues," and that we may address them in our own little groups, but they have no place on the national stage. Any candidate of color who makes it to national politics will of course have to leave their racial identity behind in order to truly represent "real" America. And there is no way that a woman of color who insists on fully representing her community and her values would ever be able to garner enough votes to win any major election.

That has long been the case. And for many years, women of color who tried to lead with truly progressive values and refused to leave the issues facing their community behind did not often win elections. Over the years, merely existing as a self-proclaimed progressive white man was considered more than enough quali-fication to win votes. It has caused many of those white men to become lazy in their politics and in their connection with their constituents.

Then a small handful of women of color took the House of Representatives, and the nation, by storm.

Few people outside of her most ardent supporters expected Al-exandria Ocasio-Cortez, a twenty-eight-year-old Democratic So-cialist and first-time candidate, to defeat long-term incumbent Joe Crowley in the Democratic primary for a seat representing New York's Fourteenth District. Ocasio-Cortez herself was so surprised that the moment she found out she had won her primary became television history: CNN cameras caught her staring, eyes wide, at a television screen, reading the poll results for the first time. "I won!" she shrieked and then clapped her hand over her mouth in amazement.

But perhaps we shouldn't have been surprised that Ocasio-Cortez was able to defeat Crowley, who was phoning it in at best. He assumed he was unbeatable. The fourth-ranking Democrat in Congress, Crowley had not faced a primary opponent in fourteen years. He had been comfortably reelected time and time again by an aging group of regular local voters who could be counted on during a primary even when nobody was running for president.

Crowley's seeming inability to consider Ocasio-Cortez as a serious competitor didn't seem to faze her. When he was a no-show to their first scheduled debate, she gamely debated an empty chair. When he skipped yet another debate, sending a representative in his place, even the *New York Times* began to wonder if he had stopped taking his role as a US congressional representative seriously.[30]

So, by knocking on doors and actually talking to people about the issues they were facing, Ocasio-Cortez was able to energize voters in a way that establishment candidates had not been able to. She decided to invest her time and energy in the voters that she thought Crowley had avoided, especially younger voters and voters from immigrant communities. Half the residents of District Fourteen were born outside the United States, and 70 percent were people of color.[31] She focused on issues that she felt connected with left-leaning younger voters in 2018: jobs, tuition-free education, the environment. Ocasio-Cortez introduced herself to people who had never had a congressional candidate knock on their door before, and she encouraged them to register as Democrats so they could vote in the primary.

"When people feel like they are being spoken directly to," Ocasio-Cortez said on *CNN Newsroom*, "I do feel like . . . they'll do things like turn out in an off-year, mid-year primary."[32]

When Ilhan Omar, a thirty-three-year-old Somali American Muslim woman who had immigrated to the United States from the war-torn country as a child, ran to represent the constituents of Minnesota's Fifth District, many people outside her local area didn't think she stood a chance. But Omar's election should have been even less of a surprise than AOC's. She was not new to Minnesota politics or to the local community, having moved there in her youth and having served as a representative in state government. Omar had already proved that she could win elections by speaking to the people that Minnesota had left behind, and unfortunately that was a lot of people. Minnesota has one of the country's worst income and wealth disparities along racial lines in the country, and 115,000 people in Omar's district—the majority of them people of color—lived at or below the poverty line.[33]

Omar quickly became known for her ability to connect with voters, regardless of age, class, or race. Some expected Omar to coast on her membership in the area's largest minority community (Minnesota has the largest number of Somali Americans in the country), but she spent time sitting face to face with as many constituents from across the district as she could. Omar talked about issues facing working-class voters, communities of color, young people, single mothers. She used her experience of being a multiple minority, a Muslim Black woman, to connect to a wide variety of Minnesotans who had been marginalized.

At a time when Trump had made it his personal mission to target Muslims and people of color as terrorists and thugs, Omar's efforts to build a broad progressive-values-based coalition paid off. She won her election with the highest percentage of votes of any woman in the history of the US House of Representatives, and the third-highest percentage of votes of any congressional candidate from Minnesota.[34]

The 2018 election also saw victory for Palestinian American and Detroit native Rashida Tlaib. Like Omar, her election should not have come as such a surprise; she was well known and respected in her prior role as a state representative, regarded as someone who would vigorously fight for Detroit. She was a thorn in the side of big businesses that tried to exploit or neglect Detroit neighborhoods and an even bigger thorn in the side of Donald Trump. When Tlaib won her bid for Congress, representing Michigan's Thirteenth District, she became the first Palestinian American to sit in Congress. She and Omar became the first two Muslim women elected to Congress.

Ayanna Pressley had already made headlines in 2009 when she became the first woman of color elected to the Boston City Council. But outside the city, broader support for her congressional run was certainly not guaranteed. Boston has a long history of racism and racial segregation, especially in politics. Like Ocasio-Cortez, Pressley took on a long-term incumbent. Michael Capuano, her opponent, had served ten terms in Congress. Pressley and Capuano were more aligned in ideology than Ocasio-Cortez and Crowley had been, making the likelihood that the young politician would be able to unseat the well-liked Capuano even smaller. Instead of confining her efforts to the city, where voters would be more inclined toward her, Pressley launched a broad campaign that focused on the entire district, reaching out to constituents of all races and ethnicities. Pressley's fresh energy, perfectly encapsulated in her campaign slogan "Change can't wait," struck a strong chord with voters, who handed Pressley a surprising double-digit primary victory, guaranteeing her election success. With no Republican challenger, Pressley became the first Black woman to represent the state of Massachusetts in Congress.

And so, four women of color who should have won their elections did. In the process they energized young voters and voters of color, and they became immediate targets of both the left and the right. They had run for office promising to represent their values and their constituents, and that's exactly what they did. House members don't get six years to adjust to life in government the way Senate members do, and women of color in the House know that they aren't guaranteed the reelections that many white men in Congress feel confident they will get, so if they were going to fulfill their promises to voters, they needed to act quickly. Rashida Tlaib showed up in Congress ready to advocate for Detroiters. She submitted 153 appropriations requests during her first four months in office and opened four neighborhood centers in her district.[35] She also joined up regularly with Ocasio-Cortez, Omar, and Pressley to push Congress on progressive positions around areas like the environment, health care, and reproductive justice.

Like Tlaib, Omar quickly got to work as well. She fast earned a reputation for being unafraid to hold members of the Trump administration accountable, and for asking the tough questions that many seasoned Democrats were afraid to ask. When Trump's new special envoy Elliott Abrams, a longtime State Department official whose work had been associated with human rights violations in El Salvador, appeared before the House, Omar asked him bluntly, "Do you think that massacre was a fabulous achievement that happened under our watch?"[36]

Within a few months Omar had worked as a strong proponent of Medicare for All, had cosponsored prounion legislation in the PRO Act, and had begun working on housing initiatives with the aim of building one million homes to "give people an opportunity to have a dignified, safe place to live." She'd also begun working with the Congressional Black Caucus to address previously unaddressed issues in the Black community like youth suicide, mental health, and the maternal mortality rate.[37]

Pressley has introduced and cosponsored multiple pieces of legislation since joining Congress. In December 2019, with Representatives Omar and Bonnie Watson Coleman, she introduced legislation aimed at stopping the criminalization and marginalization of Black and brown girls in US schools.[38] That same month, she introduced sweeping criminal-justice-reform legislation that would decriminalize sex work and end the cash bail system, solitary confinement, and the death penalty. If enacted, these changes would go far in correcting some of the ways in which our criminal-justice system has targeted people of color and marginalized people. In introducing the legislation, Pressley argued, "For far too long, those closest to the pain have not been closest to the power, resulting in a racist, xenophobic, rogue, and fundamentally flawed criminal legal system," adding, "Our resolution calls for a bold transformation of the status quo—devoted to dismantling injustices so that the system is smaller, safer, less punitive, and more humane."[39] In January of 2020, Pressley passed credit-score-reform legislation aimed at helping people recover more quickly from financial hardship with changes such as increasing protections against predatory lending, limiting the use of credit scores in job applications, and shortening the time that adverse credit events stay on credit reports.[40]

In Ocasio-Cortez's first months in office, she worked on legislation to remove restrictions against using psychedelic drugs for medical research in the hopes of better treating mental illness and depression; she cosponsored legislation for affordable insurance-covered and over-the-counter birth control. She has battled Trump's efforts to add citizenship questions to the US Census (seen by many as a way of gathering data on immigrant populations of color), was an outspoken opponent of Amazon's proposal to expand its headquarters into New York, and—most notable of all—was a cosponsor of and the most vocal voice behind the Green New Deal.

Upon her arrival in D.C., Ocasio-Cortez was both dismissed as a naïve millennial and demonized as a dangerous socialist. Her clothing was critiqued; her young, Bronx-style speech was ridiculed. But nothing targeted her with more outrage than the Green New Deal. Let's look closely at the Green New Deal so we can understand how bonkers the conservative response to it has been. The

Green New Deal is a nonbinding resolution to address our rapidly worsening global climate crisis. It consists of multiple goals to reduce greenhouse gas emissions, like moving to renewable power, upgrading energy efficiency in existing buildings, and investing in electric vehicles and light rail. The deal aimed to accomplish all of this while also protecting vulnerable communities that have economically relied on fossil fuels with job training and economic development goals.[41]

Yet even Democratic house speaker Nancy Pelosi seemed both wary and dismissive of the young Democratic Socialist's efforts: "While there are people who have a large number of Twitter followers, what's important is that we have large numbers of votes on the floor of the House," Pelosi told reporters in an apparent dismissal of Ocasio-Cortez's online popularity and the legislation she had helped put together.[42]

Republicans, of course, treated Ocasio-Cortez's Green New Deal like it was actual terrorism on paper. None of the below quotes are made up. These are real words, from grown-ass adults who were elected to represent the American people.

Senator Tom Cotton of Arkansas said that the Green New Deal would force Americans to "ride around on high-speed light rail, supposedly powered by unicorn tears." Trump claimed that it would take away everyone's "airplane rights." Wyoming senator John Barrasso issued perhaps the most bizarre of all the dire warnings about the Green New Deal, telling Americans to stock up on beef and ice cream, because under the Green New Deal, "livestock will be banned."[43]

Tlaib has also faced unprecedented amounts of scrutiny and hatred in her work, and simply for existing. She has often found herself at the crosshairs of political outrage—not only for calling the president a "motherfucker" (which was honestly one of my favorite moments of the year), but also due to her Muslim faith and her outspoken support of Palestinian people. Any time Tlaib has discussed issues regarding Israel or Palestine, she has found herself at the center of outrage from the right and the left.

Pressley faced widespread backlash for celebrating her identity, most notably in July 2019 when she dared to speak about being a proud Black woman in Congress. At a Netroots Nation convention, Pressley urged representatives from marginalized groups to truly represent their identities and culture in their work instead of sacrificing the needs of their community to the status quo:

> I don't want to bring a chair to an old table. This is the time to shake the table. This is the time to redefine that table. Because if you're going to come to this table, all of you who have aspirations of running for office. If you're not prepared to come to that table and represent that voice, don't come, because we don't need any more brown faces that don't want to be a brown voice. We don't need Black faces that don't want to be a Black voice. We don't need Muslims that don't want to be a Muslim voice. We don't need queers that don't want to be a queer voice. If you're worried about being marginalized and stereotyped, please don't even show up because we need you to represent that voice.[44]

Outrage over Pressley's asking people to represent any interests besides those of the white men who have always had massive influence in government was swift. Pressley was accused of being divisive, even racist. In a *Washington Examiner* article titled "Ayanna Pressley's Disturbing Progressive Threat," Stephen Kent used Pressley's comments to support his position that "diversity has been a threat to progressives' vision of America ever since their movement crystallized under President Woodrow Wilson," adding, "There has to be a more robust response to the radical identitarian politics of Pressley and her allies."[45] Republican representative Liz Cheney directly accused Pressley of racism, claiming that Pressley said that political voices were only legitimate if the person "espouses some preapproved set of beliefs."[46]

But of the four women, Ilhan Omar has perhaps been the most vilified by both Democrats and Republicans. Black, Muslim, and unapologetic, she has been an easy target because of her critiques of Israel and Israeli lobbyists—which have at times been sloppy and open to various interpretations. After tweeting an insinuation that the influence of the American Israel Public Affairs Committee's (AIPAC's) money was responsible for the Republican focus on her opinions regarding Israel's policies toward Palestinian people, she was accused of playing into antisemitic tropes about the power of Jewish wealth—even though the PAC ignored blatant antisemitic statements made by Republicans. Republicans had a field day with their outrage. Trump said Omar should resign. The backlash over the tweet was so severe that Omar was publicly admonished by leaders of her own party.

As Omar has continued to speak her truth and to represent the issues that matter to her and her constituents, she has also continued to be a target of hate. Trump has even spliced deceptively edited audio of one of Omar's speeches discussing the impact of the 9/11 attacks on Muslim Americans with footage of the attacks themselves in order to make Omar appear to sympathize with the attackers, igniting racist, Islamophobic rage against her. When Trump was asked if he regretted posting such an inflammatory and misleading video given the threats she had received afterward, he replied, "Not at all," and added, "She's got a way about her that's very, very bad, I think, for our country. She's extremely unpatriotic, and extremely disrespectful to our country."[47]

Ocasio-Cortez, Tlaib, Pressley, and Omar are public figures and elected representatives. Some would say that by running for office they chose a life of public scrutiny and comment. But they are also human beings, and no human should have to weather the torrent of hatred they have endured.

Sometimes it's the apathy that is most soul-crushing. In June 2019, Tlaib read one of the countless threats she had received since taking office in January of that year to FBI official Michael Garrity while questioning him on domestic terrorism: "'I was totally excited and pleased when I read about how 49 Muslims were killed and many were'"—Tlaib paused to catch her breath through tears—"'many more were wounded in New Zealand. This is a great start. Let's hope and pray that it continues here in the good ole USA. The only good Muslim is a—is a dead one.'"

She asked the official why the FBI didn't have the tools to investigate such threats. "We get so many—we get so many of them and I always find myself wondering, what happens?" she said. "What happens to these individuals? And I'm being sincere. I'm a mother. And I want to go home to my two boys."[48]

Even with the constant stream of hatred and bigotry thrown their way, Pressley, Ocasio-Cortez, Tlaib, and Omar push ahead with the progressive agendas they were elected to fight for. They continue to put forth amendments and sponsor legislation to serve their constituents. They continue to ask tough questions of the Trump administration, Republicans, and their own party. In discussing how hard the four of them have had to fight during their time in D.C., Omar sounded defiant and determined: "I think we have a beef with almost anyone here because there's a lack of courage. It seems like we're all radical because we deeply care about the people we represent and we want to throw down for them."[49]

Part of their ability to stay productive and positive through it all comes from their strong support of each other. Ocasio-Cortez, Pressley, Tlaib, and Omar have backed each other up through the controversies. At the base of their shared politics and advocacy lies a friendship that has helped get them through the worst of the harassment and threats.

"When I joined the race, I became a part of this amazing group of people who were not only speaking to the progressive values that I cared about, but who were also people I could be in solidarity with," Omar explained to Ava DuVernay. "When our day to day was filled with lots of struggle, it was good to share something or see others share and just send the positive vibes."[50]

The victories of these four young, outspokenly progressive women of color dominated news cycles in 2018 and early 2019. When I look at their elections, I'm reminded of what Lani Guinier said about the power of support for a candidate of color who truly represents their constituency, if only the representatives know that they can get enough votes to win an election by appealing so directly to the values of marginalized communities. All four districts that these women ran were safely Democratic districts with large populations of color that felt overlooked by their states and country. In all four districts, the financial disparities between people of color and the larger white population in their state showed that the sense of being overlooked had been more than a feeling.

Three of the women—Ocasio-Cortez, Omar, and Tlaib—grew up in the area they sought to represent and had built strong relationships with their communities. Pressley had lived in Boston for over fifteen years by the time she ran for Congress. Their ideas appealed to a broad coalition of underprivileged people in their constituencies. And they didn't have to sacrifice any of their people to appease a comfortable majority.

In their mission to prioritize issues most impacting the marginalized communities they serve, they've steadfastly focused on the concerns that many Democrats say they wish more representatives in their party would stand up for. They've kept their focus on the environment, health care, affordable education, reproductive justice, affordable housing, labor rights, and other core progressive causes. All while consistently fighting against lobbyists and big-money politics—as well as Trump's bigoted and increasingly authoritarian agenda.

But when I was compiling a list of their efforts and accomplishments, I had to first sort through thousands of search results that were much more focused on the controversies around them. I hope that when their constituents look to see what Ocasio-Cortez, Tlaib, Omar, and Pressley have done for them, they'll be able to find it amidst all the noise.

When I think about the trajectory our social progress is supposed to take—the way we've been taught in school that it should work—and I look at how little it tracks with how we treat women of color who dare challenge the political status quo, I am dismayed. I'm dismayed not only because it appears that women of color currently working in politics are treated with the same, if not more, disdain, blatant racism and sexism, and outright hatred that Shirley Chisholm faced—but also because the status quo they are blasted for challenging has remained so unchanged. We celebrate progress, and we talk about increased diversity within our government. Yet our Congress is still overwhelmingly white and male; our presidency is still overwhelmingly white and exclusively male. And the important advances that Shirley Chisholm fought for in 1972—issues like environmental protections, protection from government surveillance and invasion of privacy, campaign finance reform, and equal pay for women—are all changes we still fight for today. It's as if when we continuously pass up the opportunity to listen to those most affected by the shortcomings of our systems, and instead continue to reward those who benefit most from those systems, we end up making no progress at all.

## "LISTEN TO BLACK WOMEN"

The work of civil rights theorist Lani Guinier made its way back into a few headlines during the 2016 election cycle. No, not because for some reason Hillary's candidacy had everyone talking about Bill Clinton's transgressions, but because suddenly Guinier's ideas about cumulative voting—voting for more than one candidate, often ranking preference—didn't seem so outrageous.

It started on the right. It's hard to remember now, but there was a time when even Republicans were dismayed about Trump's rising popularity. Concerned with how the large Republican candidate field was spreading moderate support among multiple candidates while concentrating far-right support for Trump, people started bringing up Guinier's ideas for a voting process that would prevent such a scenario from making someone like Trump the Republican nominee.[51]

With cumulative voting, candidates who had a broad appeal wouldn't become lost among the other candidates who had broad appeal; the process would be a guardrail against electing someone who represented the fringe interests of a party. A candidate who was the first choice for some and the second and third choice for many could potentially have swung a lot of states in the primary away from Trump.

After the general election, it was the left that invoked the work of Guinier. Cumulative voting could have lessened the vitriol of the Democratic primaries and led voters to see the benefits in both Clinton and Sanders, as well as to feel like they had a say in the victory no matter who became the party's nominee. In the general election, cumulative voting would have lessened the impact of the votes for Jill Stein; people could have shown their dissatisfaction with the two-party system by putting some of their votes toward the Green Party while also hedging their bets with a vote for Clinton.[52]

In every step of the process, cumulative voting might have gotten us out of the mess we are currently in, where we have a president who lost the popular vote and brings us closer to war and authoritarianism every day.

But Guinier's ideas were seen as radical attempts to place Black voters above white voters—because she was a Black woman. If she had not been a Black woman, and if she had positioned cumulative voting as anything other than a way to increase representation for Black Americans (even though she did demonstrate multiple times that cumulative voting would help all underrepresented groups and create a more representative government for every-body), maybe she would have been listened to. Maybe her ideas would have caught on. But even for all the hand-wringing since the 2016 election, I don't think that Guinier could bring her ideas to the national stage today without being crucified in the same way she was in 1993. She would still be a Black woman making proposals that fundamentally challenge white male power. Even though ignoring her may have cost us so much, we still are in no way ready to hear her.

In 2017, four confident, talented, unapologetic young women of color were elected to US Congress, and everyone freaked the fuck out.

It sounds almost ridiculous to type that in this day and age, but when I think about the politics of recent years, it is as accurate a way as any to describe the fear, anger, and downright hatred that many Americans have toward women of color who dare reach for political power without first capitulating to white male supremacy. In 2017, forty-five years after Shirley Chisholm was accused of playing "vaginal politics" and the words "go home nigger" were hatefully scrawled across her campaign materials because she dared to believe that a Black woman could be president, and almost twenty-five years after Lani Guinier was labeled the "Quota Queen" for daring to envision an election process that didn't disenfranchise voters of color, Alexandria Ocasio-Cortez, Ilhan Omar, Rashida Tlaib, and Ayanna Pressley have been called everything from racists to terrorist sympathizers for daring to believe that their communities were worth representing and worth fighting for.

"Listen to Black women." "Listen to women of color." That has been the refrain of so many on the left since the 2016 elections. We are the group that voted against Trump more than any other. We are the ones who kept Roy Moore out of office. Almost every day I get a message from a white person saying, "Tell me what to do and I'll do it." As if I haven't been writing for years. As if Black women and women of color haven't been saying what is wrong with this country for centuries. And right now, we have women of color—strong, capable women of color—in Congress with solid progressive ideals and good ideas, and they are being lambasted as "too radical" and "too divisive." Right now we have women of color who are writing about what is needed to move this country forward, and they are being dismissed as "race-baiting" and "antiwhite." And chances are, in future elections, we will again be reaching out to them and asking, "What do we do now?" "How can we fix this?"

Studies have shown that pretty much any time a white man talks about equality and justice, he is praised. It is seen as proof of his broad leadership abilities and his magnanimousness. But women of color are never praised. They are seen as bitter, divisive, vindictive, and self-serving. This view hurts women of color in politics, in the office, and in academia. We are often the most harmed by the failures of our systems to address structural inequality; we are often the first sacrificed to political compromise; we are the vote taken for granted in every single election; we are often the only group standing between an electorate and the next white supremacist representative—and yet when we try to advocate for policies that won't have us scrambling to save everyone's asses in the eleventh hour, we are ignored or attacked.

What does it look like to respect qualified women of color as thought leaders instead of waiting to turn to them in dire times as saviors? What does it look like to recognize that the ideas we have to help our communities might just benefit all communities? What does it look like to recognize that we are more than warriors, more than survivors—we are innovators and leaders?

White men get to be respected in every step of the political process. We look to them for fresh new ideas; we look to them for the wisdom of ages; we look to them to rescue us from disaster. And yet it is women of color who are consistently tested and proven right. I hope that we will be able to recognize the talents of our current generation of women of color to lead, and to lead with courage and creativity, before it is too late for anybody—even them—to save us.

# CHAPTER 7

# GO FUCKING PLAY

*Football and the Fear of Black Men*

It may surprise you to learn that American football, a sport today known for the Black athletes who showcase their physical speed and strength every Sunday, was created to be played by wealthy white men.

There was a lot of money to be made after the Civil War and during the United States' violent expansion into Western territories in the 1800s. Families newly wealthy from the growth of railroads and trade (brought by the forced displacement of Indigenous peoples) were looking at their own sons nervously. It had taken a lot of strength and force to build their wealth and power, and it would take more strength and force to maintain them. Would their rich, spoiled offspring have what it takes to grow an American empire?

What could wealthy young men do to cultivate strength and aggression if they lived a life of ease? They could, perhaps, play a rough sport.

"The very foundation of football in this country comes out of fears of ruling-class mediocrity and [fears of] the mediocrity of their own children."

I'm sitting at a bookstore café in Washington, D.C., across a table from a noted author on the history of race and sport, Dave Zirin. It's his opening line for our conversation on football and Blackness, and it surprises me. But I shouldn't be surprised to be immediately learning from Zirin; he has written multiple bestselling books on sport, has been nominated for an NAACP Image Award for Outstanding Literary Work, and is widely recognized within the sports world as an authority on sports history and sports labor issues. He's the guy to talk to about this.

Like the mandate to "Go West, Young Man," football was born out of Muscular Christianity. Theodore Roosevelt, American cultural icon and the nation's twenty-sixth president, was, as we've seen, a big proponent of this doctrine.

"Teddy Roosevelt—he was like the prom king of this culture of toxic masculinity in sports and seeing sports as a substitute for the fight for empire and war," explained Zirin.[1]

American football had its beginnings in the Ivy League colleges, which were attended by young elites like Roosevelt. Its early days were so violent that dozens of student athletes died every year, nearly dooming the sport before it fully got off the ground. The *Smithsonian* detailed some of the injuries recorded during a particularly brutal college game in 1905: "Four concussions, three 'kicks in the head,' seven broken collarbones, three grave spinal injuries, five serious internal injuries, three broken arms, four dislocated shoulders, four broken noses, three broken shoulder blades, three broken jaws, two eyes 'gouged out,' one player bitten and another knocked unconscious three times in the same game, one breastbone fractured, one ruptured intestine and one player 'dazed.'"[2]

As outrage began to rise over the death toll of the sport, the *New York Times* placed football right alongside the lynching of Black Americans as our nation's "Two Curable Evils."[3] Through the great effort of powerful defenders like Roosevelt, who claimed that "it is mere unmanly folly to try to do away with the sport because the risk exists," football's supporters instead pressured colleges to form the NCAA to increase oversight and decrease deaths and serious injury.[4]

Although football persevered through the crisis to become one of our nation's most beloved pastimes, I am not what anybody would call a sports person. My mom signed me up for a flag football league in fifth grade, and I still haven't figured out what I (or the team that had to endure my sulky attitude and extreme lack of athletic ability) had done to warrant such punishment. I have watched a few football games (especially during my hometown Seahawks' Superbowl-winning season in 2014), but I don't think anybody could confuse me for a "fan." Instead, my interest in football has been almost entirely political, increasing with the University of Missouri protests in 2015 and continuing with the national-anthem protests started by Colin Kaepernick. To me, the idea of sitting around watching a bunch of Black bodies crash into each other to the delight of white team owners and managers is not entertaining. Even though I can respect and appreciate the great efforts the athletes put forth, the sport has long represented to me the exploitation of Black labor and Black bodies, and little else. But I have come to value (if often with dismay) the way in which we can see the reflection of American racial attitudes through the sport.

Modern-day American football has in many ways progressed and digressed racially along with American racial attitudes. While many would look at the Black millionaires it produces and think that the sport represents racial progress and Black success, it still also represents the ways in which racism and white supremacy have successfully moved out of the spotlight of violent racial terror and instead woven their way through the fabric of both the sport and society—existing and operating constantly, yet only making themselves more visible when the sport's integrity is directly threatened.

Today, Black athletes make up the majority of popular American football team rosters, but that was not always the case. My great-grandfather on my mother's side was one of the early white players. I remember my mom showing me pictures of Daddy Bud from the early 1930s in his football uniform, before a train accident crushed his foot and his professional prospects. My mom watched football in the tradition of her white family, so it did not carry the same complications for her that it carried for me— although perhaps it should have.

That American football was invented, at least in part, to create and maintain a violent white male ideal—an ideal so brutal that it claimed dozens of promising young lives each year—is a history that should perhaps be just as troubling to white Americans as the current state of football is to Black Americans. The appeal of early football was white male dominance, a hierarchy that many in the sport tried to maintain by excluding Black players. Although football was eventually integrated, that integration stopped at the surface, and it hid all the ways in which the sport still worked to maintain the ugliest of white male power. The white male dominance that was first demonstrated in how white players tackled each other on the field was diverted to how they could control the physical power of Black men. Yes, the majority of players now are Black, but those calling the shots—the owners, the managers, the quarterbacks—are primarily white men. White fans shifted their relationship to football as well. They identify with the quarterback if they identify with a player at all.

"Why is it that fantasy football is so popular?" Zirin asked rhetorically. "It's popular because, when it comes to football, fans identify with being an owner or a general manager, not with being a player. Why don't they identify with being a player? Well, a couple of reasons. One: race, without question," he explains. "And two: because being an NFL player is to be a very specific kind of athlete. You are six foot three, 280 pounds. You're running forty yards in 4.5 seconds, and fans, white fans, view these NFL players as half god, half chattel."

As white America shifted its relationship with Black America, so did football shift its relationship to Black players. Although Black players are allowed to succeed for the few years that their bodies remain healthy, they are expected to be grateful for the same success that is costing them their bodies, and—often after repeated concussions—their minds. No guarantees are given players. They have no true security. And the moment they try to wield any of the power that their fame might bring them, the punishment is swift and sharp. White fans rejoice in order restored.

The fear of the physical power and strength of men of color and their perceived threat to white male power drove the creation of a sport that began with the deaths of dozens of young white men. From there, football briefly became a tool of the exploitation of white workers. It would eventually find its way to the state it is in today—so wed to its need to hold power over Black players that it endangers the health and safety of all players and limits the potential success and popularity of the sport.

In football, I see what the fear of the perceived physicality of men of color means to a white male supremacy defined largely by its ability to maintain control through violence. I see the ways in which the need to maintain physical power over others has been translated into maintaining control over the physical power of Black men. And I also see how even fans of the sport, who only have the illusion of control over the players on their television screens, can be manipulated into helping owners maintain that control over players—even as it risks the sport they love.

But I also see opportunity to move the discussion around race and masculinity forward. I see the potential for people to come together over their love of the sport to have real dialogue on issues of justice and equality in this country. And when I look at how hard those in power in football have worked to stifle any player empowerment or solidarity around issues of justice and equality, I realize that I'm not the only one who sees that potential.

## SEGREGATED FOOTBALL NOW, SEGREGATED FOOTBALL FOREVER

*There is no more difference in compromising the*
*integrity of race on the playing field than in doing*
*so in the classroom. One break in the dike and the*
*relentless seas will rush in and destroy us.*

—*Georgia governor Marvin Griffin, 1956*[5]

Willis Ward was sitting on the bench. So was Hoot Gibson. Both Ward and Gibson were starting ends for their college teams—Georgia Tech and University of Michigan, respectively—but they were both benched for the entire game, much to the dismay of their teams' fans. Why? Because Willis Ward was Black.

Until that game in 1934, not many teams had had to deal with the issue of Black football players because, well, there just weren't that many. This is not because football wasn't popular in the Black community or because Black players weren't talented. It was because at that time, few Blacks were allowed on most college campuses, let alone on the football teams. Those Black players who persevered and were able to gain a spot on the team were often met with extreme racism and violence. When All-American player Paul Robeson joined Columbia University's team in 1918, the young Black player was quickly met with a brutal welcome.

"On the first day of practice, I was attacked by twenty-one guys," Robeson recounted. "All the guys on the defense, and all the guys on my team. They put me in the hospital for two weeks."[6]

Robeson's experience, while exceptionally violent, was not all that unique. Black players were frequently attacked and singled out, not only by opposing teams but by their own teammates. Robeson was not the only Black player to end up in the hospital due to the racist aggression of white players, and when a Black player was injured on the field, it was sometimes accompanied by chants of "kill the nigger" or "kill the coon" from the stands.

In 1923, Iowa State's lone Black team member, Jack Trice, was killed after sustaining beatings during a game against the University of Minnesota that left him with hemorrhaged lungs and internal bleeding.[7] Eleven years later, the two universities would once again feature in public racist violence; during a game between them, Iowa State's Black halfback, Ozzie Simmons, endured so many brutal hits from Minnesota players that he was forced to leave the game three times, all while enduring racist taunts from the players who had injured him.[8]

In 1934, due to the racist exclusion of Black players and the regular, violent terror visited upon those who were able to beat the odds and find a place on a college team, Georgia Tech football fans and supporters were surprised, and quite frankly appalled, to find that the University of Michigan expected them to play against Willis Ward, a Black man, in their upcoming game. While Northern teams seemed happy to maim their Black players, Southern teams simply refused to play with or against Black players. When Georgia Tech discovered that Michigan not only had a Black player, but they expected to start him, they demanded that the team pull Ward from the game.

The University of Michigan agreed with little fuss. But after Michigan students launched protests over the university's quick capitulation to open racism, the two universities came up with a compromise. Michigan would exclude Ward if Georgia Tech would also bench one of its starting players. Apparently, the disadvantage of removing one of the team's star players from the game was worth it if it meant they wouldn't have to walk on the same grass as a Black man.

Michigan won the game against Georgia Tech that day, but the real winner in the compromise was segregation: Georgia Tech and other Southern teams were so appalled that they had to go to so much trouble to avoid playing against Black athletes that they informally boycotted Northern teams until the 1970s.[9]

> *Mr. Marshall was an outspoken foe of the status quo when most were content with it. His fertile imagination and vision brought vital improvements to the structure and presentation of the game. Pro football today does in many ways reflect his personality. It has his imagination, style, zest, dedication, openness, brashness, strength and courage. We all are beneficiaries of what his dynamic personality helped shape over more than three decades.*
>
> —*NFL commissioner Pete Rozelle, in remembrance of George Preston Marshall, 1969*[10]

From 1934 to 1946, there were no Black players in the NFL. There had been a few Black players before 1934, but for a dozen years there was not a single one. No official answer exists as to why, but we do know that no Black players whose contracts were up in 1933 were renewed for 1934, and no Black players were allowed to try out for NFL teams. When scholars have dug into the reason behind this unofficial ban, they often come across one name: George Preston Marshall.

Marshall was the owner of the Boston Braves, which he later renamed the Boston Redskins, which eventually moved to D.C. and became the Washington Redskins. If you couldn't tell by the fact that this was the man behind the still highly controversial and

offensive Redskins team name, let me say without any reservation that George Preston Marshall was a fantastic racist. Not only
was he the genius behind naming his team a racial slur, but he
doubled down on the racism by having his head coach, William
Henry Dietz, dress in a headdress and war paint and dance for the
crowds during halftime. (Dietz, also known as Lone Star Dietz,
didn't seem to mind this insult to his Indigenous heritage—but
maybe that is because he was actually a white dude who had stolen
the identity of a Sioux man in order to try to cash in on the white
American fascination with Indigenous culture and the immense
star power of Indigenous players like Jim Thorpe, Gus Welsh, and
Bill Newashe.)[11]

Although Marshall's racism appeared to be far-reaching, he was
at least willing to let Indigenous people play on the team he had
named specifically to insult them. But as Black players and even
Black coaches like Fritz Pollard appeared in increasing numbers,
Marshall and others saw Black football players as a real threat to
what had been a predominantly white game. There was absolutely
no way that Marshall was going to allow Blacks anywhere near his
precious football.

"George Preston Marshall—he was a businessman," explained
Dave Zirin. "He moved the Redskins here [to Washington, D.C.]
from Boston because he wanted to appeal to the Jim Crow South."

As a committed racist and savvy businessman, Marshall saw
a great marketing opportunity in racist football fans—especially
across the South. The team fight song was sung to the tune of
"Dixie" and in fact included the line "Fight for Old Dixie" until
the 1960s. This Southern pageantry helped increase the Redskins'
popularity in the Southern areas where Marshall targeted many of
the team's radio broadcasts.[12]

Marshall, a powerful coach in the budding NFL, began pressuring other coaches in the league to make the NFL all white.
They didn't need too much convincing. This was a time when

fears of Black male physicality were being spread throughout the Jim Crow South. Black men were going to steal your women with their unchecked physical sexuality; they were going to threaten your families with their animal strength and uncontrollable rage. It is easy to see how the rise of powerful Black players in a game that had been founded to showcase white male physical superiority would be a turnoff to fans invested in shows of white male dominance. It is unlikely that Marshall was the only racist coach in the league, but he is recognized by many sports scholars as the driving force behind the unofficial ban of Black players.

The NFL couldn't stay white forever, though; its rival league, the AFL, had begun to increase the number of Black players on its teams. It turns out that some of those Black players were very good at football, even better than the white ones. The NFL started fearing the loss of fandom when they couldn't compete with the talent of the AFL's integrated teams, so the NFL's owners and coaches started recruiting Black players.

Eventually, all the NFL teams were integrated—except the Washington Redskins. Marshall, who loved racism even more than winning games, was the last owner to integrate his football team. Marshall held on to his "no-Blacks" policy so long that the coach and his team became a joke to sports commentators like Shirley Povich and Sam Lacy, who mocked Marshall's steadfast commitment to racism at the expense of his own record.

Decades after the integration of most NFL teams, Marshall's Redskins became a national embarrassment. This was not just any team; this was the team situated in the US capital. During the Cold War, the country's claim of being the defender of global freedom was severely undermined by the very public civil rights battles waging in the United States. Among many other transgressions happening in the country, Marshall's stubborn commitment to racial segregation in a uniquely American sport served to highlight the nation's hypocrisy in its ideological battle with the Soviets. As

Dave Zirin said to me, "It was embarrassing on a global propaganda scale." Finally, after the federal government threatened to take away his stadium if he didn't integrate, Marshall recruited the first Black player for the Washington Redskins, who took the field in 1962. Perhaps the strain of seeing a Black man wearing his beloved Redskins uniform was too much for Marshall to handle, for he suffered a major, debilitating stroke in 1963.

I don't think I've ever been as devoted to anything as George Preston Marshall was to his racism. While he could not hold off the integration of football, Marshall made sure that his fight for segregation would live on after him. After Marshall's death in 1969, the bulk of his estate was designated to set up a charitable foundation in his name. One of the stipulations of the money, however, was that none of it was allowed to go to "any purpose which supports or employs the principle of racial integration in any form."[13]

I do not know if Marshall would be happy with how quickly his racism was forgotten—it doesn't appear to be something he wanted to hide, in life or death. But our society likes to make heroes out of some of our biggest bigots. Marshall was inducted into the Pro Football Hall of Fame in 1983. On the Hall of Fame website page about Marshall, the only mention of his long commitment to racism and segregation is the note that he "endured his share of criticism for not integrating his team until being forced to do so in 1962."[14]

## MIZZOU AND THE RISE OF STUDENT-ATHLETE ACTIVISM

*This is not, I repeat, not, how change should come about.
I take full responsibility for the inaction, and I take full
responsibility for the frustration that has occurred.*

—*University of Missouri president Tim Wolfe,
announcing his resignation, 2015*[15]

Around two a.m. on October 24, 2015, somebody entered one of the residence halls at the University of Missouri. It was Gateway Hall, named for its mission to be a "gateway to the future of inclusive living." This person drew a swastika on the wall. With human feces.[16]

Students who did not see the swastika in situ found out via a flyer outlining the incident posted by the university's Department of Residential Life. For Jonathan Butler, a twenty-five-year-old Black graduate student at Mizzou, it was the final straw. He began a hunger strike, refusing to eat until university president Tim Wolfe either resigned or was fired.

This was not the first hate incident on campus. There had been racial slurs, homophobic slurs, and antisemitic slurs hurled at students in recent years. Students complained that the university did not take the incidents seriously and that they were made to feel unsafe by the actions. Concerned Student 1950, a student group named after the first year that Black students were allowed on campus, began staging protests shortly after the swastika was drawn. The protests quickly became heated. When students tried to engage Wolfe while he walked to his car and began to drive away, one of the students was allegedly hit by the moving vehicle, although unharmed. When Wolfe finally did meet with students, the situation went from bad to worse: students reported that he acted insulting and dismissive of their concerns.[17] A few days after the protests began, Butler, a Concerned Student 1950 member, began his hunger strike.

Meanwhile, members of Concerned Student 1950 wanted more than just a change in leadership; they wanted a change in college culture. Raising grievances that were greater in scope than slurs and swastikas, they demanded structural changes like cultural competency training for staff, an increase in teachers' diversity, and more recruitment and retention efforts of students of color. Students of multiple races and ethnicities joined the protests, camping out on campus. Soon faculty joined in, showing their support for students and also calling for Wolfe's resignation.

Although the university's administrators tried to contain the protests, they showed no sign of meeting the larger demands—especially the removal of Wolfe. They suggested that perhaps the parties could, if they were able to address the health risk to Butler arising from his hunger strike, come to a gentler compromise.

Everything changed the moment the football players joined the protest.

Butler had been friends with many of the Black players. Hearing about his hunger strike, sophomore safety Anthony Sherrils met with Butler to learn more. Then he called a team meeting. On November 7, at least thirty of the team's Black players announced that they would not play until Wolfe was gone.

The players posted a group photo to Twitter along with the following statement: "The athletes of color on the University of Missouri football team truly believe 'Injustice Anywhere is a threat to Justice Everywhere.' We will no longer participate in any football related activities until President Tim Wolfe resigns or is removed due to his negligence toward marginalized students' experiences. WE ARE UNITED!!!!!"[18]

If anyone was hoping that the players' white teammates or coach would step in to pull the Black players back in line, they were quickly disappointed. The next day, in a show of solidarity with protesting players, coach Gary Pinkel posted a team photo with the following caption: "The Mizzou Family stands as one. We are united. We are behind our players. #ConcernedStudent1950 GP."[19]

Within seventy-two hours, Wolfe had resigned.

Wolfe did not resign because the statements of the football players had convinced him or the school's board of trustees that it was the right thing to do. He resigned because Mizzou is a football school, and a football school cannot survive without football.

To say that football was a big deal at the University of Missouri would be an understatement. The Southeastern Conference champions for two years running, the Missouri Tigers were the heart and soul of the campus. They were also a major money maker for the college. If the standoff had continued into the next week, the team would have risked missing its game against Brigham Young University. That miss alone would have cost the university at least $1 million from a breach of contract with BYU. Further, missed practices and games—let alone an increase in hostility between team and school—could have cost the university its football season and its recruitment chances for the following year.

Almost immediately, the protesting players had the support of the region's Black football community. Many of the Black students on campus, including players, came from the Ferguson area and had been devastated by the killing of Michael Brown the year before. At a time when the local Black community was feeling hurt, angry, and powerless, this strong show of power by people as respected as Black college football players in the Missouri area would only become stronger the longer the protest was allowed to continue.

Anxiety around the players' protest was felt beyond the state. In recent years there had been increasing discussion about the morality of colleges and universities making hundreds of millions of dollars off the destruction of young Black bodies—especially when those students were risking their entire futures to possible injury and not getting paid for their work. Discussion around player safety, player empowerment, and player compensation was a direct threat to the college football system. Who knew how far the list of player demands might reach if the protests grew?

Wolfe later said that he did not resign because of football. He instead appealed to the anxiety of white Missourians who still felt very threatened by the unrest of the Ferguson protests. He explained to *Sports Illustrated* that he had been told that the protest had been infiltrated by "some bad characters that were in Ferguson. They were professionals; they weren't students," and he left to prevent violence instigated by these supposed outside agitators.[20] Not only were Wolfe's comments an insulting dismissal of the activism of Mizzou students; the blatant racism of his wild accusations played directly into white fears of the violence that Black unrest might bring.

Once Wolfe resigned, after eight days of starvation Jonathan Butler began to eat again. Black students and players celebrated a rare and powerful victory.

Team captain and protest leader Ian Simon read the following statement on behalf of the team after Wolfe's resignation:

> It's not about us. We just wanted to use our platform to take a stance for a fellow concerned student on an issue, especially being as though a fellow Black man's life was on the line. Due to the end of the hunger strike, we will be ending our solidarity strike to not practice and returning to our normal schedule as football players. It is a privilege to be playing on the University of Missouri's football team, and we are very thankful for this opportunity. We love the game, but [at the] end of the day, it is just that—a game.
>
> Through this experience, we've really began to bridge that gap between student and athlete in the phrase student-athlete by connecting with the community and realizing the bigger picture. We will continue to build with the community and support positive change on Mizzou's campus. Though we don't experience everything the general student body does and our struggles may look different at times, we are all #ConcernedStudent1950.[21]

It was a powerful moment for many Black people outside Missouri as well. At a time of increased racial tension and trauma around the killings of unarmed Black men by police, and the increased violence of knowing that the officers responsible for the killings would never face justice, to see children—our children—bring a powerful institution to its knees in the name of racial justice was the hope that many of us needed right then. When I read the news reports of Wolfe's resignation, I cried. I knew that the victory was small in the larger battle for Black lives, but I was so grateful for even a little hope that perhaps our children would succeed where we seemed to be failing.

There would, of course, be a price to pay for such audacity. Four days after the protests ended, Coach Pinkel announced that he had leukemia and would retire at the end of the season. The timing was horrible for a team just hitting practice again in the middle of a season filled with so much turmoil. Any coach so beloved by his team would avoid giving his players news this devastating in the middle of a season if it could at all be avoided. But the board of trustees leaked information of Pinkel's diagnosis and future retirement early.[22] Whether the information was leaked due to a lack of discretion by the board or out of spite, it is hard to imagine that the board of a football school—a school that financially depended on the success of its team—did not know how important it was to keep Pinkel's illness and retirement secret until the football season had ended.

A month after the protests, state representatives Rick Brattin and Kurt Bahr introduced a bill that would punish students and faculty for future protests. It included language stating that any "college athlete who calls, incites, supports, or participates in any strike or concerted refusal to play a scheduled game shall have his or her scholarship revoked," and "any member of a coaching staff who encourages or enables a college athlete to engage in behavior" prohibited under the bill "shall be fined by his or her institution of employment."[23]

The bill faced widespread condemnation and was quickly pulled from consideration by Brattin and Bahr, but their desire to ensure that students and universities understood the penalty for future protest—especially protest that would disturb Mizzou's or any other school's football program—was not unique. The University of Missouri would be made an example of. The following year, the state legislature cut millions of dollars from the university's budget. The message was clear: any protest and disruption on campus would be punished.

"They are there to learn, not to protest all day long. I thought we learned that lesson in the '60s. Obviously we haven't," said Republican state representative Donna Lichtenegger in support of the new budget.[24] College protest is not new; there were certainly campus demonstrations before the 1960s, and there have been every year since. I believe that getting practice in civil and political engagement through protest and other forms of political speech is one of the most important aspects of a college education, and it is dismissed and decried to our peril—but I find the imagery that Lichtenegger evoked of a 1960s campus forsaking education to hold four-year-long protests quite hilarious. Even in an era when most parents across the political spectrum want a college education for their children, though, the stereotype of the liberal-arts student forsaking practical study to major instead in macramé and social disruption is still readily believed in many conservative circles.

The following year, enrollment at Mizzou was down sharply, especially of Black students. This isn't because Black prospective students disagreed with the protests. Black students who decided not to attend the previously well-respected school said that the racism highlighted on campus had turned them off. Some Jewish prospective students said that hearing about swastikas being painted on walls kept them away. And some white prospective students said they didn't want to be associated with a university so widely known to be racist.[25] While many might like to blame the protests for the bad publicity, the truth is that it all began with racism and antisemitism on campus. The experiences that prospective students wished to avoid were real. Instead of looking at how the school's inaction had forced desperate students to launch protests, and instead of seeing the protests as the students showing their commitment to fighting racial hatred on campus, the story has become about how a group of protesters brought a university to the brink of disaster.

The reduced student enrollment, along with funding cuts from the state legislature and decreased donor funding from skittish alumni, placed the University of Missouri in financial turmoil. The chancellor had to institute a hiring and raise freeze, as well as cut some support services. The library had to ask for donations from the public for books.

While the Mizzou community still suffers painful ramifications surrounding the 2015 protest and as the administration continues to struggle to regain the confidence and support of the state legislature, many of the students of color who participated in the protests feel forever changed by the few days they stood side by side with their fellow students to stand up to powerful systems to defend equality and justice—and won.

"I thought I was just coming to college to play football and get an education," Mizzou defensive lineman Marcell Frazier said. "And all of that good stuff happened and opened up my network a lot as far as people outside of football, people outside the academic world, people in the social progress world."[26]

In the 2016 NFL draft, safety Ian Simon—one of the most vocal protestors on the Mizzou team and a well-respected player with good prospects for a professional career—met with several NFL teams but went undrafted and unsigned. Simon, who found work as a custom-suit salesman in Dallas, Texas, told *Sports Illustrated* that he had no regrets over his part in the protests, even if it might have hurt his chances at an NFL career. The protests were a success in his eyes. "There was no stumble. We had a plan, and it couldn't have gone any better," he said.[27]

## FOOTBALL TAKES A KNEE

*Wouldn't you love to see one of these NFL owners, when somebody disrespects our flag, to say: "Get that son of a bitch off the field right now? Out. He's fired. He's fired!"*

—*Donald Trump, 2017*[28]

On March 11, 2018, as Seattle Seahawks cornerbacks Neiko Thorpe and Mike Tyson left the Virginia Mason Athletic Center in Renton, Washington, they were confronted by an angry white woman. The woman had followed the two Black athletes to work in order to yell at them for protesting police brutality during the national anthem at Seahawks games.

Thorpe and Tyson recorded the interaction, and when you watch the video you can tell that they found the woman's profanity-laden tirade hilarious, if a little confusing.

Thorpe and Tyson had never protested at a Seahawks game.

Whether or not Thorpe or Tyson had ever taken a knee at a Seahawks game didn't matter to the woman yelling at them. They were Black, and they were Seahawks, so they were guilty.

"I don't care who you are," she told them while jabbing an angry finger in their direction. "All I care about is that my tax dollars pay for you to play, and go fucking play. And get off your fucking knees."[29]

The controversy that began when Black NFL players started kneeling or sitting during the national anthem before games shouldn't have come as a complete surprise to league administration. When Roger Goodell first took the job leading the NFL in 2006, he was warned that something like this could happen. At a 49ers preseason game, a sixty-four-year-old Black man named Harry Edwards sat next to him. Edwards was an advisor to the 49ers, a civil rights activist, and a sociology professor at University of California, Berkeley. He had dedicated much of his career to empowering Black athletes and was respected in academia and in football—so much so that he was often referred to as the father of athlete activism.

Edwards warned Goodell that Black athletes were becoming the preeminent stars of the NFL, and with that stardom would come power. If the NFL didn't prepare for how it was going to support and work with emboldened and empowered Black athletes, the league would find itself in direct conflict with the most prominent members of its teams.

Edwards later explained the reasoning behind his advice to Goodell: "These athletes don't leave the issues that they have in the community at the locker-room door; those come in to the locker room. . . . He was going to have to deal with some sociopolitical issues that were extrainstitutional that were going to come over the stadium wall."[30]

Edwards didn't think that Goodell understood what he was saying at the time, and it doesn't look like the league did anything to address a Black majority of players who may have wanted to use their power to address social issues. It is likely that there were not enough Black people in management meetings to tell the administrators. The disconnect between NFL administration and Black players was plain to see in the numbers. Whatever diversity had reached the NFL team rosters had certainly not reached NFL leadership. In 2006 (when Goodell became commissioner), the NFL had never had a Black team owner (it still doesn't today) and had only four Black general managers (or equivalent positions; only two Black GMs had been named in the entire NFL history). Seventy-eight percent of its head coaches were white even though 68 percent of the players were Black.[31] The league was not prepared for a rise in Black power in its ranks. But ready or not, Goodell was going to see firsthand what Edwards was talking about.

It all started in August 2016, when San Francisco 49ers quarterback Colin Kaepernick decided to sit for the national anthem during a preseason game.

"I am not going to stand up to show pride in a flag for a country that oppresses Black people and people of color," Kaepernick explained to NFL Media. "To me, this is bigger than football and it would be selfish on my part to look the other way. There are bodies in the street and people getting paid leave and getting away with murder."[32]

Kaepernick was not speaking in hyperbole when he said there were "bodies in the street and people getting paid leave and getting away with murder." The last few years had been brutal reminders for Black people across the country of how little, 150 years after the abolition of slavery, their lives mattered to broader society. Trayvon Martin, Michael Brown, Eric Garner, Tamir Rice—these names were making headlines in videos of Black bodies lying in the streets at the hands of those sworn to serve and protect. Twenty-seven percent of people who were killed by cops in 2015 were Black, even though Blacks make up only 12 percent of the overall population. In addition, cops are four times more likely to use force in their encounters with Black people than they are with whites.[33]

After sitting for two games, Kaepernick met with a military veteran. The man asked Kaepernick to kneel instead of sitting for the anthem, as a way to protest injustice against Black people in America while still showing respect for US military vets. Kaepernick took the veteran's advice and began kneeling in protest instead of sitting.[34]

After his first kneeling protest in September 2016, Kaepernick vowed to protest the entire upcoming season. He would do more than protest, though; he also pledged to donate $1 million to charitable organizations that helped marginalized communities. He was doing this because he felt it was his patriotic duty to fight injustice.

"I'm not anti-American," Kaepernick explained. "I love America. I love people. That's why I'm doing this. I want to help make America better."[35]

Kaepernick's words didn't matter. His conversation with a veteran didn't matter. It was a photo of Kaepernick kneeling during the anthem that set off the media firestorm.

Other Black players across the league began protesting. Not in huge numbers, but enough to alarm media, white fans, team owners, and NFL commissioner Roger Goodell. Dozens of players formed the Players Coalition, to support Kaepernick and to work together to advance racial justice issues in and outside the NFL. Discussions of police brutality, free speech, and respect for military veterans dominated news cycles. Opinion was sharply split on racial lines, with 62 percent of whites disapproving of the protests, and 74 percent of Blacks approving.[36] Owners began pressuring Goodell to put a stop to the protests.

"They wanted to make the problem go away real fast," explained NFL player Michael Bennett when I asked him about NFL leadership's response to the protests. "The game was the most important thing. It was winning and losing. But for a lot of the dark brothers, it was the game of life. Like, how are we supposed to tell our kids to go out into the world and be safe like our white teammates?"[37]

To many Black Americans, including me, the protests were understood and welcome. We had been marching in the streets for Black lives as video after video of the murder of unarmed Black people by police hit the internet. We saw our fathers, our sisters, our babies killed, and their killers almost without exception escaped justice. To see prominent, powerful Black athletes protest for our lives on national television during America's game—it gave us some hope that people might start paying attention.

For Donald Trump, who campaigned in 2016 on white male racial anxiety, the NFL protests were a dream come true. There is a segment of the white American population that has always viewed Black dissent as a threat to white safety and security. Since the election of Obama and the increase in protests around the country over the killing of unarmed Black people by police, white anxiety over Black empowerment had increased to a level that many of us had not seen in our lifetimes. Trump gave his angry crowds a prime target against which to vent their fury and anxiety by painting Black Americans as simply ungrateful for the opportunities they had been granted. He reframed the protests as blatant disrespect for America and American veterans, instead of as protests against police brutality. Here were some of the richest Black men in America—Black men who had been paid millions of dollars to play a game, *their* game—and they had the nerve to use that privilege to insult the troops?

Trump would insult and threaten players to raucous cheers. He promised to make sure the protests would stop and the disrespectful players (and their enabling coaches) would pay. Trump, of course, was not the only white person to benefit from stoking anger and hatred toward Black NFL players, or to capitalize on white anger at Kaepernick's audacity. Sean Hannity called Kaepernick, among other things, "a spoiled brat, out-of-touch, super-rich athlete," adding, for that special Hannity seasoning, that Kaepernick "might have converted to Islam in the off-season."[38] Equally bonkers and paranoid was Rush Limbaugh, who claimed that the protests were part of a vast left-wing conspiracy to undermine the NFL and, by extension, American manhood: "I do believe that the left wants to cause great damage to the NFL. What does the NFL stand for? Masculinity, strength, toughness. So, what are they doing to it? You go to college campuses now and you'll find classes on how to take masculinity out of men. It's actually happening. There are studies and courses in college that do this. It's patriotic, you've got the flag, you've got the anthem, you've got uniformed military personnel, all the things that the left wants to erase from this country."[39]

One of the more racist Republican congressmembers, Steve King (who once asked an interviewer from the *New York Times* with genuine confusion why it was considered bad to be a white supremacist), claimed that Kaepernick's NFL protests were "sympathetic to ISIS."[40]

After a difficult 2016 season with the 49ers, in which it was obvious that he was no longer welcome, Kaepernick opted out of his contract in March 2017 to have a better chance of getting picked up by another team than if he had been released. But by then, no team—even ones that were sympathetic to his protest—was willing to be associated with him. Why? Some were wary of the distraction that Kaepernick would bring. Perhaps others worried that the protest would gain ground with other players. But it is also clear that many refused to look at Kaepernick because they didn't want to bring the wrath of the man who was now president of the United States down on them. The protests had been a useful tool for Trump to fire up his base whenever he needed a bit of a popularity boost or a distraction from unflattering headlines. That strategy would be much harder if he couldn't be seen as the victor in the showdown with Black players. Trump absolutely needed to ensure that he could follow up on his promise to angry white voters that he would make Kaepernick pay and would bring order to the NFL. If Kaepernick were to find a happy home with another team, especially when there was every indication that he was staying in top playing shape, it would undermine Trump's appeal to white voters who wanted him to put uppity Black people in their place.

Trump's demands weren't just communicated from his podium to angry fans; he personally intervened with owners to ensure that they understood that he needed to win this battle against Black protest. President Trump called Dallas Cowboys owner Davey Jones with a message for all the NFL owners: "This is a very winning, strong issue for me," said Trump, according to Jones's deposition. "Tell everybody, you can't win this one. This one lifts me." Jones relayed Trump's remarks to the other owners: no team could afford to give Kaepernick a chance. "I thought he changed the dialogue," said Miami Dolphins owner Stephen Ross, who had been "totally supportive" of the protest until he'd gotten Trump's message.[41]

Even though far less impressive quarterbacks were picked up by teams in 2017, Kaepernick remained unsigned. Team owners and managers preferred having less effective rosters over having to deal with the backlash of allowing Black protest. In October of that year, still unsigned, Kaepernick filed a grievance with the NFL, accusing it of colluding to keep him out of the league in punishment for his national anthem protests.

Seattle Seahawks defensive end Michael Bennett decided to take a knee during the 2017 preseason. Bennett had long been vocal on racial justice issues and watched with dismay as Kaepernick was villainized and then blacklisted. That summer, Bennett was in Seattle to witness and participate in the grief and outrage after Charleena Lyles was killed by Seattle police officers in her home.

Then in late summer, a group of white supremacists held a rally in Charlottesville, Virginia, that they dubbed "Unite the Right." As swastika-wearing, angry white men marched through the city carrying torches while shouting racist and antisemitic slogans, counterprotesters arrived to fight the hate. On August 12, self-avowed white supremacist James Alex Fields Jr. plowed his car into the counterprotesters, killing thirty-two-year-old Heather Heyer and injuring nineteen others. As the nation reeled in shock at the violent protest and brutal killing of Heyer, President Trump refused to condemn the white supremacists, instead denouncing "this egregious display of hatred, bigotry and violence on many sides."[42]

Trump didn't give a full response for two days. When he did, he still refused to condemn the white supremacists. This shocked Bennett and helped galvanize him into action.

"I couldn't believe it took Trump forty-eight hours to respond, and then I couldn't believe when he said 'very fine people' were marching in an army of hate and violence," Bennett wrote in his book, *Things That Make White People Uncomfortable*. "There was no way I could stand for the national anthem, and there was no way I would, until I saw this country take steps toward common decency."[43]

Bennett reiterated that he wasn't just trying to make a political point; he was fighting for his life: "We aren't machines. We are human beings, and we aren't paid to stand for an anthem. We are paid to play football—this is our 'real world.' Maybe some people figure that being a professional athlete somehow graduates us from racism. They think we're not 'that Black.' We're in another category. But if I'm someplace where people don't know me as Michael Bennett, I am a Black man, judged by the color of my skin."[44]

Bennett knew all too well how dangerous it could be to walk around as a Black man in America. In August 2017, Bennett was leaving the Floyd Mayweather–Conor McGregor fight in Las Vegas when shots rang out. The crowd started running in every direction, and Bennett ran too. Suddenly, Bennett found himself being ordered to the ground by Las Vegas police officers with their guns drawn. As Bennett struggled to understand what was happening while getting to the ground, an officer put a gun to his head and threatened to "blow his fucking head off"; another officer jammed his knee into Bennett's back.

Las Vegas police were looking for a shooter, and Bennett had, like so many Black men before him, fit the description.

Bennett was handcuffed and put in the back of a police car. Officers soon realized that Bennett was not the shooter, and that he was in fact an NFL player. He was released without charge.[45]

"The fact is unequivocally, without question why before every game, I sit during the national anthem," Bennett said in a statement posted to Twitter, "because equality doesn't live in this country and no matter how much money you make, what job title you have, or how much you give, when you are seen as a 'Nigger,' you will be treated that way."[46]

When Bennett spoke publicly about the incident, he was met with a swift denial by the Las Vegas Metropolitan Police Department that the altercation had anything to do with his race. "Many of the folks today have called this an incident of bias-based policing, police officers focusing solely on the race of an individual that they're going to stop," said LVMPD undersheriff Kevin McMahill in a news conference addressing the events. "I can tell you as I stand here today, I see no evidence of that. I see no evidence that race played any role in this incident."[47]

Although the LVMPD tried to downplay the situation, pictures of Bennett on the floor with a gun to his head were soon published all over the internet. Seahawks coach Pete Carroll and NFL commissioner Goodell spoke in support of Bennett. "What happened with Michael is a classic illustration of the reality of inequalities that are demonstrated daily," said Carroll. "May this incident inspire all of us to respond with compassion when inequalities are brought to light and allow us to have the courage to stand for change. We can do better than this."

Goodell issued a statement saying, "The issues Michael has been raising deserve serious attention from all of our leaders in every community. We will support Michael and all NFL players in promoting mutual respect between law enforcement and the communities they loyally serve and fair and equal treatment under law."[48]

Although NFL leadership showed support for Bennett in their statements, he did not receive empathy from all of his fellow teammates. "There were some players who reached out and had a sense of compassion and empathy," Bennett told me when we talked over the phone about the events in Vegas, "and there were other sides saying, like, 'What did you expect? You were asking for it.' . . . 'Why were you there? What did you expect?'"

The realization that the camaraderie the NFL had worked so hard to instill in players stopped at the color line was a painful one for Bennett: "It was shocking, because you have the idea where you are a brotherhood. When you have an issue outside of football and you're looking for your brothers to be there for you, and when you find out they aren't, that hurts a little bit."

A few days after LVMPD cops held a gun to his head, Bennett said he planned to file a civil rights lawsuit against the department for racial profiling and excessive force. Months later, three weeks after it was announced that Bennett was going to be traded to the Philadelphia Eagles and right as he was about to launch his book tour for *Things That Make White People Uncomfortable*, police in Harris County, Texas, issued a warrant for Bennett's arrest on a felony charge of causing injury to the elderly.

According to the indictment, Bennett pushed past a sixty-six-year-old disabled female security guard at a New England Patriots game that Bennett had attended to support his brother Martellus, who played for the Patriots. Houston police chief Art Acevedo held a bizarre press conference demonizing Bennett. "You're morally corrupt when you put your hands on a little old lady in a wheelchair," he said. "That is morally corrupt . . . morally bankrupt. He's morally bankrupt. There's no excuse for that."[49]

Much about the indictment and the theatrics around it seemed suspect to Bennett and many observers. The alleged incident had occurred over a year earlier, and yet the matter was shelved by police until Bennett came forward about his altercation with Las Vegas police in September 2017. It was only then that police in Houston began investigating the complaint and, with no video or photo evidence tying Bennett to the assault against the security guard, decided to press charges—just as he was about to release his book, which discussed in detail his assault by Las Vegas police officers.[50]

Equally disturbing was Acevedo's press conference itself. Police are not supposed to make disparaging comments about defendants in public, lest they taint the jury trial. And yet here was the chief of police in a major city calling Bennett "morally corrupt." The level of vitriol was also unusual for a crime that appears to have only wounded a person's shoulder. Acevedo exaggerated the assault for the cameras, stating that Bennett deliberately pushed an elderly woman and her wheelchair to the floor in his haste to get to his brother. Officers had to later clarify that, no, the woman had not been pushed to the floor, and that with her motorized wheelchair weighing eight hundred pounds, doing so would have been almost impossible.

To many, myself included, it appeared as if Bennett had been made a target by a police department for daring to speak out against police brutality. Bennett, however, saw what had happened to him as simply part of what happens to Black people around the country.

"At first it felt like a conspiracy, but it just happens to be what a lot of Black people go through in America—especially Black men," Bennett explained to me. "We get charged, and if you have a great lawyer you can win and if you don't you end up in jail. I think I was just part of the system and part of what happens to a lot of Americans.

"Your freedom is everything, and if you don't have freedom, what are you supposed to do? You won't be able to take care of you kids. . . . It was just a heavy weight," he continued, reflecting on the year and a half he spent in legal limbo. "When I look back—I think it's just overwhelming when I look back and think about all that."

When Black people threaten white authority, even mildly, there is often a price to be paid. I do believe that Bennett was targeted by police in Harris County. Whether it was because of his protests, or because he spoke out about his treatment by Las Vegas police, or a combination of both, I don't know. But I know that the police in Harris County were willing to waste a lot of money and resources to publicly take on a case that never had any real standing, when the only potential benefit to them would be the damage it would do to Bennett's name and career.

Bennett would live in legal uncertainty until April 3, 2019, when all charges were dropped, citing insufficient evidence. While Bennett was fighting for his freedom, the NFL was still struggling to find a way to get players to stop protesting. With every new protest, Trump would take to Twitter, firing up his angry supporters to attack the NFL. He started telling football lovers to walk out of games if any players protested. Goodell was trying to figure out how to get the league to support racial justice in a way that would make players feel like they could stop protesting.

Although a lot of white commentators decried the athletes' protests, demanding that the athletes "focus on the game," it is important to remember that social causes are not new to professional sports. Professional leagues, including the NFL, have given money and time to raise breast cancer awareness, to fight hunger, and to provide toys to poor children. When we look at the response to peaceful, unobtrusive protests against the killing of unarmed Black men, we need to ask ourselves why so many white Americans saw these protests as an insult.

Kaepernick took a knee to protest a racist system that devalued Black lives. His specific targets were our social and political systems, which were harming people of color. Black athletes who joined the protest spoke repeatedly about the reasons why they were participating—and the reasons pretty much all revolved around their need for equality and safety in a world that was harming them. That this was so easily reinterpreted as an attack on America and therefore an attack on whiteness speaks to how closely many white Americans identify with our racist, oppressive systems.

Members of the Players Coalition met with Goodell, and they began discussing an $89 million commitment from team owners toward social justice issues. It is natural that some players would be skeptical of the NFL's motives for offering up the money, given the way that Kaepernick continued to be treated. Goodell assured the players that it wouldn't be contingent on the cessation of protests, but he stated a hope that players would be satisfied enough to begin standing for the anthem again.

Protests continued, if to a lesser degree, throughout the negotiations, and Trump continued to place public and private pressure on team owners to stop them.

The skepticism that some players had toward the NFL was justified when league leadership suddenly reversed course on the player protests. Many players felt stunned and betrayed when the NFL announced in May 2019, with no consultation with the players' union, that they were banning protests. Any player who protested the national anthem would be fined or suspended. Players and the National Football League Players Association (NFLPA) were outraged at this violation of players' rights of free speech and of their collective-bargaining ability.

Although Goodell called the new rule a "compromise" that all owners had agreed to, there was clearly some dissent. Jets owner Christopher Johnson said shortly after the rules were announced that he would not punish his players for peaceful protests and would pay any fines they incurred for doing so. Jed York of the 49ers said that his team had abstained from the vote on the new policy.

Whatever the reason behind the NFL's sudden decision, the league appeared to have overstepped its bounds. Banning protest of any kind raised red flags with the NFLPA, as the right to protest and speak freely in the workplace has long been a foundation of union power. While the NFL could punish one man to set an example, any broad rules limiting player protest could also restrict union strikes down the line. The Players Association filed a grievance with the NFL, and the press lambasted the league's poorly thought-through rules that were, in most legal experts' opinions, unconstitutional.

The NFL quickly backed down, stating that it would continue to discuss a solution with players before implementing any new rules.

More than a year after leaving the 49ers, Kaepernick was still unsigned. Even the Seattle Seahawks, who had staged team-wide protests and whose coach had been vocally supportive of his players, canceled a scheduled practice with Kaepernick when he wouldn't assure the team that he would quit protesting.

But Kaepernick did not back down, and he did not forget his promises. On January 31, 2018, Kaepernick announced that he had reached his goal of giving $1 million to organizations serving oppressed communities. Kaepernick had paired up with celebrities and community leaders, pledging to match their donations to boost the overall amount of his own contributions. Usher, Meek Mill, Serena Williams, Snoop Dogg, and Jesse Williams were each inspired to give $20,000 to $40,000 to community organizations.[51]

"With or without the NFL's platform, I will continue to work for the people," Kaepernick said when accepting *Sports Illustrated*'s Muhammad Ali Legacy Award in December 2017. "Because my platform is the people."[52]

I asked Michael Bennett why he continued to protest and speak out, even after dealing with hostile management and teammates, angry fans and press, and possible police retaliation.

"At some point the silence is a sin against God—because you are required to be the person you want to be, you are required to speak up," he explained. "We might run a mile in 4.2 minutes. We might run the hundred-yard dash in 9.6 seconds. But I think the true legacy is how we leave our people—what we do. What is really our obligation as human beings is to change humanity and change society. So as athletes we have to realize that we do have the power—more power than just dunking the ball."

Many fans of football who were dismayed over Kaepernick's protests may be quite pleased that he has been kept from their beloved game. But in punishing Kaepernick, and in stifling player protest, the NFL has maintained a status quo that has harmed all NFL players, of all races. The reactions to the protests at the University of Missouri and to the NFL protests have nothing to do with respect or patriotism. They have to do with power.

"It wasn't about kneeling during the anthem, gimme a break," said Dave Zirin with a chuckle when I asked him about the NFL's reaction to Kaepernick. "It wasn't even fear of alienating white fans or ratings, because their money is locked in from TV—from public money. They didn't give two shits about that."

Football is unique to American sport in that it can make superstars and millionaires out of its players while also fundamentally disempowering them by ensuring that the majority of money and power in the sport will always go to the institutions that own it. It begins in college football, where for many schools, the sport keeps the lights on. College coaches can make tens of millions of dollars a year at big football schools. Players are recruited with the promise of a chance at stardom, the education itself offered by the college often given a lower priority in courting these talents. Student athletes are asked to carry their class load, keep in peak physical condition, and risk life-altering injury every week—and they do it without receiving a cut of the hundreds of millions of dollars that their blood, sweat, and talent bring in. When the majority of the players are Black, it is hard to not see the racial implications of Black men physically toiling for free in order to make white institutions millions of dollars.

As Dave Zirin noted, "These football players at the collegiate level are both completely powerless and have so much power—and both of these things exist side by side. It's all about whether or not they exercise that power."

When Black student athletes at Mizzou seized control of the social power that their work and talent had provided them, how can
we be surprised that the institutional power that seeks to harness
the athletes' physical power worked to ensure that student athletes
would not attempt to exercise their power again? As with so many
other institutions that were built to maintain white male authority,
any change that threatens the power dynamic must be stopped—
even if that change would also benefit white men.

Both the University of Missouri protests and the NFL protests were about labor—more specifically, about a controlled labor
force. Entire college and university budgets are built off of the exploitation of football players, regardless of race. Players of all races
are being injured, are having their lives irrevocably altered at the
young age of nineteen and twenty, all for the remote chance that
they might break into the pros. They are breaking their bodies—
and often their minds—in order to make millions, even billions,
for schools that will give them little in return.

If these athletes make it into the NFL, they will find themselves
in some of the most exploitative contracts in professional sports.
They will endure workouts at levels of intensity and frequency that
doctors say are unsafe. They may suffer multiple concussions that
could leave them permanently disabled, violent, or suicidal in later
years. They will make good money for the few years they can play
before they are injured. With no guaranteed contracts, they will
be sent packing when the injuries are too inconvenient, or when a
younger player comes along who is willing to risk injury for a little
less pay. Then, they will be forgotten.

But sometimes the ones who aren't forgotten use their legacies
to try to change the game. In the fall of 2018, a group of football greats—including legends like Jim Brown, Joe Namath, and
Lawrence Taylor—threatened to boycott the annual hall-of-fame
ceremony in 2020. In their letter to the NFL Hall of Fame, they
discussed the great sacrifices they had made to help earn the league

billions of dollars, and they demanded health insurance and an annual salary in return:

> We, the undersigned Pro Football Hall of Famers, were integral to the creation of the modern NFL, which in 2017 generated $14 billion in revenue. But when the league enshrined us as the greatest ever to play America's most popular sport, they gave us a gold jacket, a bust and a ring—and that was it.
>
> People know us from our highlight reels. They see us honored and mythologized before games and at halftime, and it would be reasonable if they thought life was good for us. But on balance, it's not. As a group we are struggling with severe health and financial problems. To build this game, we sacrificed our bodies. In many cases, and despite the fact that we were led to believe otherwise, we sacrificed our minds. We believe we deserve more.[53]

They do deserve more. I think any fan of the game could see that. For the joy they give fans, for the money they bring to the industry and to the cities they play in—all at such great risk to their physical and mental health—they deserve more than a few years in the spotlight and a lifetime of financial and medical struggle.

Student athletes at the University of Missouri were protesting for a better labor deal. They had signed on to play football, and in return they wanted the university to provide a more racially diverse, healthy, and safe educational and living environment.

Colin Kaepernick wanted to bring attention to the issues of systemic racism impacting his life and the lives of many of his teammates of color. But he was also fighting for the ability to control his image and decide what issues his celebrity would be used for. He wanted to be able to determine how to spend his social capital in a profession that regularly requires its athletes to use that capital for NFL benefit through interviews and public appearances.

College football players have been asking for years why they can't get a cut of the billions of dollars they bring in to their institutions. Players from high school through the NFL have been asking for better safety protections and greater transparency around the medical risks of repeated concussions. Professional football players wonder why their contracts are less secure than those in the NBA and MLB, even though they are at greater risk of career-ending injury. They bristle at the media requirements placed on them outside the game to help sell the league to the public. Retired professional players are asking for a little care for their bodies that have been broken for the sport.

The Mizzou and NFL protests did not happen in a vacuum. At the time of the NFL protests, there had been increased talk about the exploitation of college players, the autonomy and career security of NFL players, and the racial power dynamics in both settings. Meanwhile, the NFL was preparing for upcoming contract negotiations during a very high-profile year: the hundredth anniversary of the league in 2020. American football could not afford to have a player body that realized the power it wielded over both public opinion and the NFL's earning potential.

These are labor disputes. This is workers asking if they are being compensated fairly for the work they are doing and if their labor conditions are safe and healthy. In keeping tight control over its athletes—tighter than is exercised in just about any other professional sport in the country—American football can continue to capitalize on its vast popularity and on the athletes that make it so popular, while avoiding ceding any power to those athletes.

This manipulation is unsurprising when we remember that many NFL teams started as company teams as a way to pacify and control workers. Teams like the Decatur Staleys (which became the Chicago Bears) were developed to keep workers busy and happy, and to foster company loyalty during times of union upheaval.[54]

According to Dave Zirin, those teams were encouraged "as something for workers to do after work to keep them away from union meetings, to keep them away from political meetings, to give them a social space that doesn't involve rebellion." Today, where businesses once used football to distract white workers from their labor grievances, American football leadership now uses race to distract the public from the labor grievances of the players.

American football was founded as part of the elite white male preoccupation with maintaining physical power over a nation and its people. When that preoccupation cost too many lives, the sport became a tool for maintaining elite white male power by distracting dissatisfied white working-class men. It is now a tool used to control the football players who risk their bodies and their brains to make rich white men even richer. And through it all, an adoring public has embraced the sport as a symbol of American power and masculinity. When we look at how the sport has embraced violence, undermined workers, and exploited people of color—what could be more American than that?

# CONCLUSION

## *Can White Manhood Be More Than This?*

I was hiding away in a relative's cabin in the woods trying to write when my phone lit up with a news alert. There had been another mass shooting. I had been up to my neck in white male violence while researching this book, and that day, August 3, 2019, my phone told me that a gunman had opened fire in a Walmart in El Paso, Texas, killing twenty-two people. The gunman, a white, twenty-one-year-old man named Patrick W. Crusius, confessed to police on the scene that he had been targeting Mexicans. Prior to his deadly rampage, he wrote a four-page manifesto, declaring that he was going to carry out the attack in "response to the Hispanic invasion of Texas."[1]

The process of writing this book, analyzing the worst of violent racism and sexism in our history, all while living as a Black woman in this country, had been slowly wearing away at my soul. Reading stories of families fleeing another terrorist who was shooting and hoping to hit someone with brown skin felt like too much to bear.

In my heartbreak, rage, and weariness I fired off a simple message online talking about how heartsick I was and begging for
a shift in how we address white male terrorism and white male
identity.

A few hours after posting my message, I received a short and
straightforward email: "My name is Carrah Quigley. I am the
daughter of a school shooter. I would love to provide any information I can share with you about white male aggression and American culture. I was literally raised by this subject."[2]

Quigley offered to send me links to articles about her and offered to be of assistance to my book project.

A few days later, we spoke over Skype. I was immediately struck
by how sincere and warm Quigley seemed, and how obviously
passionate she was about the issue of mass shootings. She sat on
the couch in her living room while her dogs walked up occasionally, looking for affection. I huddled in front of my computer in
the tiny cabin. We talked for over an hour.

Carrah Quigley had, by all accounts, a happy childhood. She
and her siblings adored their father, Bob Bechtel, who was a loving father and a respected teacher. Quigley described Bechtel as a
man who would hug you so tight he'd leave you gasping for air.
Her image of her dad came crashing down when she was nineteen.
Bechtel sat her down and told her his biggest secret: he had murdered someone decades earlier.

Bob Bechtel was a twenty-two-year-old student at Swarthmore
College in 1955. He was bright, but was an outsider who didn't
make friends easily. He was poorer than most of the other students
at the elite school, and he felt like they looked down on him for
it. He told his daughter that a few students had bullied him at
college, adding to the trauma of the teasing he had experienced
throughout primary school. According to Bechtel, the trauma
from the bullying caused him to briefly lose his mind. Whenever
Quigley asked him what he was thinking on January 11, 1955, he

insisted, "I wasn't thinking. You're not understanding. I was temporarily insane." He would say this over and over again.

"I think he was so used to a level of anxiety, threat, and PTSD all the time due to bullying that I don't think he would have even known how close he was to exploding," Carrah explained to me. "I think this was just the next logical step, because he couldn't somehow shift or change his belief that blaming the world would solve everything. The world is against you. It's you against the world. Even if five guys bullied you throughout high school, just five guys, you would perceive it as the whole world."

Bechtel entered his dorm hallway at three a.m. on January 11, 1955, with a gun and enough ammunition to kill every person in the building. He walked to the room of eighteen-year-old Francis Holmes Strozier, took a shot in the dark, and struck Strozier in the head while he slept, killing him instantly.

Bechtel told his daughter that the moment he knew he had killed Strozier, he came to, and he no longer wanted to go through with his plan to kill everyone in the dorm. "There was this instantaneous squeezing of his heart," Quigley told me, "and he gasped for air and he stopped. He said in that moment he realized he was loved far more than he ever thought he was hated."

Bechtel emptied his gun, shooting into the floor instead of at his fellow students, and waited for the police to arrive.

Bechtel was found not responsible for the murder of Francis Strozier by reason of insanity and was sent to the Fairview State Hospital for the Criminally Insane.

Reading the court transcripts from Bechtel's appeal of his sentencing for the murder of Strozier, I see a slightly different picture of Bob Bechtel than the one he painted for his daughter. Bechtel had long shown signs of extreme paranoia and a proclivity toward violence. In high school he had been hospitalized for psychiatric treatment and said he had thoughts of killing a classmate who he claimed had threatened him, stating, "It was either he or I."

Bechtel was discharged from the Air Force after only forty-three days with a diagnosis of "anxiety reaction, schizoid personality, paranoid personality, paranoid delusions" after he attacked a fellow soldier who he believed had stolen his records.

At Swarthmore, he regularly quarreled with his classmates. Unhappy, Bechtel left college and returned home, but he was upset to find that his mother was not as sympathetic as he had expected. Upset at his mother's response, Bechtel took two guns from his home and headed back to campus. He entered his dorm prepared to kill all 120 students, and shot Francis Strozier in the head.

Whereas Bechtel had described to his daughter an immediate clarity and remorse upon killing Strozier, the testimony he gave in his appeal shows a different frame of mind: "He stated that he has no feelings about the killing, feels no remorse, and is neither sorry or glad he did it. He could see no difference between war . . . and his action."[3]

After less than five years at Fairview, Bechtel was found to be sane and was released. Still in his twenties, Bechtel was able to rebuild his life. He went back to school, married, had kids, and became a professor at the University of Arizona.

Years after confessing his secret to Quigley, Bechtel began to speak publicly about the shooting in order to raise awareness of the impact of bullying in schools. Bechtel was, by all accounts, passionate about breaking the cycle of violence that he himself had once been caught up in.[4] To Bechtel, these young white men opening fire in classrooms and shopping malls were perpetrators, but also victims themselves, of violence. In order to stop them from lashing out in such devastating ways, he argued, society needed to show them love and connection.

Quigley described hearing news of another school shooting, when Eric Harris and Dylan Klebold killed thirteen of their classmates at Columbine High School in 1999: "I came home and looked at my dad, and he said, 'You realize that this could have been prevented.' He said, 'All anyone ever had to do was just listen to these children, and just be with these children.'"

I pointed out to Quigley that young white men are more likely to carry out these shootings than anyone else, and asked her why she thought that was the case. She described the pressures her father felt to achieve a white male definition of success, and how easy it was to compare himself to others and to blame others whenever he fell short: "It's in a constant state of anxiety, so to speak. Something can be taken away because it's all lack, lack, lack. It's all about how you compare to other people because you can't exist on your own. . . . So much of what makes a white male angry is the climb and the hierarchy."

But I think it's more than just the climb. It's the expectation that many white men have that they shouldn't have to climb, shouldn't have to struggle, as others do. It's the idea not only that they think they have less than others, but that they were *supposed* to have *so much more*. When you are denied the power, the success, or even the relationships that you think are your right, you either believe that you are broken or you believe that you have been stolen from. White men who think they have been stolen from often take that anger out on others. White men who think they are broken take that anger out on themselves. There were 47,173 suicides in 2017. Of those, 70 percent were white men, and the rate of white male suicides is rising.[5] Across the country, people are mourning the losses of sons, fathers, husbands, and friends who have chosen this particularly devastating way out.

Right now, white men are the biggest domestic terror threats in this country. They are shooting up schools, shopping malls, and casinos. Seventy percent of school shooters are white males.[6] In the years since the terror attacks on September 11, 2001, white male terrorists have killed more Americans than Jihadi terrorists.[7] In a world where many people of many different races and genders are bullied, where many people feel left out and overlooked, it is white men who are choosing to turn that pain and fear into self-harm and murderous rage far more frequently than almost anybody else in America.

Whatever is happening with white men that causes them to open fire on innocents, I'm not sure how much of it can be prevented by simply listening to them.

I do believe that love can solve many problems. I believe that love can guide us through some of the darkest times. But what does it mean to truly love white men who are violently enforcing white male supremacy? What does it mean to truly love white men who feel entitled to status and are angry at the world when they do not get it? And what would it mean to love the same people whom those white men seek to harm?

The emails started coming in 2018. They would usually arrive after I had posted an article on race or gender, but sometimes they would appear at random. I still remember the first one, which shook me.

"I know you think I should kill myself because I voted for Donald Trump, because I'm white, because I'm a male, so I'm just going to, since that is the only ethical conclusion."

The email listed the various hardships the sender had endured. Poverty, mental illness, discrimination. But none of that mattered, because I had shown him that the problem was that he was a white man and he should die. And so his death would be on my hands.

"I'm going to kill myself because that's exactly what you want and will make you happy and I will teach you a lesson when the whole world learns about it."

The email continued, describing how he was going to kill himself (with a Glock that he kept at home) and reiterating that it would be my fault. He then ended with a racist tirade, calling me a "worthless monkey bitch."

I have received many violent emails from white men over the years, but I sat with this one for a while. I tried to process what

I was reading and tried to figure out what I should or could do about it. In the end, I placed it in the same folder as all the death and rape threats.

A few weeks later I received another email from a different sender. The message, with slight wording differences, was essentially the same. This white man was going to kill himself and I was to blame. A few days later I got a similar message via Twitter messenger. A few days after that, another email.

As the threats of suicide piled up, I began to see a coordinated campaign to harass me, and as disturbing as it was, it was also sadly fascinating in what it revealed. These men were trying to terrorize me with what they saw as the only logical conclusion to my anti-racist, feminist work: the mass suicide of white men. They wanted me to know that they saw my work to end violent misogyny and white supremacy, and they saw that it was a threat, not only to their norms and their status but to their very lives.

These men wanted me to know that they were miserable, they felt screwed over, and they felt demonized. They wanted me to know that the only option available to address white male patriarchy was either to maintain the status quo that was making us all miserable, or death. They wanted me to know that they were not capable of growth or change and that any attempts to bring about that growth or change would end them.

Nobody is more pessimistic about white men than white men.

I am the mother of two boys. Two beautiful young men who were born as beautiful babies full of endless possibility. It was shocking to watch how quickly the patriarchy came to claim my sweet little boys. They weren't even in preschool before I had to battle a world that wanted to take everything that was soft and kind and generous about them and turn those traits into hardness, cruelty, and dominance. I watched my older son, who had the most brilliant smile I have ever seen, struggle under the weight of being repeatedly told by society that his loving, open nature was a weakness.

The teenage brain can be a very dangerous place. As young people grow and get ready for adulthood, their world is rapidly changing—as are their hormones. A great day is often the best day of their life and a bad day is often the worst. And if you ask a teen how they are doing on a bad day, if they are willing to talk to you at all, you may hear that every day they've ever had is bad, and every day they *will* ever have will be bad. Teenagers often have difficulty projecting themselves into a different, better future. It can be a very scary time, and the consequences can be very real.

I could have lost my son, the driving force of my heart and soul, to this despair. I'm forever grateful that part of him wanted to live, and that part decided to reach out for help.

It has been years since that terrifying time for my family. We worked with some great therapists, spent a lot of time healing together, and my son grew out of his hardest phase. Not all families are so lucky. Sometimes there is no intervention that can save our children from the claws of anxiety and depression. It has only been in the last two years or so that I've been able to relax somewhat—feeling confident that we made it through the worst of it, that I was going to see my baby grow into a man.

Then, early in the morning on August 14, 2019—two weeks from my son's eighteenth birthday—I got a call from the King County sheriff's office that there had been a report of shots fired at my house. I was across the country, getting ready to head home from a conference. We do not own any guns, and my son doesn't have any friends who own guns, so I knew there was a strong chance this was a hoax. But what if. They were going to send officers to my home.

What if?

I sent a neighbor to go knock on the door, then on my son's window. My son had been sound asleep, unharmed. But the police had received a call from someone pretending to be my son and stating that he had killed two people in the house. They were going to send an armed response. To my home, where my son was alone and barely awake and very confused.

What if we had fought so hard to save my son only to lose him because an angry white man decided to send armed cops to our house at six a.m.?

When I read the emails I receive from white men threatening suicide, I read them as someone who knows what the despair of suicidal thoughts looks like. And when I look at the threats and harassment that I and so many women and people of color have received from angry white men, I know what that despair looks like when it's mixed with the entitlement and bitter disappointment of white male mediocrity.

I don't know if the men who emailed me were actually considering suicide; I doubt they were. I think they were just having some sick, twisted version of fun. But when I look at white male identity in America, I see it all. I see the desperation, the disappointment, the despair, the rage.

White male identity is in a very dark place. White men have been told that they should be fulfilled, happy, successful, and powerful, and they are not. They are missing something vital—an intrinsic sense of self that is not tied to how much power or success they can hold over others—and that hole is eating away at them. I can only imagine how desolately lonely it must feel to only be able to relate to other human beings through conquer and competition. The love, admiration, belonging, and fulfilment they have been promised will never come—it cannot exist for you when your success is tied to the subjugation of those around you. These white men are filled with anger, sadness, and fear over what they do not have, what they believe has been stolen from them. And they look at where they are now, and they cannot imagine anything different. As miserable as they are, they are convinced that no other option exists for them. It is either this, or death: ours or theirs.

I don't want this for white men. I don't want it for any of us. When we look at the history of white male identity in this country, it becomes clear that we are only stuck in these cycles of reactionary violence and oppression because we have not tried anything new. We have become convinced that there is only one way for white men to be. We are afraid to imagine something better.

I do not believe that these white men are born wanting to dominate. I do not believe they are born unable to feel empathy for people who are not them. I do not believe they are born without any intrinsic sense of value. If I did, this would be a very different book. I believe that we are all perpetrators and victims of one of the most evil and insidious social constructs in Western history: white male supremacy.

The constraints of white male identity in America have locked white men into cycles of fear and violence—where the only success they are allowed comes at the expense of others, and the only feelings they are allowed to express are triumph or rage. When white men try to break free from these cycles, they are ostracized by society at large or find themselves victims of other white men who are willing to fulfill their expected roles of dominance. When women and people of color try to free themselves from the oppression of white male supremacy, they are viewed as direct threats to the very identity of white men, and the power structure upholding that identity works swiftly to eliminate the threat.

White male supremacy protects itself not only through the expected violence of white men, but also through control of societal norms that keep us invested in the perpetration of white male power. Think of how the white male glorification of violence has saturated our action films, in which the hero can only maintain or gain freedom through use of a gun. Think of how many career advice books tell women to cooperate less and compete more in order to succeed. Think of how often people of color are expected to abandon their regional and racial dialects in order to be seen as "eloquent" in school and work. Think of how whenever a white man in a nice suit and bold tie, with salt and pepper hair, a strong handshake, and an allergy to apology stands behind a podium— we want to elect him to office.

We have to investigate the way in which all of us, regardless of race or gender, have been conditioned to uphold white male supremacy. We are expected to support white male supremacy in order to get a promotion, to be respected by our peers, for our children to succeed in school. We must ask ourselves what we are willing to give up in order to be free. We must question what we value as individuals and as a society. Leadership should not look like one race or gender; power shouldn't either. We must look at how our votes, our money, and our individual privilege are tied to making sure that white men remain in power over us.

And we must look at what we have been missing out on, at our inability to truly value people who are not white men or who are unable to mimic white men to achieve success. What can women and people of color accomplish in a world that doesn't see us as fundamentally lacking? What can we accomplish in a world that sees difference as an opportunity instead of a threat? What other paths to success have been open to us this entire time that we've refused to embark upon?

We need to do more than just break free of the oppression of white men. We also have to imagine a white manhood that is not based in the oppression of others. We have to value the empathy, kindness, and cooperation that white men, as human beings, are capable of. We have to define strength and leadership in ways that don't reinforce abusive patriarchy and white supremacy. We have to be honest about what white male supremacy has cost not only women, nonbinary people, and people of color—but also white men.

We must start asking what we want white manhood to be, and what we will no longer accept. We must stop rewarding violence and oppression. We must stop confusing bullies with leaders. We must stop telling women and people of color that the only path to success lies in emulating white male dominance. And those of us with privilege of race or status have to divorce ourselves from the lure of proximity to white male power—whether that privilege comes from being a white woman, a light-skinned person of color, or a wealthy person of color—even when those white men are our friends, our husbands, our fathers, or our sons. Instead of seeing humanity as a competition for status, we could all have faith that full equality can allow for esteem and respect to be spread universally.

The path we are on right now is the same one that has brought us only death and despair for hundreds of years. I have seen where this path leads, and nothing is worth continuing in this direction, for anyone. We must break free. We must start making better and more informed choices—with our votes, our wallets, our media, our societal expectations.

Does this sound like too large a task? Too monumental a shift? I can see that. But I can also see how much work it has taken to create and maintain a system of white male mediocrity in this country. I've seen all the creative justifications our society has come up with for the continuation of white male power. I've seen all the effort that our society has put forth in order to keep women and people of color from rising to a status that would threaten the comfort of white male mediocrity. And I've seen how many people we are willing to sacrifice toward those efforts. I look at how much has gone into maintaining a definition of toxic white manhood, and I do not think that we lack the strength or endurance needed to create a new, healthier version of white male identity. We just seem to lack the imagination.

Right now white manhood is on a suicide mission. It is standing at the edge of disaster with a gun in its hands, and it's willing to take us all down with it. For centuries, violent definitions of

white manhood have cost countless lives of women, disabled people, queer and transgender people, people of color—and plenty of
cis, straight, abled, white men themselves. Now, as we reach the
apex of hypercapitalism that makes it harder and harder for white
men to hold out hope that all they've been promised will actually
be theirs, we see their desperation lead to terrorism, self-harm, and
the catastrophic destruction of our environment.

How many more mass shootings will we be able to endure?
How many more economic recessions? How much more climate
crisis? How many more wars? How many more pandemics? How
many more people can live in poverty? How many more of us can
go without health care? How many more can be locked away in
prisons? I don't think we can withstand much more. I don't think
we are withstanding what is happening right now. We are coming
apart as we grow increasingly polarized and as our power structures work to further insulate themselves from any responsibility
to the people they claim to serve. We are running out of time to
fix this. I have to believe that it's not too late, and I hope you believe that too, because we have so much to do.

But this is a human problem. These expectations of violent
white manhood were set by people. The centering of white manhood at the expense of everyone else was done by people. These
systems of power guaranteeing that a few white men will maintain
power over us all, and that the remaining white men will spend
their lives clawing toward whatever little power is left, have been
built by people. People who were the first to use violence and oppression. People who have worked very hard to convince us that
there has never been a time when they were not in charge, and
there never will be. But these people were no smarter or more special than us, and they depend on us, on our continued partici-
pation in the systems of oppression they have built to maintain
their power. We have to find where we have been bonded to these
systems, both individually and collectively, and we have to sever

those bonds. I believe we can. I believe it because even after centuries of oppression and conditioning, we are still here pushing and fighting against it. After centuries of being told that the cost of standing up to white male supremacy is too high, we still stand.

We have to have more than just the desire to fight; we have to have the bravery to look at ourselves and see our complicity in the violence of white male supremacy. We have to not only believe that we deserve better; we have to have faith that we can do better. And we have to start now.

# ACKNOWLEDGMENTS

The inspiration for this book hit me like a bolt of lightning. When it struck, the first person I told was my agent, Lauren Abramo. I'm so grateful to you, Lauren, for taking a feverishly dashed-off email and running with it. Your faith in my work and your unending support—matched with your unparalleled skills and knowledge in your advocacy for your clients—are the bedrock on which our success has been built. I am so grateful for you, and you are absolutely stuck with me.

There is no way I would have been able to write a book about two hundred years of white male supremacy in America and have it be (a) less than ten thousand pages or (b) just a bunch of blank, tear-stained pages if it weren't for my amazing research assistants, Tina Catania and Taylor McCadney. Thank you for your hard work on this project.

I want to give a special thanks to some of the brilliant experts who spoke to me for this book. Dave Zirin, Betsy Gaines Quammen, Michael Bennett, Ellen Pao, Russell K. Brooks, Carrah Quigley, Imani Gandy, and Robin DiAngelo: You have all made this book measurably better than it would have been without your contributions. Thank you for gracing me with your time and knowledge.

When I first proposed this book, I was very naïve about the toll this project would take on me. I know it sounds silly to think that, as a Black woman, spending two years delving into centuries of racist and sexist violence and oppression wouldn't negatively impact me. But having already spent years writing and speaking on contemporary racism in America, I thought I had built a thick enough skin to take on such a task fairly easily. Boy was I wrong. The cumulative effect of this work was compounded by the regular racist harassment that I and my family endured this past year and a half. My work was defined by white male violence, and for a time, so was my home. This one hurt, and will hurt for a while. I'm so grateful for the patience and care that my agent, Seal Press, my publicist, Sharon Kunz, and my editors, Laura Mazer, Emi Ikkanda, and Claire Potter, have shown as I worked to balance this important work and my own self-preservation.

Thank you to my business manager, Ebony Arunga, for answering every email and scheduling every call and conference that I avoided while working on this book. Now that the book is done, I will . . . continue to avoid all of those things as usual. You are a gem and the wheels would fall off this entire operation without you.

When people ask me how I keep going when this work seems like too much, I always point to my kids. Even if you've spent all day researching hatred and violence, and you've been crying for hours, a kid will knock on your door and remind you that you are out of snacks. Malcolm and Marcus: thank you for keeping me grounded and whole. Thank you for the guidance of your pure hearts. Thank you for your humor and talent and love. This work is all for you and because of you. I want this world to be worthy of your potential.

Mom, Jacque, Aham, Basil, Lindy—thanks for being the best and funniest family in the world. I love you.

The month before I was to begin working on this book full-time, I decided on a whim to take a trip to Stockholm. I took a deep breath and asked a friend I had long had a crush on if he wanted to go with me. He did, and we fell in love. He has stayed up late at night researching with me. He has listened to me moan and complain about how writing is the worst thing in the world and I'm never going to do it again. He has driven kids to school while I worked to meet deadlines. He has held space for my fear and grief. He has held his own fear and grief for me. We have been locked in through a pandemic together. He has made me laugh at least once every single day. I have never been bold when it comes to my love life and was quite content to be single forever, until the moment that I decided that I was going to ask a guy to fly halfway around the world with me for our first date. There are few risks I've taken that have provided such great rewards. Gabriel: I love you. You're my guy.

# NOTES

## 1. COWBOYS AND PATRIOTS

1. M. Elias, "Sikh Temple Killer Wade Michael Page Radicalized in Army," Southern Poverty Law Center, November 11, 2012, www.splcenter.org /fighting-hate/intelligence-report/2012/sikh-temple-killer-wade-michael -page-radicalized-army.

2. E. Blakemore, "The Truth Behind Buffalo Bill's Scalping Act," JStor Daily, February 26, 2017, https://daily.jstor.org/the-truth-behind-buffalo -bills-scalping-act/; R. Slotkin, *Gunfighter Nation: The Myth of the Frontier in Twentieth-Century America* (Norman: University of Oklahoma Press, 1998).

3. B. Madley, "Reexamining the American Genocide Debate: Meaning, Historiography, and New Methods," *American Historical Review* 120, no. 1 (2015): 98–139.

4. "Scalping in America," Indian Country Today, October 2, 2017, https:// newsmaven.io/indiancountrytoday/archive/scalping-in-america-AvU3W-1ae0 W3AjR4BHCvEg.

5. J. W. Phippen, "Kill Every Buffalo You Can! Every Buffalo Dead Is an Indian Gone," *The Atlantic*, May 13, 2016, www.theatlantic.com/national /archive/2016/05/the-buffalo-killers/482349/.

6. R. Brooks, interview with author, March 23, 2020.

7. Phippen, "Kill Every Buffalo You Can!"; G. King, "Where the Buffalo No Longer Roamed," *Smithsonian*, July 17, 2012, www.smithsonianmag.com /history/where-the-buffalo-no-longer-roamed-3067904/.

8. Slotkin, *Gunfighter Nation*.

9. P. L. Hedren, "The Contradictory Legacies of Buffalo Bill Cody's First Scalp for Custer," *Montana: The Magazine of Western History*, Spring 2005; Slotkin, *Gunfighter Nation*.

10. R. B. Smith, "Buffalo Bill's Skirmish at Warbonnet Creek," HistoryNet, December 1996, www.historynet.com/buffalo-bills-skirmish-at-warbonnet-creek.htm.

11. L. North, "Man of the Plains: Recollections of Luther North," in *Pioneer Heritage Series*, vol. 6 (Norman: University of Oklahoma Press, 1961), 128.

12. S. M. Underhill, *The Manufacture of Consent: J. Edgar Hoover and the Rhetorical Rise of the FBI* (East Lansing: Michigan State University Press, 2020).

13. P. J. Barrish, *The Cambridge Introduction to American Literary Realism* (Cambridge, UK: Cambridge University Press, 2011).

14. G. Cooper, "Two Rough Riders Make for a Rocky Relationship," *Chautauquan Daily*, July 25, 2014, https://chqdaily.wordpress.com/2014/07/25/two-rough-riders-make-for-a-rocky-relationship/.

15. W. G. Moss, "Which Presidents—If Any—Did Right by Native Americans?," History News Network, October 7, 2018, https://historynewsnetwork.org/article/170123.

16. A. Townsend EagleWoman, "The Ongoing Traumatic Experience of Genocide for American Indians and Alaska Natives in the United States: The Call to Recognize Full Human Rights as Set Forth in the UN Declaration on the Rights of Indigenous Peoples," *American Indian Law Journal* 3, no. 2 (2015): 437.

17. G. Gerstle, "Teddy Roosevelt's Complicated Legacy 100 Years After His Death," interview by J. Hobson, *Here and Now*, WBUR, March 21, 2019, www.wbur.org/hereandnow/2019/03/21/teddy-roosevelt-legacy-100-years.

18. "Teddy Roosevelt and the Indians," Native American Netroots, October 10, 2011, http://nativeamericannetroots.net/diary/1093.

19. L. S. Warren, *Buffalo Bill's America: William Cody and the Wild West Show* (New York: Vintage Books, 2006), 215.

20. "August 26, 1902: Buffalo Bill's Wild West Makes Oregon Debut," Dave Knows Portland, August 26, 2011, http://portland.daveknows.org/2011/08/26/august-26-1902-buffalo-bills-wild-west-makes-oregon-debut/.

21. Warren, *Buffalo Bill's America*.

22. K. Repanshek, *Re-Bisoning the West: Restoring an American Icon to the Landscape* (Salt Lake City: Torrey House Press, 2019), 139.

23. D. Nesheim, "How William F. Cody Helped Save the Buffalo Without Really Trying," *Great Plains Quarterly* 27, no. 3 (2007): 163–175, https://digitalcommons.unl.edu/greatplainsquarterly/1504.

24. B. G. Quammen, *American Zion: Cliven Bundy, God and Public Lands in the West* (Salt Lake City: Torrey House Press, 2020), 84.

25. "Testimony in Trials of John D. Lee," Mountain Meadows Association, accessed February 2020, www.mtn-meadows-assoc.com/johnson.htm.

26. "Last Confession and Statement of John D. Lee," Mountain Meadows Association, accessed February 2020, www.mtn-meadows-assoc.com /jdlconfession.htm.

27. Quammen, *American Zion*, 87

28. S. Levin, "Rebel Cowboys: How the Bundy Family Sparked a New Battle for the American West," *The Guardian*, August 29, 2016, www .theguardian.com/us-news/2016/aug/29/oregon-militia-standoff-bundy-family.

29. J. Pogue, "The Religious Ideology Driving the Bundy Brothers," *Outside*, May 17, 2018, www.outsideonline.com/2308761/religious-ideology-driving -bundy-brothers.

30. B. Gaines Quammen, interview with author, February 25, 2020.

31. Levin, "Rebel Cowboys."

32. A. Nagourney, "A Defiant Rancher Savors the Audience That Rallied to His Side," *New York Times*, April 23, 2014, www.nytimes.com/2014/04/24 /us/politics/rancher-proudly-breaks-the-law-becoming-a-hero-in-the-west .html.

33. Quammen, *American Zion*.

34. L. Sottile, "Trump's Pardoning of Two Oregon Ranchers Is a Victory for the Bundys—And an Ominous Loss for Public-Lands Advocates," *Pacific Standard*, July 11, 2018, https://psmag.com/environment/trumps-pardoning -of-oregon-ranchers-is-a-victory-for-the-bundys-and-a-loss-for-public-lands -advocate.

35. Levin, "Rebel Cowboys."

36. Levin, "Rebel Cowboys."

37. Quammen, *American Zion*.

38. A. Templeton, "LaVoy Finicum's Family Remembers Him as a Man Driven by Family and Faith," OPB, February 6, 2016, www.opb .org/news/series/burns-oregon-standoff-bundy-militia-news-updates /lavoy-finicums-family-remembers-him-as-a-man-driven-by-family-and-faith/.

39. K. Galbraith, "What Will Happen if the Oregon Militia Gets Its Demands?," *The Guardian*, January 8, 2016, www.theguardian.com /us-news/2016/jan/08/oregon-militia-standoff-demands-what-comes-next.

40. C. Sherwood and K. Johnson, "Bundy Brothers Acquitted in Takeover of Oregon Wildlife Refuge," *New York Times*, October 27, 2016, www .nytimes.com/2016/10/28/us/bundy-brothers-acquitted-in-takeover-of -oregon-wildlife-refuge.html.

41. Sottile, "Trump's Pardoning of Two Oregon Ranchers Is a Victory for the Bundys."

42. M. Nijhuis, "How Fire, Once a Friend of Forests, Became a Destroyer," *National Geographic*, November 22, 2015, www.nationalgeographic.com /news/2015/11/151122-wildfire-forest-service-firefighting-history-pyne -climate-ngbooktalk/.

43. "The Bannock War," Native American Netroots, December 27, 2010, http://nativeamericannetroots.net/diary/814.

44. Quammen, *American Zion*.

45. S. Levin, "Fresh Outrage After Militia Seen Rifling Through Tribal Artifacts at Oregon Refuge," *The Guardian*, January 21, 2016, www.theguardian .com/us-news/2016/jan/21/oregon-militia-standoff-malheur-wildlife -refuge-native-american-artifacts-paiute-tribe.

## 2. FOR YOUR BENEFIT, IN OUR IMAGE

1. A. Wald, "When Max Eastman Was Young," *Jacobin*, November 2018, www.jacobinmag.com/2018/11/max-eastman-masses-eugene-debs -canton-speech.

2. E. Arnesen, "The Passions of Max Eastman," *Dissent*, Winter 2018, www.dissentmagazine.org/article/passions-max-eastman-biography-review.

3. "Floyd Dell: A Respectable Radical," Postscripts, October 23, 2012, http://notorc.blogspot.com/2012/10/floyd-dell-respectable-radical.html.

4. "Backwards Glance: Feminism for Men in 1914," *Voice Male*, July 9, 2013, https://voicemalemagazine.org/feminism-for-men-in-1914/.

5. E. K. Trimberger, "Feminism, Men, and Modern Love: Greenwich Village, 1900–1925," in *Powers of Desire*, ed. A. Snitnow, C. Stansell, and S. Thompson (New York: Monthly Review Press, 1983), 131–152.

6. "Floyd Dell: A Respectable Radical."

7. Trimberger, "Feminism, Men, and Modern Love."

8. J. Neuman, "Who Won Women's Suffrage? A Case for 'Mere Men,'" *Journal of the Gilded Age and Progressive Era* 16, no. 3 (2017): 347–367.

9. E. Francis, "From Event to Monument: Modernism, Feminism and Isadora Duncan," *American Studies* 35, no. 1 (1994): 24–45.

10. M. C. Jones, *Heretics and Hellraisers: Women Contributors to* The Masses, *1911–1917* (Austin: University of Texas Press, 1993), 22.

11. F. Dell, "Feminism for Men," *The Masses*, July 1914, http://omeka .ursinus.edu/files/original/36e5c6312e00e0bf06cc21dfa6796f89.pdf.

12. Trimberger, "Feminism, Men, and Modern Love."

13. Trimberger, "Feminism, Men, and Modern Love."

14. J. P. Diggins, *Up from Communism: Conservative Odysseys in American Intellectual History* (New York: Columbia University Press, 1994 [1975]), 219.

15. Diggins, *Up from Communism*.

16. J. Allen, "New Details Revealed About Biden's Busing Record: Why Was He So Strongly Opposed?," NBC News, July 6, 2019, www .nbcnews.com/politics/2020-election/biden-s-mastery-backlash-politics -takes-center-stage-n1025931.

17. "Wilmington Integration Order Poses the Possibility of Busing," *New York Times*, July 13, 1974, www.nytimes.com/1974/07/13/archives /wilmington-integration-order-poses-the-possibility-of-busing.html.

18. J. Sokol, "How a Young Joe Biden Turned Liberals Against Integration," *Politico*, August 4, 2015, www.politico.com/magazine/story/2015/08/04 /joe-biden-integration-school-busing-120968.

19. Sokol, "How a Young Joe Biden Turned Liberals Against Integration."

20. D. B. Taylor, S. G. Stolberg, and A. W. Herndon, "A Brief History of Joe Biden and School Busing," *New York Times*, July 15, 2019, www.nytimes .com/2019/07/15/us/joe-biden-busing-timeline.html.

21. Sokol, "How a Young Joe Biden Turned Liberals Against Integration."

22. Taylor, Stolberg, and Herndon, "A Brief History of Joe Biden and School Busing."

23. A. W. Herndon and S. G. Stolberg, "How Joe Biden Became the Democrats' Anti-Busing Crusader," *New York Times*, July 15, 2019, www.nytimes .com/2019/07/15/us/politics/biden-busing.html.

24. Sokol, "How a Young Joe Biden Turned Liberals Against Integration."

25. Sokol, "How a Young Joe Biden Turned Liberals Against Integration."

26. Sokol, "How a Young Joe Biden Turned Liberals Against Integration."

27. J. Biden, *Promises to Keep* (New York: Random House, 2007), 125.

28. J. Biden, "Joe Biden Full Interview," interview by J. Favreau, J. Lovett, T. Vietor, *Pod Save America*, March 2019, https://youtu.be/Tcev9dcFDkw.

29. K. Glueck, "Biden, Recalling 'Civility' in Senate, Invokes Two Segregationist Senators," *New York Times*, June 19, 2019, www.nytimes .com/2019/06/19/us/politics/biden-segregationists.html.

30. R. A. Caro, *The Years of Lyndon Johnson: Master of the Senate* (New York: Knopf, 2002), 767.

31. K. Glueck and A. W. Herndon, "Joe Biden and Democratic Rivals Exchange Attacks over His Remarks on Segregationists," *New York Times*, June 19, 2019, www.nytimes.com/2019/06/19/us/politics/biden-eastland .html?module=inline.

32. D. Gunn, "Non-White School Districts Get $23 Billion Less Funding Than White Ones," *Pacific Standard*, February 26, 2019, https://psmag.com /education/nonwhite-school-districts-get-23-billion-less-funding-than-white -ones.

33. "Delaware's School Resegregation Increasing After Dissolution of Its Groundbreaking Metropolitan Desegregation Plan," Civil Rights Project, December 18, 2014, www.civilrightsproject.ucla.edu/news /press-releases/2014-press-releases/ucla-report-finds-delaware2019s-school-resegregation-increasing-after-dissolution-of-its-groundbreaking-metropolitan -desegregation-plan.

34. J. Bies, "Lawsuit: Delaware Schools Are Leaving Children in Poverty Behind," *Delaware Online*, May 23, 2018, www.delawareonline.com/story/news/education/2018/05/23/lawsuit-would-change-way-delaware-schools-funded/590963002/.

35. I. Oluo (@ijeomaoluo), "I dreamt last night," Twitter, May 27, 2019, 8:46 a.m., https://twitter.com/IjeomaOluo/status/1133036856033988608.

36. S. Doyle, "Not About Gender," Tumblr, 2016, https://sadydoyle.tumblr.com/post/132899987688/not-about-gender.

37. Jeanne Shaheen, "I was honored to introduce my friend Hillary Clinton," Facebook, January 22, 2016, www.facebook.com/jeanneshaheenNH/photos/a.10151236112888293.495154.6691963292/10153925284253293/?type=3.

38. I. Gandy, interview with author, May 28, 2019.

39. P. Bump, "Here's What Happened at Saturday's Dramatic Nevada Democratic Convention," *Washington Post*, May 17, 2016, www.washingtonpost.com/news/the-fix/wp/2016/05/15/heres-what-happened-at-saturdays-dramatic-nevada-democratic-convention/.

40. J. Ralston, "Sample of Voicemails Left for State Democratic Chairwoman Roberta Lange," *Ralston Reports*, May 16, 2016, www.ralstonreports.com/blog/sample-voicemails-left-state-democratic-chairwoman-roberta-lange.

41. S. Ember, "Bernie Sanders Stumbled with Black Voters in 2016. Can He Do Better in 2020?," *New York Times*, February 17, 2019, www.nytimes.com/2019/02/17/us/politics/bernie-sanders-black-voters-outreach.html.

42. T. J. Starr, "How Bernie Sanders Lost Black Voters," *Splinter News*, July 10, 2016, https://splinternews.com/how-bernie-sanders-lost-black-voters-1793860129.

43. Starr, "How Bernie Sanders Lost Black Voters."

44. Starr, "How Bernie Sanders Lost Black Voters."

45. S. Ember and K. Benner, "Sexism Claims from Bernie Sanders's 2016 Run: Paid Less, Treated Worse," *New York Times*, January 2, 2019, www.nytimes.com/2019/01/02/us/politics/bernie-sanders-campaign-sexism.html?module=inline.

46. S. Ember and J. Martin, "Bernie Sanders Apologizes Again to Women Who Were Mistreated in 2016 Campaign," *New York Times*, January 2, 2019, www.nytimes.com/2019/01/10/us/politics/sanders-sexism-apology.html.

47. G. E. Curry, "In Vermont, Socialist Makes Congressional Election Hot," July 29, 1990, www.chicagotribune.com/news/ct-xpm-1990-07-29-9003030805-story.html.

48. B. Sanders, "NYT: Learning from the Ferguson Tragedy," Sanders senatorial website, August 21, 2014, www.sanders.senate.gov/newsroom/recent-business/nyt-learning-from-the-ferguson-tragedy.

49. L. Kreutz, "Hillary Clinton Knocks Bernie Sanders over Response to Donald Trump's Abortion Comments," ABC News, March 31, 2016,

https://abcnews.go.com/Politics/hillary-clinton-knocks-bernie-sanders
-response-donald-trumps/story?id=38063205.

50. B. Griffiths, "Sanders Slams Identity Politics as Democrats Figure Out
Their Future," *Politico*, November 21, 2016, www.politico.com/story/2016/11
/bernie-sanders-democrats-identity-politics-231710.

51. R. Graham, "What's It Like to Be a 'Bernie Bro' Heading into
2020?," *Slate*, March 4, 2019, www.evernote.com/l/AZ7rzFMUe9ZJKapsd9
_So-kYf644n1Ow_eA/.

52. Quoted in E. Morrissey, "Sanders: My Primary Opponents Care
Only About Identity Politics and False Diversity," *Hot Air*, January 25,
2019, https://hotair.com/archives/2019/01/25/sanders-primary-opponents
-care-identity-politics-false-diversity/.

53. T. J. Starr, "Bernie Sanders Is Not a Real Progressive," *The Root*, November 6, 2017, www.theroot.com/bernie-sanders-is-not-a-real-progressive
-1820122317.

54. "Bernie Sanders at Black Forum MN: Full Discussion w/Sanders," You-
Tube, February 13, 2016, www.youtube.com/watch?v=GsI3-2VgF1U.

55. R. D. Francis, "Him, Not Her: Why Working-Class White Men Reluctant About Trump Still Made Him President of the United States," *Socius* 4,
no. 11 (2018): 1–11.

56. D. Kurtzleben, "Here's How Many Bernie Sanders Supporters Ultimately Voted for Trump," NPR, August 24, 2017, www.npr.org
/2017/08/24/545812242/1-in-10-sanders-primary-voters-ended-up-supporting
-trump-survey-finds.

57. "Exit Polls: Obama Wins Big Among Young, Minority Voters," CNN,
November, 4, 2008, https://web.archive.org/web/20081108082743/http://
www.cnn.com/2008/POLITICS/11/04/exit.polls/.

58. R. DiAngelo, interview with author, May 3, 2019.

## 3. THE IVY LEAGUE AND THE TAX EATERS

1. M. Kennedy, "Princeton Will Keep Woodrow Wilson's Name on
School Buildings," NPR, April 4, 2016, www.npr.org/sections/thetwo-way
/2016/04/04/472985937/princeton-will-keep-woodrow-wilsons-name-on
-school-buildings.

2. S. Svrluga, "Princeton Protesters Occupy President's Office, Demand
'Racist' Woodrow Wilson's Name Be Removed," *Washington Post*, November 18, 2015, www.washingtonpost.com/news/grade-point/wp/2015/11/18
/princeton-protesters-occupy-presidents-office-demand-racist-woodrow
-wilsons-name-be-removed/.

3. D. Matthews, "Woodrow Wilson Was Extremely Racist—Even
by the Standards of His Time," *Vox*, November 20, 2015, www.vox.com
/policy-and-politics/2015/11/20/9766896/woodrow-wilson-racist.

4. A. Neklason, "Elite-College Admissions Were Built to Protect Privilege," *The Atlantic*, March 18, 2019, www.theatlantic.com/education/archive/2019/03/history-privilege-elite-college-admissions/585088/.

5. Neklason, "Elite-College Admissions Were Built to Protect Privilege."

6. Neklason, "Elite-College Admissions Were Built to Protect Privilege."

7. I. Shapira, "Before Asian Americans Sued Harvard, the School Once Tried Restricting the Number of Jews," *Washington Post*, October 15, 2018, www.washingtonpost.com/news/retropolis/wp/2018/09/14/before-asian-americans-sued-harvard-the-school-tried-restricting-the-number-of-jews/?noredirect=on.

8. Neklason, "Elite-College Admissions Were Built to Protect Privilege."

9. Neklason, "Elite-College Admissions Were Built to Protect Privilege."

10. S. S. Avi-Yonah and D. R. Franklin, "Renovated Lowell House Will Not Display Portrait of Controversial Former University President Abbott Lawrence Lowell," *Harvard Crimson*, March 26, 2019, www.thecrimson.com/article/2019/3/26/lowell-portraits-removed/.

11. A. DenHoed, "The Forgotten Lessons of the American Eugenics Movement," *New Yorker*, April 27, 2016, www.newyorker.com/books/page-turner/the-forgotten-lessons-of-the-american-eugenics-movement.

12. J. Weissglass, "For Equality's Sake, the SAT Should Be Abolished," *Los Angeles Times*, January 24, 2000, www.latimes.com/archives/la-xpm-2000-jan-24-me-57241-story.html.

13. M. Viera, "The History of the SAT Is Mired in Racism and Elitism," *Teen Vogue*, October 1, 2018, www.teenvogue.com/story/the-history-of-the-sat-is-mired-in-racism-and-elitism.

14. C. Brigham, "Intelligence Tests of Immigrant Groups," *Psychological Review* 37 (1930): 158–165.

15. Viera, "The History of the SAT Is Mired in Racism and Elitism."

16. "Land-Grant Universities," *Encyclopaedia Brittanica*, accessed May 2020, www.britannica.com/topic/land-grant-university.

17. C. W. Young, *Background for Developing a System of Hispanic-Serving Land-Grant Colleges*, Hispanic Association of Colleges and Unversities, accessed May 2020, www.hacu.net/images/hacu/young.pdf.

18. "Farm Bill Reauthorization Workplan," Hispanic Association of Colleges and Universities, acessed May 2020, www.hacu.net/hacu/Reauthorization_workplan.asp.

19. M. Lazerson, "The Disappointments of Success: Higher Education After World War II," *Annals of the American Academy of Political and Social Science* 559 (1998): 64–76.

20. "Ethnic Studies 50th Anniversary Commemoration Week," San Francisco State University, 2019, https://ethnicstudies.sfsu.edu/50th.

21. Lazerson, "The Disappointments of Success."

22. Lazerson, "The Disappointments of Success."

23. Lazerson, "The Disappointments of Success."

24. D. Fergus, "My Students Pay Too Much for College. Blame Reagan," *Washington Post*, September 2, 2014, www.washingtonpost.com /posteverything/wp/2014/09/02/my-students-pay-too-much-for-college -blame-reagan/?noredirect=on&utm_term=.9401a2038ec4.

25. J. Kahn, "Ronald Reagan Launched Political Career Using the Berkeley Campus as a Target," *UC Berkeley News*, June 8, 2004, www.berkeley.edu /news/media/releases/2004/06/08_reagan.shtml.

26. "The 1980's," History.com, June 7, 2019, www.history.com/topics /1980s/1980s.

27. K. Sullivan and M. Jordan, "'Elitists, Crybabies and Junky Degrees': Educators See Growing Disdain for Universities," *Chicago Tribune*, November 25, 2017, www.chicagotribune.com/nation-world/ct-college-education -critics-20171125-story.html.

28. Sullivan and Jordan, "'Elitists, Crybabies and Junky Degrees.'"

29. M. Balingit and D. Douglas-Gabriel, "Trump Seeks to Slash $8.5 Billion from Education Department Budget," *Washington Post*, March 11, 2019, www.washingtonpost.com/local/education/trump-seeks-to-slash-85-billion -from-education-department-budget/2019/03/11/69ab930e-441f-11e9-8aab -95b8d80a1e4f_story.html?utm_term=.0b221cac52db.

30. Z. Friedman, "What Trump's Student Loan Forgiveness Plan Means for You," *Forbes*, March 27, 2019, www.forbes.com/sites/zackfriedman/2019/03 /27/what-trumps-latest-proposals-mean-for-your-student-loans/#6f8c1af 9508f.

31. Balingit and Douglas-Gabriel, "Trump Seeks to Slash $8.5 Billion from Education Department Budget."

32. "Median Incomes v. Average College Tuition Rates, 1971–2016," Pro-Con.org, April 20, 2017, https://college-education.procon.org/view.resource .php?resourceID=005532.

33. J. Selingo, "States' Decision to Reduce Support for Higher Education Comes at a Cost," *Washington Post*, September 8, 2018, www.washington post.com/education/2018/09/08/states-decision-reduce-support-higher -education-comes-cost/; J. Marcus, "Americans Don't Realize State Funding for Higher Ed Is Falling, New Poll Finds," *Hechinger Report*, February 25, 2019, https://hechingerreport.org/americans-think-state-funding-for-higher -ed-has-held-steady-or-risen-survey-finds/.

34. S. Stebbins, "Choosing a Degree? These College Majors Are Likely to Pay Off the Least," *USA Today*, January 19, 2020, www.usatoday .com/story/money/2020/01/19/jobs-college-degrees-education-arts-pay-off -the-least/41006589/.

35. B. Auguste, "Failing by Degrees: Why College Grads Need Non-College Grads to Succeed," *Forbes*, March 14, 2019, www.forbes.com/sites /byronauguste/2019/03/14/failing-by-degrees-why-college-grads-need-non

-college-grads-to-succeed/#38ea75316c5b; "View Talent Shortages Around the World," Manpower Group, 2018, https://go.manpowergroup.com /talent-shortage-2018#shortagebycountry-globaldata.

36. A. Graves, "How Many Times Has Trump Mentioned His Wharton Education? We Crunched the Numbers," *Daily Pennsylvanian*, January 17, 2018, www.thedp.com/article/2018/01/trump-penn-wharton -data-education-times-ivy-league-business-finance-philadelphia-campaign; J. Glenza, "Trump Makes 'Blood' Truce with Fox Then Says He Is Top Candidate for Women," *The Guardian*, August 11, 2015, www.theguardian .com/us-news/2015/aug/11/donald-trump-megyn-kelly-fox-women.

37. R. D. Francis, "Him, Not Her: Why Working-Class White Men Reluctant About Trump Still Made Him President of the United States," *Socius* 4, no. 11 (2018): 1–11.

38. A. Tyson and S. Maniam, "Behind Trump's Victory: Divisions by Race, Gender, Education," Pew Research Center, November 9, 2016, www .pewresearch.org/fact-tank/2016/11/09/behind-trumps-victory-divisions -by-race-gender-education/.

39. C. Ingraham, "Three Quarters of Whites Don't Have Any Non-White Friends," *Washington Post*, August 25, 2014, www.washingtonpost.com/news /wonk/wp/2014/08/25/three-quarters-of-whites-dont-have-any-non-white -friends/?utm_term=.669393795a9d.

40. "Income and Wealth in the United States: An Overview of Recent Data," Peter G. Peterson Foundation, October 4, 2019, www.pgpf.org /blog/2019/10/income-and-wealth-in-the-united-states-an-overview-of-data.

41. "Completing College—National by Race and Ethnicity—2017," National Student Clearinghouse Research Center, April 26, 2017, https://nsc researchcenter.org/signaturereport12-supplement-2/.

42. Sullivan and Jordan, "'Elitists, Crybabies and Junky Degrees.'"

## 4. WE HAVE FAR TOO MANY NEGROES

1. C. Ingraham, "Three Quarters of Whites Don't Have Any Non-White Friends," *Washington Post*, August 25, 2014, www.washingtonpost.com/news /wonk/wp/2014/08/25/three-quarters-of-whites-dont-have-any-non-white -friends/?utm_term=.669393795a9d.

2. S. A. Reich, *The Great Black Migration: A Historical Encyclopedia of the American Mosaic* (Santa Barbara, CA: Greenwood, 2014), 148.

3. I. X. Kendi, *Stamped from the Beginning: The Definitive History of Racist Ideas in America* (New York: Nation Books, 2016), 243.

4. M. Berman, "Even More Black People Were Lynched in the U.S. Than Previously Thought, Study Finds," *Washington Post*, February 10, 2015, www .washingtonpost.com/news/post-nation/wp/2015/02/10/even-more-black -people-were-lynched-in-the-u-s-than-previously-thought-study-finds/?utm _term=.ee0d39576e53.

5. E. J. Scott, "Letters of Negro Migrants of 1916–1918," *Journal of Negro History* 4, no. 3 (1919): 317.

6. I. Wilkerson, "The Long-Lasting Legacy of the Great Migration," *Smithsonian*, September 2016, www.smithsonianmag.com/history /long-lasting-legacy-great-migration-180960118/.

7. "Top 10 Poorest States in the U.S.," Friends Committee on National Legislation, September 18, 2018, www.fcnl.org/updates/top-10-poorest-states -in-the-u-s-1630.

8. "Top 10 Hungriest States in the U.S.," Friends Committee on National Legislation, September 18, 2018, www.fcnl.org/updates/top-10-hungriest -states-in-the-u-s-1629.

9. U. Akcigit, J. Grigsby, and T. Nicholas, *The Rise of American Ingenuity: Innovation and Inventors of the Golden Age*, Working Paper 17-063, Harvard Business School, June 7, 2017, www.hbs.edu/faculty/Publication %20Files/17-063_e55d07c8-c1db-4e59-b935-37a7701e0839.pdf.

10. T.-N. Coates, "What This Cruel War Was Over," *The Atlantic*, June 22, 2015, www.theatlantic.com/politics/archive/2015/06/what-this -cruel-war-was-over/396482/.

11. "Wealth and Culture in the South: Slavery and the White Class Structure," Lumen Learning, accessed May 2019, https://courses.lumenlearning .com/ushistory1os2xmaster/chapter/wealth-and-culture-in-the-south/.

12. J. Hammond, "Document: Cotton Is King (March 4, 1858)," republished on the website Teaching American History, accessed May 2020, https:// teachingamericanhistory.org/library/document/cotton-is-king/.

13. Kendi, *Stamped from the Beginning*, 238.

14. Coates, "What This Cruel War Was Over."

15. J. N. Gregory, "Southernizing the American Working Class: Post War Episodes of Regional and Class Transformation," *Labor History* 39, no. 2 (1998): 135–154, http://faculty.washington.edu/gregoryj/southernization.pdf.

16. Seattle Civil Rights and Labor History Project, "Racial Restrictive Covenants," University of Washington, accessed May 2020, https://depts .washington.edu/civilr/covenants.htm.

17. Scott, "Letters of Negro Migrants of 1916–1918."

18. Wilkerson, "The Long-Lasting Legacy of the Great Migration."

19. "World War I and the Great Migration," History, Art, and Archives, United States House of Representatives, accessed April 7, 2019, https:// history.house.gov/Exhibitions-and-Publications/BAIC/Historical-Essays /Temporary-Farewell/World-War-I-And-Great-Migration/.

20. "Targeting Black Veterans: Lynching in America," Equal Justice Initiative, 2017, https://eji.org/reports/online/lynching-in-america-targeting -black-veterans/red-summer.

21. M. Ihejirika, "'Chicago 1919' Explores Racial Tension, from Eugene Williams to Laquan McDonald," *Chicago Sun-Times*, March 10, 2019,

https://chicago.suntimes.com/2019/3/10/18313804/chicago-1919-explores
-racial-tension-from-eugene-williams-to-laquan-mcdonald.

22. "The Red Summer of 1919," History.com, last updated July 26, 2019,
www.history.com/topics/black-history/chicago-race-riot-of-1919.

23. Ihejirika, "'Chicago 1919' Explores Racial Tension, from Eugene Williams to Laquan McDonald."

24. O. B. Waxman, "The Forgotten March That Started the National Civil
Rights Movement Took Place 100 Years Ago," *Time*, July 28, 2017, https://
time.com/4828991/east-saint-louis-riots-1917/.

25. A. Keyes, "The East St. Louis Race Riot Left Dozens Dead, Devastating a Community on the Rise," *Smithsonian*, June 30, 2017, www
.smithsonianmag.com/smithsonian-institution/east-st-louis-race-riot-left-
dozens-dead-devastating-community-on-the-rise-180963885/.

26. Waxman, "The Forgotten March."

27. "1920s–1948: Racially Restrictive Covenants," Fair Housing Center of
Greater Boston, accessed June 17, 2019, www.bostonfairhousing.org/timeline
/1920s1948-Restrictive-Covenants.html.

28. "Power, Politics, and Pride: Dr. King's Chicago Crusade," WTTW
.com, accessed May 2020, https://interactive.wttw.com/dusable-to-obama
/dr-kings-chicago-crusade.

29. D. T. Carter, "What Trump Owes George Wallace," *Gulf News*, January 12, 2016, https://gulfnews.com/opinion/op-eds/what-trump-owes-george
-wallace-1.1652614.

30. B. Lyman, "George Wallace: A Segregationist Stand for America," *USA
Today*, August 16, 2018, www.usatoday.com/story/news/nation-now/1968
-project/2018/08/16/stand-up-america-george-wallaces-chaotic-prophetic
-campaign/961043002/.

31. D. McCabe and P. Stekler, dirs., *George Wallace: Settin' the Woods on
Fire*, 2000, Vimeo.com.

32. Lyman, "George Wallace."

33. K. Nodjimbadem, "The Racial Segregation of American Cities Was Anything but Accidental," *Smithsonian*, May 30, 2017, www
.smithsonianmag.com/history/how-federal-government-intentionally
-racially-segregated-american-cities-180963494/; R. Rothstein, "Public Housing: Government-Sponsored Segregation," *American Prospect*, October 11,
2012, https://prospect.org/article/public-housing-government-sponsored
-segregation.

34. J. R. Thomas, "Separated by Design: How Some of America's Richest Towns Fight Affordable Housing," *ProPublica*, May 22, 2019, www
.propublica.org/article/how-some-of-americas-richest-towns-fight-affordable
-housing.

## 5. FIRE THE WOMEN

1. R. Ebert, "Nine to Five," December 19, 1980, republished on RogerEbert .com, accessed June 2020, www.rogerebert.com/reviews/nine-to-five-1980.

2. V. Canby, "'Nine to Five,' Office Comedy," *New York Times*, December 19, 1980, https://timesmachine.nytimes.com/timesmachine/1980/12/19 /111324357.pdf?pdf_redirect=true&ip=0.

3. R. S. McElvaine, *The Great Depression: America 1929–1941* (New York: Crown/Archetype, 2010), 176.

4. McElvaine, *The Great Depression*, 10.

5. McElvaine, *The Great Depression*, 11.

6. McElvaine, *The Great Depression*, 176.

7. McElvaine, *The Great Depression*, 176.

8. R. L. Boyd, "Race, Labor Market Disadvantage, and Survivalist Entrepreneurship: Black Women in the Urban North During the Great Depression," *Sociological Forum* 15, no. 4 (2000): 647–670.

9. S. Terkel, *Hard Times: An Oral History of the Great Depression* (New York: New Press, 2000 [1970]), 82–83.

10. M. McDonald Way, *Family Economics and Public Policy, 1800s–Present: How Laws, Incentives, and Social Programs Drive Family Decision-Making and the US Economy* (Babson Park, FL: Springer, 2018), 152.

11. E. Blakemore, "Why Many Married Women Were Banned from Working During the Great Depression," History.com, July 21, 2019, www.history .com/news/great-depression-married-women-employment.

12. McElvaine, *The Great Depression*, 176.

13. M. Honey, *Creating Rosie the Riveter: Class, Gender and Propaganda During World War II* (Amherst: University of Massachusetts Press, 1984), 150.

14. Blakemore, "Why Many Married Women Were Banned from Working During the Great Depression."

15. A. Hoffman, *Unwanted Mexican Americans in the Great Depression: Repatriation Pressures, 1929–1939* (Tucson: University of Arizona Press, 1974), 39–41, 64–68.

16. S. J. Loza, *Barrio Rhythm: Mexican American Music in Los Angeles* (Champaign: University of Illinois Press, 1993), 36–37.

17. K. R. Johnson, "The Forgotten Repatriation of Persons of Mexican Ancestry and Lessons for the War on Terror," *Pace Law Review* 26, no. 1 (2005): 6.

18. T. L. Bynum, "'We Must March Forward!': Juanita Jackson and the Origins of the NAACP Youth Movement," *Journal of African American History* 94, no. 4 (2009): 487–508.

19. R. Freedman, *Children of the Great Depression* (New York: Houghton Mifflin Harcourt, 2005), 49.

20. McElvaine, *The Great Depression*, 268.

21. Honey, *Creating Rosie the Riveter*, 18.

22. K. T. Anderson, "Last Hired, First Fired: Black Women Workers During World War II," *Journal of American History* 69, no. 1 (1982): 82–97.

23. Honey, *Creating Rosie the Riveter*, 3–4.

24. Honey, *Creating Rosie the Riveter*, 19–20, 136.

25. Honey, *Creating Rosie the Riveter*, 147.

26. Honey, *Creating Rosie the Riveter*, 6–10.

27. C. Kirkpatrick, "EM 31: Do You Want Your Wife to Work After the War? (1944)," republished on the website of the American Historical Association, accessed May 2020, www.historians.org/about-aha-and-membership/aha-history-and-archives/gi-roundtable-series/pamphlets/em-31-do-you-want-your-wife-to-work-after-the-war-(1944).

28. "GI Rountable Series: Introduction," American Historical Association, accessed November 29, 2019, www.historians.org/about-aha-and-membership/aha-history-and-archives/gi-roundtable-series/gi-roundtable-series-introduction.

29. S. M. Hartmann, "Women and World War II," Metropolitan State University of Denver, accessed August 21, 2019, https://msudenver.edu/camphale/thewomensarmycorps/womenwwii/; "American Women in World War II," History.com, updated February 28, 2020, www.history.com/topics/world-war-ii/american-women-in-world-war-ii-1.

30. C. Le Faucheur, "Should Women War Workers Be Fired?," National WWII Museum, accessed November 29, 2019, www.nationalww2museum.org/war/articles/should-women-war-workers-be-fired.

31. Honey, *Creating Rosie the Riveter*, 4–5.

32. Le Faucheur, "Should Women War Workers Be Fired?"

33. K. Weisul, "Where Are All the Missing Veteran-Owned Businesses?," *Inc.*, October 2016, www.inc.com/magazine/201610/kimberly-weisul/missing-veteran-owned-businesses.html.

34. J. Bellefaire, "History Highlight: Women Veterans and the WWII GI Bill of Rights," Women in Military Service Memorial Foundation, November 2006, www.womensmemorial.org/history-highlight.

35. "After the War: Blacks and the G.I. Bill," Smithsonian American Art Museum, February 2015, https://americanexperience.si.edu/wp-content/uploads/2015/02/After-the-War-Blacks-and-the-GI-Bill.pdf.

36. Washington Paid Family and Medical Leave, *Parents' Guide to Paid Family and Medical Leave*, March 2020, https://paidleave.wa.gov/app/uploads/2020/04/Parents-guide-V.3-FINAL.pdf.

37. L. Kane, "Sweden Is Apparently Full of 'Latte Dads' Carrying Toddlers—And It's a Sign of Critical Social Change," *Business Insider*, April 4, 2018, www.businessinsider.com/sweden-maternity-leave-paternity-leave-policies-latte-dads-2018-4.

38. C. Miller, K. Quealy, M. Sanger-Katz, "The Top Jobs Where Women Are Outnumbered by Men Named John," *New York Times*, April 24, 2018, www.nytimes.com/interactive/2018/04/24/upshot/women-and-men-named-john.html.

39. L. Dishman, "What Is the Glass Cliff, and Why Do So Many Female CEOs Fall Off It?," Fast Company, July 27, 2018, www.fastcompany.com/90206067/what-is-the-glass-cliff-and-why-do-so-many-female-ceos-fall-off-it.

40. J. Berman, "When a Woman or Person of Color Becomes CEO, White Men Have a Strange Reaction," MarketWatch, March 3, 2018, www.marketwatch.com/story/when-a-woman-or-person-of-color-becomes-ceo-white-men-have-a-strange-reaction-2018-02-23.

41. D. Byers, "Turbulence at the *Times*," *Politico*, April 23, 2013, www.politico.com/story/2013/04/new-york-times-turbulence-090544?o=1.

42. E. Pao, interview with author, May 13, 2019.

43. F. Garza, "The Only People Who Aren't Penalized for Promoting Diversity at Work Are White Men," *Quartz*, March 25, 2016, https://qz.com/647512/the-only-people-who-arent-penalized-for-promoting-diversity-at-work-are-white-men/.

44. Byers, "Turbulence at the *Times*."

45. A. Fitzgerald, "Female-Led Companies More Likely to Be Targeted by Activist Investors, MU Research Finds," *Mizzou News*, April 17, 2018, https://munews.missouri.edu/news-releases/2018/0417-female-led-companies-more-likely-to-be-targeted-by-activist-investors-mu-research-finds/.

## 6. SOCIALISTS AND QUOTA QUEENS

1. "The Counted: People Killed by Police in the US," interactive database, *The Guardian*, accessed June 28, 2020, www.theguardian.com/us-news/ng-interactive/2015/jun/01/the-counted-police-killings-us-database.

2. C. Sweda, "Police Officers Convicted for Fatal Shootings Are the Exception, Not the Rule," NBC News, March 13, 2019, www.nbcnews.com/news/nbcblk/police-officers-convicted-fatal-shootings-are-exception-not-rule-n982741.

3. S. Chisholm, "Shirley Chisholm's Presidential Announcement Speech Transcript," Common Lit, accessed September 2019, www.commonlit.org/texts/shirley-chisholm-s-presidential-announcement-speech-transcript.

4. E. M. Simien, *Historic Firsts: How Symbolic Empowerment Changes U.S. Politics* (Oxford, UK: Oxford University Press, 2016), 32.

5. "This Day in History: Jan. 25, 1972: Shirley Chisholm Began Historic Campaign for President," Zinn Education Project, accessed September 2019, www.zinnedproject.org/news/tdih/shirley-chisholm-announces-campaign/; Chisholm, "Shirley Chisholm's Presidential Announcement Speech Transcript."

6. R. L. Madden, "Mrs. Chisholm Defeats Farmer, Is First Negro Woman in House," *New York Times*, November 6, 1968, accessed September 2019, https://timesmachine.nytimes.com/timesmachine/1968/11/06/91291879.html?pageNumber=1.

7. J. Landers, "'Unbought and Unbossed': When a Black Woman Ran for the White House," *Smithsonian*, April 25, 2016, www.smithsonianmag.com/smithsonian-institution/unbought-and-unbossed-when-black-woman-ran-for-the-white-house-180958699/.

8. J. Freeman, "Shirley Chisholm's 1972 Presidential Campaign," February 2005, reproduced on the website of the University of Illinois at Chicago, accessed November 11, 2014, www.uic.edu/orgs/cwluherstory/jofreeman/polhistory/chisholm.htm.

9. Chisholm, "Shirley Chisholm's Presidential Announcement Speech Transcript."

10. A. Diekman, "Covering the 1972 Chisholm Campaign: Shaping Perceptions and Postponing Progress," *Journal of Undergraduate Research at Minnesota State University, Mankato* 9, no. 1 (2009): 1–12.

11. E. Blakemore, "Here's What People Once Said About How a Woman Would Never Be the Democratic Nominee," *Time*, June 7, 2016, https://time.com/4359610/shirley-chisholm-nominee/?amp=true.

12. A. Tully, "No 'Women's Lib' for Negro Congresswoman," *Beaver County Times*, February 2, 1972, reproduced in the Google news archive, accessed September 2019, https://news.google.com/newspapers?id=J7AiAAAAIBAJ&sjid=ErMFAAAAIBAJ&pg=2935%2C941954.

13. Landers, "'Unbought and Unbossed.'"

14. L. Raatma, *Shirley Chisholm* (New York: Marshall Cavendish, 2011), 69.

15. B. Obama, "Remarks by the President at Medal of Freedom Ceremony," website of the White House, November 24, 2015, https://obamawhitehouse.archives.gov/the-press-office/2015/11/24/remarks-president-medal-freedom-ceremony.

16. Landers, "'Unbought and Unbossed.'"

17. G. F. Will, "Sympathy for Guinier," *Newsweek*, June 13, 1993, www.newsweek.com/sympathy-guinier-194016.

18. A. Lewis, "The Case of Lani Guinier," *New York Review of Books*, August 13, 1998, www.nybooks.com/articles/1998/08/13/the-case-of-lani-guinier/.

19. J. Levin, "The Welfare Queen," *Slate*, December 19, 2013, www.slate.com/articles/news_and_politics/history/2013/12/linda_taylor_welfare_queen_ronald_reagan_made_her_a_notorious_american_villain.html.

20. L. Weymouth, "Lani Guinier: Radical Justice," *Washington Post*, May 25, 1993, www.washingtonpost.com/archive/opinions/1993/05/25/lani

-guinier-radical-justice/1b4d4e4d-30d1-47d1-b1ab-cb5c77125987/?utm
_term=.381eb432e545.

21. Weymouth, "Lani Guinier: Radical Justice."

22. Quoted in D. Harris, *Black Feminist Politics from Kennedy to Clinton* (New York: Palgrave Macmillan, 2009), 125.

23. L. Guinier, "Lani Guinier on Her Interactions with Bill Clinton," interview by P. Slen, C-SPAN, March 2, 2015, www.c-span.org/video/?c4529828 /lani-guinier-interactions-bill-clinton.

24. C. I. King, "Bill Clinton's Treatment of Lani Guinier," *Washington Post*, June 6, 1993, www.washingtonpost.com/archive/opinions/1993/06/06 /bill-clintons-treatment-of-lani-guinier/412b72d0-d823-4ac2-8bc3 -2619c447d6e5/?noredirect=on&utm_term=.880bec21aba0.

25. D. Lauter, "Clinton Withdraws Guinier as Nominee for Civil Rights Job," *Los Angeles Times*, June 4, 1993, www.latimes.com/archives/la-xpm-1993 -06-04-mn-43290-story.html.

26. Guinier, "Lani Guinier on Her Interactions with Bill Clinton."

27. B. Milano, "'If You Stop There . . .': Celebrating Guinier in the Spirit She Has Inspired," *Harvard Law Today*, February 23, 2018, https://today.law .harvard.edu/stop-celebrating-guinier-spirit-inspired/.

28. Milano, "'If You Stop There. . . .'"

29. J. Lemon, "Democrats Alexandria Ocasio-Cortez, Ilhan Omar Want to 'Make Us Slaves to Socialism,' GOP Congresswoman Accuses," *Newsweek*, April 14, 2019, www.newsweek.com/democrats-alexandria-ocasio-cortez -ilhan-omar-want-make-us-slaves-socialism-1395584.

30. Editorial Board, "If You Want to Be Speaker, Mr. Crowley, Don't Take Voters for Granted," *New York Times*, June 19, 2018, www.nytimes .com/2018/06/19/opinion/joseph-crowley-alexandria-ocasio-cortez.html.

31. E. Godfrey, "A Shocking Insurgent Victory in New York," *The Atlantic*, June 27, 2018, https://www.theatlantic.com/politics/archive/2018/06/a -latina-democratic-socialist-beat-the-king-of-queens/563861/.

32. G. Krieg, "Who Is Alexandria Ocasio-Cortez?" CNN, February 8, 2019, www.cnn.com/2018/06/27/politics/who-is-alexandria-ocasio-cortez /index.html.

33. A. Herrera, P. Majerle, "'In Love with Democracy,' Ilhan Omar Draws Diverse Supporters in Bid for Congress," *The World*, November 1, 2018, www.pri.org/stories/2018-11-01/love-democracy-ilhan-omar-draws-diverse -supporters-bid-congress.

34. E. Ostermeier, "Ilhan Omar Nearly Breaks Minnesota US House Electoral Record," Smart Politics, November 13, 2018, https:// editions.lib.umn.edu/smartpolitics/2018/11/13/ilhan-omar-nearly-breaks -minnesota-us-house-electoral-record/; A. DuVernay, "Ilhan Omar Tells

Ava DuVernay About the (Good) Trouble She's Making in Congress," *Interview Magazine*, April 3, 2019, www.interviewmagazine.com/culture /conversation-with-congresswoman-ilhan-omar-and-ava-duvernay.

35. J. Nichols, "Rashida Tlaib: There's a 'Real Human Impact of Doing Nothing,'" *The Nation*, June 11, 2019, www.thenation.com/podcast/rashida -tlaib-next-left/.

36. DuVernay, "Ilhan Omar Tells Ava DuVernay About the (Good) Trouble She's Making in Congress."

37. G. Solomon, "The Omar Effect: On the Pulse of Controversy and Change," *Minnesota Spokesman-Recorder*, June 12, 2019, http://spokesman -recorder.com/2019/06/12/the-omar-effect-on-the-pulse-of-controversy-and -change/.

38. M. Harriot, "Ayanna Pressley Introduces Legislation to End the 'Pushout' of Black Girls," *The Root*, December 11, 2019, www.theroot.com /ayanna-pressley-introduces-legislation-to-end-the-push-1840346412.

39. "Rep. Ayanna Pressley's 'People's Justice Guarantee' Is the Most Sweeping Weed Legislation Proposal Yet. But Will It Pass?" *Greenwich Time*, December 11, 2019, www.greenwichtime.com/business/article/Rep -Ayanna-Pressley-s-People-s-Justice-14896636.php.

40. N. DeCosta-Klipa, "The House Passed Ayanna Pressley's Credit Score Reform Bill. Here's What It Would Do," *Boston*, January 30, 2020, www.boston .com/news/politics/2020/01/30/ayanna-pressley-house-credit-reporting-bill.

41. L. Friedman, "What Is the Green New Deal? A Climate Proposal, Explained," *New York Times*, February 21, 2019, www.nytimes.com/2019/02/21 /climate/green-new-deal-questions-answers.html.

42. S. Tarlo, "House Speaker Nancy Pelosi Appears to Mock Rep. Alexandria Ocasio-Cortez's Following on Twitter," *Salon*, April 9, 2019, www .salon.com/2019/04/09/house-speaker-nancy-pelosi-appears-to-mock-rep -alexandria-ocasio-cortezs-following-on-twitter/.

43. Friedman, "What Is the Green New Deal?"

44. I. Schwartz, "Rep. Ayanna Pressley: 'We Don't Need Any More Brown Faces That Don't Want to Be a Brown Voice,'" Real Clear Politics, July 14, 2019, www.realclearpolitics.com/video/2019/07/14/rep_ayanna_pressley_we _dont_need_any_more_brown_faces_that_dont_want_to_be_a_brown _voice.html.

45. S. Kent, "Ayanna Pressley's Disturbing Progressive Threat," *Washington Examiner*, July 17, 2019, www.washingtonexaminer.com/opinion /ayanna-pressleys-disturbing-progressive-threat.

46. J. Bowden, "Liz Cheney Calls Ayanna Pressley's Comments at Netroots Nation 'Racist,'" *The Hill*, July 16, 2019, https://thehill.com/homenews /house/453342-liz-cheney-calls-ayanna-pressleys-comments-at-netroots -nation-racist.

47. Z. Beauchamp, "It's Time for Ilhan Omar's Critics to Stand with Her Against Trump's Attacks," *Vox*, April 18, 2019, www.vox.com/policy -and-politics/2019/4/18/18410662/ilhan-omar-trump-911-islamophobia.

48. "Rep. Tlaib Tears Up While Reading Death Threat," CNN, June 4, 2019, www.cnn.com/videos/politics/2019/06/04/rashida-tlaib-mcgarrity -domestic-terrorism-emotional-sot-vpx.cnn.

49. S. Grasso, "Stop Calling AOC, Ilhan Omar, and Rashida Tlaib 'Radical,' Start Calling Everyone Else Cowards," *Splinter*, February 22, 2019, https://splinternews.com/stop-calling-aoc-ilhan-omar-and-rashida-tlaib -radical-1832814428.

50. DuVernay, "Ilhan Omar Tells Ava DuVernay About the (Good) Trouble She's Making in Congress."

51. P. Rosenberg, "The Republican Nomination Process Is Dramatic Evidence of the Failure of Our Voting Rules. Instant Runoff Fixes It," *Salon*, March 26, 2016, www.salon.com/2016/03/26/this_one_reform_defeats _donald_trump_and_saves_democracy_too_bad_the_gerrymandering_gop _never_listened_but_maybe_they_will_now/; K. Eberhard and M. Morales, "How Trump Is Winning—Even Though Most Republicans Aren't Voting for Him," Sightline Institute, March 7, 2016, www.sightline.org/2016/03/07 /how-trump-is-winning-even-though-most-republicans-arent-voting-for -him/.

52. G. Guilford, "Maine Is Adopting a Voting System That Will Make It Easier for Third Party Candidates to Get Elected," *QZ*, November 9, 2016, https://qz.com/828585/maine-is-adopting-a-voting-system-that-will-make-it -easier-for-third-party-candidates-to-get-elected/; K. Budech, "Alternative Voting Systems Can Save Democracy," Sightline Institute, December 1, 2016, www .sightline.org/2016/12/01/alternative-voting-systems-can-save-democracy/.

## 7. GO FUCKING PLAY

1. D. Zirin, interview with author, April 26, 2019.

2. K. Abbott, "Score One for Roosevelt," *Smithsonian*, September 20, 2011, www.smithsonianmag.com/history/score-one-for-roosevelt-83762245/.

3. Editorial Board, "Two Curable Evils," *New York Times*, November 23, 1897, https://timesmachine.nytimes.com/timesmachine/1897/11/23/10 2065399.pdf.

4. Abbott, "Score One for Roosevelt."

5. R. O. Davies, *Sports in American Life: A History*, 3rd ed. (Hoboken, NJ: John Wiley and Sons, 2016), 210–214.

6. K. L. Shropshire, *In Black and White: Race and Sports in America* (New York: NYU Press, 1996), 26.

7. "Jack Trice, ISU Football Legend," African American Registry, accessed April 23, 2019, https://aaregistry.org/story/jack-trice-isu-football-legend/.

8. M. Steil, "The Origin of Floyd of Rosedale," Minnesota Public Radio, November 17, 2005, http://news.minnesota.publicradio.org/features/2005/11/14_steilm_floydofrosedale/.

9. Davies, *Sports in American Life*.

10. "The Coffin Corner: Vol. 6, Nos. 11 and 12 (1984): G.P.M.: George Preston Marshall," Pro Football Hall of Fame, accessed April 23, 2019, http://profootballresearchers.com/archives/Website_Files/Coffin_Corner/06-12-202.pdf.

11. L. M. Waggoner, "On Trial: The Washington R*dskins' Wily Mascot: Coach William 'Lone Star' Dietz," *Montana: The Magazine of Western History*, Spring 2013.

12. Shropshire, *In Black and White*, 29–31.

13. M. Goodpaster, "The Shame That Is the Washington Redskins and Daniel Snyder (The Racism of George Preston Marshall)," The Grueling Truth, March 3, 2018, https://thegruelingtruth.com/football/nfl/shame-washington-redskins-daniel-snyder-racism-george-preston-marshall/.

14. "Founder-Owner: George Preston Marshall," website of the Pro Football Hall of Fame, accessed August 2019, www.profootballhof.com/players/george-preston-marshall/.

15. K. Briquelet, "How Mizzou Football Sacked President over Racism on Campus," *Daily Beast*, November 10, 2015, www.thedailybeast.com/articles/2015/11/09/striking-mizzou-football-team-wants-president-out-over-wave-of-racism.

16. RHA Mizzou (@RHAMizzou), "We will not stay silent," Twitter, October 29, 2015, 6:54 p.m., https://twitter.com/RHAMizzou/status/659911318309212161.

17. B. Trachtenberg, "The 2015 University of Missouri Protests and Their Lessons for Higher Education Policy and Administration," SSRN, July 24, 2018, http://ssrn.com/abstract=3217199.

18. The Legion of Black Collegians (@MizzouLBC), "We are no longer taking it. It's time to fight," Twitter, November 7, 2015, 6:14 p.m., https://twitter.com/MizzouLBC/status/663177684428566532.

19. Coach Gary Pinkel (@GaryPinkel), "The Mizzou Family stands as one," Twitter, November 8, 2015, 9:39 a.m., https://twitter.com/GaryPinkel/status/663410502370856960.

20. "One Year After Protest Rocked Missouri, the Effects on the Football Team and University Remain Tangible," *Sports Illustrated*, November 8, 2016, www.si.com/college-football/2016/11/08/how-missouri-football-has-changed-1-year-after-boycott.

21. D. Matter, "Former MU Player Ian Simon Accepts ESPN Award," *St. Louis Post-Dispatch*, July 16, 2016, www.stltoday.com/sports/college

/mizzou/eye-on-the-tigers/former-mu-player-ian-simon-accepts-espn-award
/article_3ff6a26e-aea3-58fd-b5f9-fc21ae30bb76.html.

22. "One Year After Protest Rocked Missouri."

23. R. Felton, "Missouri Bill Aims to Strip Scholarships from College
Athletes Who Refuse to Play," *Washington Post*, December 14, 2015, www
.theguardian.com/us-news/2015/dec/14/missouri-bill-scholarships-college
-athletes-protest.

24. T. Kingkade, "Missouri Lawmakers Push to Punish Mizzou Because
Students Protested," *Huffington Post*, February 12, 2016, www.huffpost
.com/entry/missouri-lawmakers-mizzou-student-protest_n_56be1eb4e4b08f
fac124ff95.

25. A. Hartocollis, "Long After Protests, Students Shun the University of
Missouri," *New York Times*, July 9, 2017, www.nytimes.com/2017/07/09/us
/university-of-missouri-enrollment-protests-fallout.html.

26. P. Baugh, "Athletics and Activism: Looking Back on a Historic Football Boycott," *The Maneater*, October 22, 2016, www.themaneater.com/stories
/sports/athletics-and-activism-looking-back-historic-footb.

27. "One Year After Protest Rocked Missouri."

28. N. Bierman, "For Years, Trump Bashed the NFL and Players Who
Protested Racial Injustice. Here's Why He Stopped," *Los Angeles Times*, February 3, 2019, www.latimes.com/politics/la-na-pol-trump-nfl-20190201-story
.html.

29. KIRO 7 News Staff, "Seahawks Players Berated by Driver Never
Staged Public Protests During National Anthem," KIRO 7 News, March 12,
2018, www.kiro7.com/news/local/seahawks-players-berated-by-driver-never
-staged-public-protests-during-national-anthem/714923210.

30. J. Trotter and J. Reid, "Irreconcilable Differences: Why the Players Coalition Split Apart," The Undefeated, February 2, 2018, https://theundefeated
.com/features/irreconcilable-differences-why-the-nfl-players-coalition
-split-apart/.

31. R. Lapchick, B. Ekiyor, and H. Ruiz, "The 2006 Racial and Gender Report Card: The National Football League," September 26, 2007,
https://43530132-36e9-4f52-811a-182c7a91933b.filesusr.com/ugd/7d86e5
_7232193e48f64e90af2cdf09e65a8a94.pdf.

32. S. Wyche, "Colin Kaepernick Explains Why He Sat During National Anthem," website of the NFL, August 27, 2016, www.nfl.com/news
/story/0ap3000000691077/article/colin-kaepernick-explains-protest-of
-national-anthem.

33. I. Oluo, *So You Want to Talk About Race* (New York: Seal Press, 2018).

34. P. Holloway, "Colin Kaepernick Warned Players Who Kneeled
with Him They May Not Work Again," Niners Nation, February 20, 2019,

www.ninersnation.com/2019/2/20/18232588/colin-kaepernick-settlement
-kneeling-players-michael-wilhoite.

35. V. Mather, "A Timeline of Colin Kaepernick vs. the N.F.L.," *New York Times*, February 15, 2019, www.nytimes.com/2019/02/15/sports/nfl
-colin-kaepernick-protests-timeline.html.

36. B. Lacina, "Since the NFL Anthem Protests, White Fans Like the White Players More—and the Black Ones Less," *Washington Post*, January 19, 2019, www.washingtonpost.com/news/monkey-cage/wp/2019/01/19
/happy-nfl-playoffs-since-the-anthem-protests-white-football-fans-like-white
-players-more-and-black-ones-less/?utm_term=.be8d18623bff.

37. M. Bennett, interview with author, June 30, 2019.

38. Media Matters Staff, "Sean Hannity Speculates That Kaepernick Protested National Anthem Because 'He Might Have Converted to Islam,'" Media Matters, August 29, 2016, www.mediamatters.org/sean-hannity/sean
-hannity-speculates-kaepernick-protested-national-anthem-because-he-might
-have.

39. Media Matters Staff, "Rush Limbaugh: NFL Protests Are a Leftist Plot 'to Cause Great Damage to the NFL' Because It Stands for 'Masculinity,'" Media Matters, September 28, 2017, www.mediamatters.org/sean-hannity
/rush-limbaugh-nfl-protests-are-leftist-plot-cause-great-damage-nfl-because-it
-stands.

40. T. Gabriel, "Before Trump, Steve King Set the Agenda for the Wall and Anti-Immigrant Politics," *New York Times*, January 10, 2019, www.nytimes.com/2019/01/10/us/politics/steve-king-trump-immigration
-wall.html; J. Yomtov, "GOP Rep. Steve King on Kaepernick: 'This Is Activism That's Sympathetic to ISIS,'" *USA Today*, September 15, 2016, www
.usatoday.com/story/sports/nfl/2016/09/15/steve-king-colin-kaepernick
-activism-sympathetic-to-isis/90399954/.

41. E. Rosenberg, "'You Can't Win This One,' Donald Trump Told NFL Owners About Anthem Protests. They Believed Him," *Chicago Tribune*, May 30, 2018, www.chicagotribune.com/sports/ct-spt-trump-nfl-anthem-protests
-20180530-story.html.

42. A. Parker, "How Trump Has Attempted to Recast His Response to Charlottesville," *Washington Post*, May 7, 2019, www.washingtonpost.com
/politics/how-trump-has-attempted-to-recast-his-response-to-charlottesville
/2019/05/06/8c4b7fc2-6b80-11e9-a66d-a82d3f3d96d5_story.html?utm
_term=.dda383279216.

43. M. Bennett and D. Zirin, *Things That Make White People Uncomfortable* (Chicago: Haymarket Books, 2018), 15.

44. Bennett and Zirin, *Things That Make White People Uncomfortable*, 16–17.

45. C. Boren, "'Terrified and Confused': Seahawks' Michael Bennett Tells of Traumatic Police Encounter," *Washington Post*, September 7, 2017, www .washingtonpost.com/news/early-lead/wp/2017/09/06/im-going-to-die-for -no-other-reason-than-i-am-black-michael-bennett-tells-of-police-encounter /?utm_term=.44f66fd34bff.

46. M. Bennett (@mosesbread72), "Equality," Twitter, September 17, 2017, 7:01 a.m., https://twitter.com/mosesbread72/status/90543070159565 2096.

47. K. Spain, "Las Vegas Police: 'No Evidence' Race Played Role in Michael Bennett Incident," KHOU, September 7, 2017, www.khou.com/article/news /las-vegas-police-no-evidence-race-played-role-in-michael-bennett-incident /285-471794348.

48. Boren, "'Terrified and Confused.'"

49. D. Barron, "Charges Against Michael Bennett Dropped Because of Insufficient Evidence," *Houston Chronicle*, April 3, 2019, www.houston chronicle.com/sports/texans/article/Charges-against-Michael-Bennett -dropped-because-13739414.php.

50. J. Breech, "Eagles' Michael Bennett Indicted on Felony Charge, Has Warrant Out for Arrest," CBS Sports, March 23, 2018, www.cbssports.com/nfl /news/eagles-michael-bennett-indicted-on-felony-charge-has-warrant-out-for -arrest/.

51. A. Willingham, "While You Were Arguing About the Anthem, Colin Kaepernick Just Finished Donating $1 Million," CNN, January 31, 2018, www.cnn.com/2018/01/31/sport/colin-kaepernick-million-dollar-donation -pledge-anthem-nfl-trnd/index.html.

52. D. Rapaport, "Kaepernick Vows to Continue Combating Racial Injustice 'With or Without the NFL,'" *Sports Illustrated*, December 5, 2017, www.si.com/nfl/2017/12/06/colin-kaepernick-sports-illustrated-muhammad -ali-award-acceptance-speech.

53. Letter, E. Dickerson, Chairman, Hall of Fame Board, et al. to R. Goodell et al., n.d. (2018), reproduced on the website of ESPN, accessed May 2020, http://a.espncdn.com/pdf/2018/0918/HOFLetter.pdf.

54. D. A. Gilbert, "The Gridiron and the Gray Flannel Suit: NFL Football and the Modern U.S. Workplace," *Journal of Sport and Social Issues* 42, no. 2 (2018): 132–148.

## CONCLUSION

1. N. Bogel-Burroughs, "'I'm the Shooter': El Paso Suspect Confessed to Targeting Mexicans, Police Say," *New York Times*, August 9, 2019, www .nytimes.com/2019/08/09/us/el-paso-suspect-confession.html.

2. C. Quigley, email correspondence with author, August 3, 2019.

3. "Commonwealth v. Bechtel," February 6, 1956, reproduced on Justia .com, accessed June 2020, https://law.justia.com/cases/pennsylvania /supreme-court/1956/384-pa-184-0.html.

4. "Professor Shares Story of His 1955 Murder Case," *Arizona Daily Sun*, November 19, 2004, https://azdailysun.com/professor-shares-story-of-his -murder-case/article_cf711db1-2fce-5b93-a9bb-da64ae513b57.html.

5. S. Rodrick, "All-American Despair," *Rolling Stone*, May 30, 2019, www.rollingstone.com/culture/culture-features/suicide-rate-america-white -men-841576/.

6. W. Cai and J. K. Patel, "A Half-Century of School Shootings like Columbine, Sandy Hook and Parkland," *New York Times*, May 11, 2019, www .nytimes.com/interactive/2019/05/11/us/school-shootings-united-states .html.

7. D. Byman, "Right-Wingers Are America's Deadliest Terrorists," *Slate*, August 5, 2019, https://slate.com/news-and-politics/2019/08/right-wing -terrorist-killings-government-focus-jihadis-islamic-radicalism.html.

# INDEX

310 Index

Eastman, Max, 53–55, 56–58,
60–62, 63
Ebert, Roger, 150
economic inequality
disparities in net worth, 4
income inequality, 172, 178
Sanders on, 79–80
wage gaps, 4, 172, 178
wealth gaps, 135, 146, 157
education
admissions criteria and, 102,
104–105
affirmative action programs and,
107
assault on higher, 95–121
costs of, 108–110, 112–113
cuts/inequality in funding for,
69–70, 110–111
GI Bill and, 170
at historically Black colleges and
universities, 78, 106
land-grant schools, 105–106
Scholastic Aptitude Test (SAT)
and, 104–105, 118
school segregation and, 63–71
voting trends and, 114–118
*See also individual institutions*
Edwards, Harry, 245–246
El Paso shooting, 265
equality, slow implementation of, 7–8
ethnic studies departments, 107
eugenics, 103–104
Eugenics Advisory Council, 103
Evergreen State College, 97

Facebook, 181
fake news, 95–96
family leave, 172
fear
of "feminizing" of young men,
25–26
of people of color, 125–126

federal grazing restrictions and fees,
36–37, 38–39, 40
feminism
male feminists and, 49, 51–63
problems within, 51–52
socialist, 53–55, 57
"Feminism for Men" (Dell), 58
"feminizing" of young men, fear of,
25–26
Ferguson, Missouri, 80, 119, 144,
240–241
FHA loans, 145–146
Fields, James Alex, Jr., 251
5th Cavalry, 23
financial net worth, disparities in, 4.
*See also* economic inequality
Finicum, LaVoy, 40–41
Fletcher, Duncan, 132
Flint, Michigan, 191
Fonda, Jane, 149
football, American
fantasy, 231
founding of, 262–263
history of, 227–229
Mizzou protests and, 239–240
modern-day, 229–230
NFL (National Football League),
235–236, 244, 245–263
physicality of, 231–232
segregation of, 232–237
unofficial ban on Black players
from, 234–237
*See also* NFL (National Football
League)
Frazier, Marcell, 244

Gage, B. Marie, 59
Gandy, Imani, 71–72, 75, 88
Garner, Eric, 134, 247
Garrity, Michael, 219
gender wage gap, 4. *See also*
economic inequality

314                                   Index

"Unite the Right" rally, 251
University of California, Berkeley,
    107, 109
University of Michigan football,
    232–234
University of Missouri protests, 229,
    237–244, 259–260, 261
University of Pennsylvania, 113–114
US Census, 215
Usher, 258

veterans
    Black, 170–171
    GI Bill for, 106, 146, 170, 171
Vietnam War, 195
villains, fabricated, 17–19
violence, incitement of, 186–187
Vorse, Mary Heaton, 57
voter suppression, 141
voting, cumulative system for,
    204–206, 221–223
voting rights
    Reconstruction and, 127
    Wilson's opposition to, 99
    for women, 51, 56–57
Voting Rights Act, 201
voting trends, education and,
    114–118

wage gaps, 4, 172, 178. See also
    economic inequality
Wall Street, 157
Wallace, George, 66, 139–142
War Department, 167
Ward, Willis, 232–234
Warner, Susan, 26
Warren, Elizabeth, 207
Washington Redskins, 234–235,
    236–237
Watergate scandal, 199
wealth gaps, 135, 146, 157. See also
    economic inequality

welfare system, 202
Welsh, Gus, 235
Western Washington University,
    119–120
westward expansion
    brutality of, 13–14
    Native people and, 20–22
    Roosevelt and, 27–28
Weymouth, Lally, 203
Wharton School of Finance,
    113–114
White Buttes, Battle of, 25
White Citizens' Council, 69
white culture, normalization of, 3
white feminism, 52
White Fragility (DiAngelo), 87
white male anger, diversity as
    leading to, 5
white male identity
    constraints of, 274
    as construct, 11
    darkness of, 273
    violence and, 276–277
white male supremacy
    as root source, 3
    upholding of, 274–275
white migration, 132–134
white nationalists, Obama and, 37
white supremacy, as pyramid
    scheme, 131
"white trash," 132
whiteness, threats to, 49–50
Will, George, 201
Williams, Eugene, 136
Williams, Jesse, 258
Williams, Patricia, 207
Williams, Serena, 258
"Willie Horton ad," 126
Wilson, Woodrow, 98–100, 217
winner-take-all elections,
    203–204
Woermer, William, 146

**Ijeoma Oluo** is the author of the *New York Times* bestseller *So You Want to Talk About Race*. Her work on race has been featured in the *New York Times* and the *Washington Post*. She has twice been named to the Root 100, and she received the 2018 Feminist Humanist Award from the American Humanist Association. She lives in Seattle, Washington.